BAD INDIANS

"Essential for all of us who were taught in school that the 'Mission Indians' no longer existed in California. . . . Miranda takes us on a journey to locate herself by way of the stories of her ancestors and others who come alive through her writing. It's such a fine book that a few words can't do it justice."

**—Leslie Marmon Silko, author of *Ceremony*, *The Turquoise Lodge*,
and *Storyteller***

"For so long, Native writers and readers have opened books of our tribal history, archaeology, and anthropology and found that it is not the story we know. . . . From the voice of the silenced, the written about and not written by, this book is groundbreaking not only as literature but as history."

**—Linda Hogan, author of *A History of Kindness* and *The Radiant
Lives of Animals***

"With insight and compassion, Deborah A. Miranda has written and compiled a potent history, an engaging family story, and a memoir of extraordinary depth. *Bad Indians* has become a classic."

**—Debra Magpie Earling, author of *Perma Red* and *The Lost
Journals of Sacajewea***

"In its first decade, *Bad Indians* has inspired a generation of readers, students, and scholars with its poetic force and with its searing indictments of the discourses of Indian vanishing and the practices of Indian erasure. Perhaps more profoundly, *Bad Indians* has modeled a new method for writing Indigenous histories: one that fully articulates the personal within the communal and the affective within the political. Just imagine what this book, its beauty, and its provocations will accomplish in the decades to come."

**—Chadwick Allen, author of *Earthworks Rising: Mound Building in
Native Literature and Arts***

"Ten years in, *Bad Indians* remains a brilliant tour de force. At times memoir, other times searing history, other times literary experimentation, Miranda's work shatters the sunny California mythos so many of us were raised to believe along with our childhood mission projects. Bad Indians unflinchingly takes aim at the quotidian violences that mark California's colonial histories, and more importantly, foregrounds the immense and beautiful work of Indigenous resistance, healing, and survival."

**—T. J. Tallie, author of *Queering Colonial Natal: Indigeneity and the
Violence of Belonging in Southern Africa***

"This book is healing. This book is medicine. . . . This beautifully-wrought memoir should be mandatory as a text in every American history class."

—Pamela Uschuk, author of *Crazy Love* and *Refugee*

"In *Bad Indians: A Tribal Memoir*, we learn about the Indigenous people of California from the 16th century to the present. What was and is day-to-day life for them? How much has been erased from our history books? How do we begin to dispel the myth that Native Americans are a people of the past? We start here."

—Brea Baker, *ELLE*

"Miranda locates Native women's voices in the archives, exhuming them from anthropological documents and newspapers so their words can accompany hers in this robust rejection of dominant narratives of Native absence. . . . At times playful, at other times tender, *Bad Indians* is a powerful read."

—Anne Mai Yee Jansen, *Book Riot*

"Miranda's research into her family history, Indigenous Californians, is the grounding cable for her to tell their collective tribal story. The book is full of photo slides, obtained through her meticulous research, as she writes to humanize the people within them; some of them her direct ancestors. Through Miranda's poetic lyricism and objective research we cannot help but feel them through the lens."

—Marlena Gates, *Electric Literature*

"This multi-genre memoir uses archives in all senses of the word, as well as imaginative writing, to render a prismatic and complex story about her own family and the history of colonization in California from the Spanish missions of the 1700s to present."

—Sarah Neilson, *Mental Floss*

"No other history of California's Indigenous communities that I know of presents such a moving, personal account of loss and survival."

—Frederick E. Hoxie, professor emeritus at University of Illinois, Urbana-Champaign

"For anyone and everyone who likes to listen to and tell stories and who believes in the liberating power of story."

—Jonah Raskin, *Anderson Valley Advertiser*

"A searing indictment of the ravages of the past and a hopeful look at the courage to confront and overcome them."

—*Kirkus Reviews*

"Miranda's is an emotional, powerfully told story that contributes greatly to her goal of 'killing the lies' about her people."

—Deborah Donovan, *Booklist*

BAD INDIANS

A Tribal Memoir

10TH ANNIVERSARY EDITION

Deborah A. Miranda

Heyday, Berkeley, California

Parts of this collection have previously been published in slightly different forms in the following: *Yellow Medicine Review*; *News from Native California*; *Native Bruin*; *"Bad Girls"/"Good Girls": Women, Sex and Power in the Nineties*; *Ahani: Indigenous American Poetry*; *Intertexts*; *Native Literatures*; *Generations*; *The Zen of La Llorona*; *West Trestle Review*; *High Desert Journal*; *World Literature Today*; and *Bad NDNS*.

Library of Congress Cataloging-in-Publication Data

Names: Miranda, Deborah A., author.
Title: Bad Indians : a tribal memoir / Deborah A. Miranda.
Description: 10th anniversary edition. | Berkeley, California : Heyday,
    [2022] | Includes bibliographical references.
Identifiers: LCCN 2022018375 (print) | LCCN 2022018376 (ebook) | ISBN
    9781597145862 (hardcover) | ISBN 9781597145879 (epub)
Subjects: LCSH: Indians of North America--California--History. | Indians of
    North America--California--Missions. | Indians, Treatment
    of--California--History. | Miranda, Deborah A.,--Family. | Esselen
    Indians--Biography. | California--Social conditions. | California--Race
    relations.
Classification: LCC E78.C15 M6 2022 (print) | LCC E78.C15 (ebook) | DDC
    305.8009794 [B]--dc23/eng/20220518
LC record available at https://lccn.loc.gov/2022018375
LC ebook record available at https://lccn.loc.gov/2022018376

Cover photo: Deborah Miranda, circa 1964, Los Angeles, California. Courtesy of the author

Cover and Interior Design: Lorraine Rath and Marlon Rigel

Published by Heyday
P.O. Box 9145, Berkeley, California 94709
(510) 549-3564
heydaybooks.com

Printed in East Peoria, Illinois, by Versa Press, Inc.

10 9 8 7 6 5 4 3 2 1

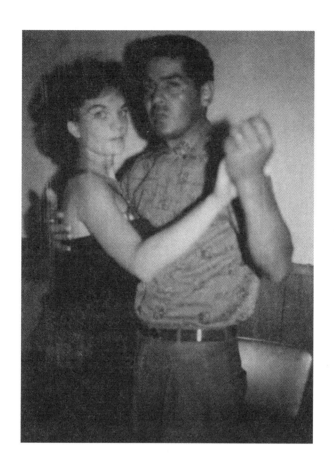

For my mother and father,
who survived each other

"I am the result of the love of thousands."

—Linda Hogan

Contents

The Light from the Carrisa Plains: Reinvention
1900–1961   91

Teheyapami Achiska: Home
1961–present   123

Las Otno Ayam, Las Metx, Las Iapa, Las Ewshai, let salewa iyu. Atsa jatan Las Ewshai ka amumut lakam let lala ma'ali manaleneipa. Let kia'alpa ahik iniwa welel ta'a neku tuxus laka masianex jatan kominan efexe. Let taheiya neku Las Ewshai ahik, tamakapa sasipi let papia cha'a. Let toxesa iniwa alpa pami lex panna laka lax panna. Let alpa ahik kominan kinia ta'a iniwa alpa machi ahik lex efexe cha'a. Let kia'alpa ahik lex panna ewaimitano machi kinia lachs ka laka keya lax maxana shansha.

Kia Las Otno Ayam Taxawi Name Kominan.

Honorable Creator, Honorable Grandfathers, Honorable Grandmothers, Honorable Ancestors, we come in a good way. Days of Ancestors are gone but we will not forget. We ask that these words find the ears and hearts of all people. We honor the Ancestors that suffered so that we could live. We give these stories to our Children and their Children. We pray that all who find these stories know that our people exist. We ask that our Children forever know who they are and where their blood runs.

Creator protect you all.

—prayer composed by Louise Miranda Ramirez,
Chairwoman, Ohlone/Costanoan-Esselen Nation

Preface to the 10th Anniversary Edition

How do we tell our Indigenous stories in the colonizer's language? Joy Harjo and Gloria Bird tell us that because many Indigenous people of North America no longer speak our native languages (and even if we do, the dominant culture certainly does not), we must use the colonizer's languages—English, Spanish, French—to speak and be heard. But, the two poets add, we don't just "use" those languages: we *reinvent* them. And the mixed-genre, hybrid structure of *Bad Indians: A Tribal Memoir* became my way of "reinventing the enemy's language" in order to tell our story with the truth that has been missing from the colonizer's version.

The nature of hybrid literature is a paradox: it is made up from fractured pieces that create a new whole. As one shard feeds into still another, where once there seemed to be only brokenness becomes a more complete story that continues to grow in detail and depth. In fact, I found that even as *Bad Indians* was about to go to print in 2013, pieces of the larger story continued to demand expression. The first draft of "Ularia's Curse," for example, was written in one day, and a polished version emailed to Heyday editors a week later, just in time to be included in the book before it went to print!

In the years since publication, other pieces that clearly belong within the covers of *Bad Indians* have come into the world, and I am happy to be able to include them here. The canonization of Junípero Serra in 2015 took me back to a collection of Serra's writings from 1769, where I used a poetic device called "erasure" to spotlight Indian voices. The prose poem "Juliana, 1803" was written partly from a dream that continues to haunt me; I found some peace in telling harsh truths about the forced imprisonment of young Indian girls in *monjerios*. "The People Before" is a "found" poem that I wrote while teaching at the inaugural Indigenous Nations Poets gathering at the Library of Congress in April 2022. The photograph of Victor (in "Cousins") was a lucky find, bringing my relative's beautiful face into our line of vision. The poem "tsa'a kakalu / uncle crow" evolved from Isabel Meadows's stories about my ancestor Ventura, a cantor at Mission Carmel. Other new poems were born on a train trip I took down the California coast visiting missions ("Namo'esa," "San Zombie de los Muertos Vivientes," "San Amnesia de la Lobotomía," "San Mariposa de las Piedras," "Santa Grita de los Dioramas").

Longer pieces connected to my own life continue the more traditional memoir aspect of *Bad Indians*: "Dear Sonora" speaks directly to a young fourth-grade student who wrote looking for direction on her mission project. "Transplant" explores the healing aspects of a beloved place from my childhood, while "Tuolumne" explores my understanding of a brief but powerful moment in my father's relationship with his own father. And I've added a new final essay titled "Surfing the Tsunami" about the experience of writing *Bad Indians* and how the book has been received by various audiences in the past ten years.

This new edition also gives me the opportunity to clarify the legal name of my tribe: the Ohlone/Costanoan-Esselen Nation of the Greater Monterey Bay Area. Among ourselves, we say Esselen, the Esselen Nation, or OCEN. However, many people mistake us for Ohlone, which is not surprising, given that's literally part of our name. Of course, the Ohlone are a San Francisco Bay Area tribe.

Why, then, do we have another tribe's identity as part of our name? The short answer: because we are petitioning for federal re-recognition, we must use the names by which we have historically been identified, and Euro-Americans usually did not actually know the names by which we called ourselves. Names used historically to identify us have included the Monterey Band of Monterey County, San Carlos Indians, Mission San Carlos Indians, Costanoan, Carmeleños, Ohlone, and Esselen. When we organized to petition for re-recognition, having been accidentally dropped from the federal government's rolls (another long story), we were advised to go with the names that appear most prominently in the archives of our history—to support our assertion that we are still the same people.

In addition, while we share the same ancestral connections, we are a separate entity from the Esselen Tribe of Monterey County, which was recently gifted a piece of our shared homeland by an outside benefactor. The similarity of the tribal names is confusing, and our relations with this other branch of the Esselen are complicated; again, much of this confusion finds its roots in the powerful aftershocks of colonization, missionization, and US government mismanagement of Indigenous identities and lives. However, I have faith that the ancestors recognize, love, and depend on all their descendants, no matter what we must or choose to call ourselves.

There you have it. For the full story, visit our tribal website at http://www.ohlonecostanoanesselennation.org/.

In closing, I freely admit that even with this tenth-anniversary edition, I am not finished reinventing the stories of my people. But then, I suspect that my people are not done reinventing themselves.

Deborah A. Miranda

Introduction
California Is a Story

> They love their children to excess (if that can be said), but they give
> them no education whatever. They merely recount to them the fables
> which they heard in their pagan state. They do this to entertain and
> satisfy the children. The latter believe these things as if they really
> happened, for a certain period. They held and do hold those as wise
> men who knew and could relate more of these fables. This is their
> chief knowledge.
>
> —Mission San Juan Bautista, response to the
> Interrogatorio (Questionnaire) sent by the Spanish
> viceroy in Mexico to all California missions, 1812

CALIFORNIA IS A STORY. California is many stories. As Leslie Silko tells us, don't be fooled by stories! Stories are "all we have," she says. And it is true. Human beings have no other way of knowing that we exist, or what we have survived, except through the vehicle of story.

One of the stories California tells is this: In 1959, my mother met my father. Madgel Eleanor Yeoman encountered Alfred Edward Miranda. She was twenty-five years old, he was thirty-three. She had been born and raised in Beverly Hills; he had been born on the Tuolomne Rancheria (a California Indian reservation) and raised on the mean streets of Santa Monica. Her father ("Yeoman") was of English descent, her mother ("Gano" or "Genaux") of French ancestry and possibly Jewish. Al was Chumash and Esselen, his mother from the Santa Barbara/Santa Ynez Mission Indians, his father from the Carmel Mission Indians. Midgie was fair-skinned, black-haired, and blue-eyed. Al was so dark his gang nickname was "Blackie."

His skin was decorated with various homemade gang and Navy tattoos, along with the name of his first wife. Soon "Miche," his nickname for my mother, would join that collection.

My mother was still trying to recover from the aftermath of her first, disastrous marriage, which had included the birth of three children and the wrenching, accidental death of one of them. But Miche still had a dancer's body: 5'2", one hundred pounds, able to dance tango and flamenco in high heels and tight dresses. She'd trained at Hollywood Professional High School with Eduardo Cansino, movie star Rita Hayworth's father. The highlight of my father's formal education came in the eighth grade of his Catholic school, when he took a bet from one of his friends that nuns were bald beneath their wimples, snatched the head covering off of Sister Theresa Anthony, and was promptly expelled. Somehow, I don't think this was his first strike.

As a young man, my father married Marcelina, a beautiful young woman he'd grown up with, though the marriage didn't last. By the time my parents met, Al already had four daughters: Rose Marie, Louise, Lenora, and Pat.

I would be his fifth—not his hoped-for son.

Miche and Al: colonizer and Indian; European and Indigenous; nominal Christian and lapsed Catholic; once-good girl and twice-bad boy. Heaven on earth, and hell, too.

It was Miche's dancing that captivated my father. He met her in an East L.A. bar. Together—my father slim and muscular in his pressed light chinos and crisp shirt, my mother glowing in spaghetti-strap black nightclub best—they made a striking couple, full of passion and mutual joy. All the pieces fit, despite the fact that none of the pieces were even remotely from the same puzzle. They fulfilled each other's romantic fantasies: he was strong, macho, *suave;* she was Hollywood lipstick and mascara, a classy, albeit wounded, dove.

Two worlds collided, just like in a good old sci-fi movie produced at one of the studios my mother had hung around all her young life. Miche knew how to dress, how to draw on eyebrows with a perfect arch, the exact deep blood-red shade of lipstick to apply. She was beautiful, on fire with suicidal depression, desperate for love. The death of her baby, Jenny, haunted her every day. It had happened just a few years before when a pregnant Midgie and her then-husband Mike drank and fought, fought and drank, leaving two toddler girls to fend for themselves; now, Midgie used alcohol and heroin to dull the visceral pain, speed to get up the next morning and get my half-siblings off to school.

Al told me once, "She gave up heroin for me." He said it in a half-wondering tone of voice, as if he still couldn't quite believe it. I do.

Theirs was the kind of desire that happens only once in a lifetime, the kind of desire that eventually leaves you wishing you'd never tasted its soul-thieving mouth, the kind of desire you pray to forget. Desire that demands like demonic possession. Desire you wouldn't wish on your worst enemy; desire you hope to God your own children never know.

No wonder Midgie could give up heroin for my father: she always went for the most destructive drug she could find.

Romeo and Juliet had nothing on my parents. In the era before the civil rights movement, even in lascivious Southern California, a darkly handsome Indian man and a white woman were not easily tolerated. Although antimiscegenation laws had been declared unconstitutional in California in 1948 (the case involved a Mexican American woman and an African American man—Mexican Americans were, at that time, generally classified as "white"), ten years later it was still unusual to see an interracial couple, even in Los Angeles. "I got into a fight once in Santa Monica," my father remembered, "with this white guy who kept asking your mother why she was with a black man. I wanted to beat the shit out of him, but your mother wouldn't let me."

My mother's parents, white farm kids from Nebraska who had moved to Los Angeles in the early 1930s and found their own private paradise, were horrified, enraged, and devastated. Although for all the wrong reasons, given the outcome of their daughter's marriage, that turned out to be an appropriate response. I'm pretty sure they had never even seen a black man in the flesh before arriving in L.A. as married adults; I don't think they'd seen what they thought of as an "Indian" until they took a trip through the Southwest when my mother was a child. As far as they knew, people of color—especially *men* of color—were practically another species, people you hired or saw doing manual labor, like their Japanese gardener (sent to an internment camp during World War II and never seen again). A colored man was not fit to marry their daughter, even if she was a divorcée with two young children, a tattered reputation, a shattered heart.

By 1961, my father's family had been enduring and/or celebrating mixed-race unions for about two hundred years in one form or another: California Indian with Mexican Indian, Chumash with Esselen, Spaniard with Indian, and rich variations thereof. By force, by choice, or by love, mixed-race unions were a tradition for those who survived the California missions. Those who will not change do not survive; but who are we, when we have survived?

Out of this particular union, then, comes my story: in the form of a small, light brown baby with dark eyes and wispy brown hair. And dimples. "The first thing I did was look to see if you had dimples," my mother said in one of her many retellings of the birth, "like your father." My father insisted that all his kids had dimples; checking for them was a kind of paternity test on his part. And into this body of mine came the full force of two separate streams of human history and story.

This California story dovetails with another: as a mixed-blood "Mission Indian," I have spent a lifetime being told I'm not a "*real* Indian"—in large part because I do not have the language of my ancestors, and much of our culture was literally razed to the ground. I refused to believe that the absence of language meant my culture was nonexistent, but since even other Indians thought "all you California Indians were extinct," it's been a tough road. Along the way, I've learned a lot about stories, their power to rebuild or silence.

I'm not saying the old adage "language is culture" is completely off-track. Reclaiming our languages is a sacred and beautiful act. But it is deceptive to pin our survival on language. If a language is destroyed, as many Native American languages have been, that does not decimate the culture. Culture is ultimately lost when we stop telling the stories of who we are, where we have been, how we arrived here, what we once knew, what we wish we knew; when we stop our retelling of the past, our imagining of our future, and the long, long task of inventing an identity every single second of our lives.

Culture is lost when we neglect to tell our stories, when we forget the power and craft of storytelling. Native Americans did not enter the canonical field of American literature until 1969, when Kiowa author N. Scott Momaday won the Pulitzer Prize for fiction. It would be fifty-two more years before Mojave poet Natalie Diaz and Turtle Mountain Ojibwe novelist Louise Erdrich received Pulitzers in 2021. (Linda Hogan's novel *Mean Spirit*

From my mother, the French Huguenots fleeing to the New World to escape religious persecution. English peasants looking for land. Starving Irish trying to outrun famine. Traumatized Sephardic Jews looking for yet another new start. The Baptist minister, John Gano, who baptized George Washington as an adult. The Confederate general, Richard Montgomery Gano, who, during the War Between the States, commanded Brig. Gen. Stand Watie's First Indian Brigade (consisting of Cherokee, Creek, and Seminole) at the second Battle of Cabin Creek.

My father's genealogy of genocide, smallpox, enslavement, loss of language, religion, culture, health, land; his inheritance of violence and struggle and fear, alcoholism, diabetes, poverty. The Indian languages his mother and grandmother spoke together; the Christmas parties in his grandfather's house out at Big Sur; relatives lynched from the infamous oak in Monterey. His "street" Spanish, his Indian accent, his taste for acorn mush, salmon straight out of the Santa Ynez River, his memories of the old people who helped raise him.

was a finalist in 1990.) Scott Momaday wasn't the first published Indian author. He was just the first one who managed to jam his foot in the door long enough so those behind him could scramble through a little easier. The gatekeepers of "literature" have kept us outside by making education and literacy so undesirable and so painful (boarding schools, punishment for the slightest Indianness) and by making our own stories so unacceptable (you had to write like a white man or, conversely, write the way Tonto spoke if you wanted to be published) that it took all that time for us to even approach the door.

Prior to 1969, who was telling our story? Non-Indians, for the most part. Self-representation was almost unheard of, stereotypes and biases were bleeding into American culture freely. So *who* tells a story is a mighty piece of information for the listeners; you must know what that storyteller has at stake. Demanding to know who is telling your story means asking, "Who is inventing me, for what purpose, with what intentions?"

Europeans told stories about Indigenous people in North and South America long before any of them ever left European shores in their small boats and actually met a Native person. Cannibals, human-animal offspring, mutated monsters, bloodthirsty devils—the names and stories sank into the minds and identities of Europeans and made them fearful, defensive, righteous. The stories that had been told about inhabitants of other lands created, in turn, the stories that played out at First Contact—stories about savages, heathens, pagans, barbarians, and other lesser, inferior beings.

Story is the most powerful force in the world—in our world, maybe in all worlds. Story *is* culture. Story, like culture, is constantly moving. It is a river where no gallon of water is the same gallon it was one second ago. Yet it is still the same river. It exists as a truth. As a whole. Even if the whole is in constant change. In fact, *because* of that constant change.

All my life, I have heard only one story about California Indians: godless, dirty, stupid, primitive, ugly, passive, drunken, immoral, lazy, weak-willed people who *might* make good workers if properly trained and motivated. What kind of story is that to grow up with?

The story of the missionization of California.

In 1769, after missionizing much of Mexico, the Spaniards began to move up the west coast of North America in order to establish claims to rich resources and land before other European nations could get a foothold. Together, the Franciscan priests and Spanish soldiers "built" a series of twenty-one missions along what is now coastal California. (California's Indigenous peoples, numbering over one million at the time, did most of the actual labor.) These missions, some rehabilitated from melting adobe, others in near-original state, are now one of the state's biggest tourist attractions; in the little town of Carmel, Mission San Carlos Borromeo de Carmelo is *the* biggest attraction. Elsewhere, so-called Mission décor drenches Southern California, from restaurants to homes, apartment buildings, animal shelters, grocery stores, and post offices. In many neighborhoods, a bastardized Mission style is actually required by cities or neighborhood associations. Along with this visual mythology of adobe and red clay roof tiles comes the cultural storytelling that drains the missions of their brutal and bloody pasts for popular consumption.

In California schools, students come up against the "Mission Unit" in fourth grade, reinforcing the same lies those children have been breathing in most of their lives. Part of California's history curriculum, the unit is entrenched in the educational system and impossible to avoid, a powerfully authoritative indoctrination in Mission Mythology to which fourth graders have little if any resistance. Intense pressure is put upon students (and their parents) to create a "Mission Project" that glorifies the era and glosses over both Spanish and Mexican exploitation of Indians, as well as American enslavement of those same Indians during American rule. In other words, the Mission Unit is all too often a lesson in imperialism, racism, and Manifest Destiny rather than actually educational or a jumping off point for critical thinking or accurate history.

Can you imagine teaching about slavery in the South while simultaneously requiring each child to lovingly construct a plantation model, complete with happy darkies in the fields, white masters, overseers with whips, and human auctions? Or asking fourth graders to study the Holocaust by carefully designing detailed concentration camps, complete with gas chambers, heroic Nazi guards, crematoriums?

I left California after kindergarten and completed my schooling in Washington State (where I suffered through the "Oregon Trail Unit" instead, but that's another story), so I never had to produce a Mission Project. This book is, in a way, my belated offering at that particular altar.

Visiting the missions as an adult, proud, mixed-blood California Indian woman, I found myself unprepared for gift shops well stocked with CDs of pre-researched Mission Projects, xeroxed pamphlets of mission terms, facts, and history (one for each mission), coloring books, packaged models of missions ("easily assembled in 10 minutes!") and other project paraphernalia for the discerning fourth grader and their worried parents. Large, elaborate dioramas are featured within many of the missions for fourth graders and tourists to view while imagining the same rote story, "the olden days" when the padre stood in the shade of the church doorway and watched the Indians—men, women, children—go meekly about their daily work, clothed, Christianized, content.

For many years, the Carmel Mission store maintained a "fourth-grade corner" with mission kits, pamphlets, and other materials specifically targeting fourth-grade mission projects. Other websites offer "easy," "quick," "guaranteed A+!!!" Mission Projects, targeting those anxious parents, for a price.

Generations of Californians have grown up steeped in a culture and educational system that trains them to think of Indians as passive, dumb, and disappeared. In other words, the project is so well established, in such a predictable and well-loved rut, that veering outside of the worn but comfortable mythology is all but impossible.

On my visit to Mission Dolores, I found that out in a particularly visceral way.

It was over winter break, 2008. I was in San Francisco for a conference, and my friend Kimberly and I had hopped on a streetcar to visit Mission Dolores. As we emerged from the mission church via a side door into a small courtyard (featuring one of those giant dioramas behind glass), we inadvertently walked into video camera range of a mother filming her daughter's fourth-grade project.

Excusing ourselves, we studiously examined the diorama while the little girl flubbed her lines a few times. She was reading directly from the flyer given tourists in the gift shop and could say "basilica" but not "archdiocese," but she maintained her poise through several takes until she nailed it.

Both mothers ourselves, Kimberly and I paused to exchange a few words of solidarity about school projects with the mother, which gave Mom the chance to brag about how she and Virginia were trying to "do something a little different" by using video instead of making a model.

"That's great!" I said, giving them both a polite smile. "I'll bet your teacher will be glad to have something out of the ordinary." Contrary to what many believe, I do not attack unsuspecting white women and children; I am not a Political Correction Officer prowling the missions, hoping to ruin some hardworking child's day.

"Well, it *is* different actually being right here," Mom said excitedly. "To think about all those Indians and how they lived all that time ago, that's kind of impressive."

I could not resist. "And better yet," I beamed, "still live! Guess what? I'm a member of the Ohlone/Costanoan-Esselen Nation myself! Some of my ancestors *lived* in this mission. I've found their names in the Book of Baptism." (See? I didn't mention that they are also all listed in the Book of Deaths soon afterward.)

The mother was beside herself with pleasure, posed me with her daughter for a still photo, and wrote down my name so she could Google my work. Little Virginia, however, was literally shocked into silence. Her face drained, her body went stiff, and she stared at me as if I had risen, an Indigenous skeleton clad in decrepit rags, from beneath the clay bricks of the courtyard. Even though her mother and I talked a few more minutes, Virginia the fourth grader—previously a calm, articulate news anchor in training—remained a shy shadow, shooting side glances at me out of the corners of her eyes.

As Kimberly and I walked away, I thought, "That poor kid has never seen a live Indian, much less a 'Mission Indian'—she thought we were all dead!" Having me suddenly appear in the middle of her video project must have been a lot like turning the corner to find the (dead) person you were talking about suddenly in your face, talking back.

Kimberly, echoing my thoughts, chortled quietly, "Yes, Virginia, there really are live Mission Indians."

The problem is, thanks to Mission Mythology, most fourth graders will never know that.

That's why it's time for the Mission Fantasy Fairy Tale to end. This story has done more damage to California Indians than any conquistador, any priest, any *soldado de cuera* (leather-jacket soldier), any smallpox, measles, or influenza virus. This story has not just killed us, it has taught us how to kill ourselves and kill each other with alcohol, domestic violence, horizontal racism, internalized hatred. This story is a kind of evil, a kind of witchery. We have to put an end to it now.

But where to start? What's the best way to kill a lie? Like bad spirits, they are notoriously immune to arrows—in fact, they are often known to rise after being killed, even after being buried. We must know where to aim, pick our targets, remain clear-sighted.

I say "we" because my efforts here are part of a much wider circle of California Indian peoples and allies talking back to mythology, protesting, making waves.

We each have our chosen weapons. My sister Louise chooses language: pulling the Esselen words out of field notes, off wax cylinders, singing the words over the bones of those she reburies with intimate tenderness, writing new stories in an old tongue. My friend Georgiana Valoyce Sanchez (Chumash) chooses storytelling and song, clappersticks and rhythm, teaching and education. James Luna (Luiseño, Puyukitchum, Ipi, and Mexican American, 1950–2018) created live and video performances that turn stereotypes on their heads, inventing new ceremonies to reclaim ancient identities. L. Frank (Tongva/Ajachmem) reenvisions mission history through her infamous Coyote cartoons, her museum research, and recreation of Indigenous California arts.

Many other California Indians weave baskets, harvest acorns, write poems, sing Bird Songs, document museum holdings, string abalone shell, construct tule boats and *tomols,* carve stone bowls, create visual art, work for repatriation of bones and belongings.

I choose to make this book: to create a space where voices can speak after long and often violently imposed silence. Constructing this book has been hard, listening to those stories seep out of old government documents, BIA forms, field notes, the diaries of explorers and priests, the occasional writings or testimony from Indians, family stories, photographs, newspaper articles; it's been painful, dreaming of destruction, starved children, bones that cry. But at the end of it, I feel voices present that the world hasn't heard for a long, long time. Voices telling the antidote to lies.

My ancestors, collectively, are the story-bridge that allows me to be here. I'm honored to be one of the bridges back to them, to their words and experiences.

"Stories are their chief knowledge," wrote the padre from Mission San Juan Bautista.

Yes—and they are, still. May it always be so.

The End of the World: Missionization 1770–1836

The Genealogy of Violence, Part I

Los Pájaros

based on writings by Junípero Serra, May 1773 and June 1774

Seeing your people come through the fields
we noticed a great flock of birds
of various and beautifully blended colors
such as we had never seen before.

We noticed a great flock of birds
swooping out of the heavens just ahead
such as we had never seen before
as if they came to welcome our newly arrived guests.

Swooping out of the heavens just ahead
six or more soldiers set out together on horseback
as if they came to greet their newly acquired hosts
in the far distant rancherias even many leagues away.

Six or more soldiers set out together on horseback.
Both men and women at sight of them took to their heels
in the far distant rancherias even many leagues away,
fleeing the soldiers, clever as they are at lassoing cows.

Both men and women at sight of them took to their heels
but the women were caught with Spanish ropes.
The soldiers, clever as they are at lassoing cows
preyed on the women for their unbridled lust.

The women were caught with Spanish ropes.
Indian men defended their wives—
prey for the Spaniards' unbridled lust—
only to be shot down with bullets.

The Indian men tried to defend their wives
of various and beautifully blended colors
only to be shot down with bullets
seeing your people come through the fields.

Fisher of Men

based on writings by Junípero Serra

They are entirely naked,
as Adam in the garden before sin.
Not for one moment could we notice
the least sign of shame.

Before long, they will be caught
in the apostolic and evangelical net.
To God alone be all the honor
and glory! I dread to think

that such a plentiful harvest, ripe
for the reapers, remain untouched.
They are entirely naked,
as Adam in the garden before sin.

Though I find it hard—a sinner like me—
to be left all alone, nearest priest
more than eighty leagues away, nothing
in between but savages and rough roads,

before long they will be caught
in the apostolic and evangelical net.
More naked people than these
cannot be found in the whole world.

His Divine Majesty be pleased,
in his infinite mercy, give me
a holy death; they are entirely naked,
as Adam in the garden before sin.

When arrows were raining everywhere,
I held the Virgin's picture in one hand,
Her Divine Crucified Son in the other.
Pray for me as I move amidst

dangers from naked and barbarous men.
Before long, they will be caught
in the apostolic and evangelical net.
Those who are to come here put up

with hardships for the love of God
and the salvation of souls . . .
but to a willing heart all is sweet,
amanti suave est.

They are naked as Adam
in the garden before sin.
Before long, they will be caught
in the apostolic and evangelical net:

such a plentiful harvest, ripe
for the reapers.

Erasure **Poem**

The tract through which **we** passed is generally very good land, with plenty of water; and there, as well as **here**, the country is neither rocky nor overrun with brush-wood. There are, however, many hills, but they **are composed of earth**. The road has been good in some places, but the greater part bad. About half-way, the **valleys and** banks of **rivulets** began to be delightful. We found **vines** of a large size, and in some cases quite **loaded with grapes**; we also found **an abundance of roses**, which appeared to be like those of Castile.

We have seen **Indians** in immense numbers, and all those **on this coast** of the Pacific contrive to make a good subsistence on various seeds, and by fishing. The latter they **carry on** by means of rafts or canoes, made of tule (bullrush) with which they go a great way to sea. They are **very civil**. All the males, **old and young**, go naked; the women, however, and the female children, are **decent**ly covered from their breasts downward. We found **on our journey**, as well as in the place where **we** stopped, that they **treat**ed us **with** as much **confidence and good-will** as if they had known us **all** their **lives**. But when we offered them any of our victuals, they **always** refused them. All they **care**d **for** was cloth, and only for something of this sort would they exchange their fish or whatever else they had. During **the whole** march we found hares, rabbits, some deer, and a **multitude** of berendos (**a kind of** a **wild** goat).

I pray **God** may preserve your health and life many years.

From this port and intended Mission of San Diego, in North California, third July, 1769. FRIAR MIGUEL JOSE JUNÍPERO SERRA

A Poem

We   here
are composed of earth
valleys and   rivulets
vines   loaded with grapes
an abundance of roses
We   Indians   on this coast
carry on
very civil,   old and young
decent   on our journey
we treat with   confidence and good-will
all lives   always care for
the whole
multitude
a kind of wild
God

s   o   n   g   o   f

I I ' U R*
[*one of the Kumeyaay words for *Juniperus californica*]

My Mission Glossary

(excerpts from a very late fourth-grade project)

For many decades, all California schoolchildren have been required to take part in the "Mission Unit" during their fourth-grade year. Because I left California after kindergarten, I never participated in this rite of passage. Till now.—dm

Deby's mission

Deby Miranda, fourth-grade picture

Adobe Bricks

Figure 1

Recipe: Gather your Indians from the mission. Try to catch them between their regular chores of tending the fields, chasing cattle, cooking, weaving, mandatory prayers, and catechism instruction.

Then you need dirt, water, straw, sometimes horse manure. Make sure it's good dirt, not too much clay or the bricks will crack as they dry. Your Indians might have to haul some dirt in, which could take days, and no mules, a cart if they're lucky, baskets if not.

Tell them to dig a big round basin in the ground, soak it well with water, throw everything in. That water has to come from someplace. River, spring, rain barrels maybe. Indian women make some baskets good as a bucket. Keep some of the men running back and forth for water, while the others jump into the pit and start mixing with their feet. (Shovels are valuable and hard to come by; make sure the iron is not stolen for weapons.) This is where good legs are a blessing. The work keeps their dancing muscles in shape, and they seem to like dirt, aren't concerned about the ripe odor.

Mission building is smelly business.

Now, when it's all mixed they'll start the rhythm of scoop and slap. Scoop up that mud, slap it into a wooden form. Pack it in good and tight. Repeat till the form is full, move on to the next. (Oh—wooden forms. Before beginning, you must assign Indians to cut down trees and make lumber for the forms, and then make the forms. Few nails to be had, but they're clever with rope and vine once you get the idea across.)

Anyhow, as soon as the whole form is full, have the Indios check and see if they can lift it right off those bricks so you can reuse it. In an hour, perhaps a day, the bricks should just stand alone, mixed right. Now, if the weather holds you can leave the wet bricks right there, turn them once in a while, let the air and heat bake them hard. When rain threatens, the Indians must weave reeds and grasses as they do for their own mats.

Adobe takes three to four weeks to cure. So you want to build up a good supply before you start building anything like a mission. Dried, each brick weighs about sixty pounds. Stacking one upon the other requires strong Indians, especially when climbing ladders and makeshift scaffolding.

All in all, adobe is cheap—the ingredients free for the taking—but you will certainly go through a lot of Indians. More lazy creatures on earth we have never seen.

Bells

From the start, the hollow stones with voices. Made in their own land, hard beyond rock or bone or abalone shell, shaped by hands of unseen beings we thought must be gods.

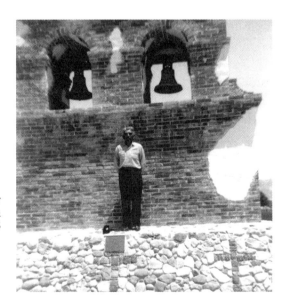

Figure 2. Tom Miranda (my grandfather) at Mission San Miguel *campanario,* circa 1955

Soldiers brought them from the ships, hung them first from trees, then on wooden frames. At last, the bells sounded from the *campanario* in the church itself—after we made it, after we built the church.

The voice of the bell is the voice of the padres. We try, but we cannot always obey.

Bells at dawn, keening. Bells ordering us to prayer; the alcaldes stand over us with cudgels and long canes, invoke silence. Bells direct us to breakfast, gruel of *atole* quickly swallowed. Bells tell us to scatter to our work, we women to laundry and looms, grinding corn or acorns or wheat, the gardens, harvesting, storing, preparing, cooking; men to the fields to plow, plant, slaughter cattle, adobe, plaster, tile, paint our designs inside the church.

Men work their leather, repair soldiers' saddles, plait reins or the cords of whips they use on us. Seamstresses cut, stitch, clothe our naked shame. Blacksmiths practice the art of heated metal, beating until the acceptable shape emerges. Vaqueros herd and skin the cattle for the hides the Spaniards love so, swimming in blood day after day till Indian skins smell like death too.

Bells for midday meal. *Atole* again. Bells return us to our labors, bells demand prayers or instruction in prayer, bells determine evening meal, maybe *posole* with meat. Bells give us permission to sleep.

Once, the bells hung silent. The padres told us to put all else aside, join in gathering a great tide of sardines. Oh, what pleasure while we brought in that slippery harvest! For many days we waded in the surf with our baskets, salty water bathing us of dust and blood, sun claiming our bare backs. We sang lusty songs out beyond the padres' hearing; I heard laughter all around me as the young unmarried men and women, separated in day by work and at night by lock and key, exchanged more than looks. We ate sardines fresh, we roasted them in coals, wrapped in seaweed, we hung them over the fire, their rich fat dripping onto embers.

Some of us caught as much as ten barrels, but when the barrels ran out and still the sardines came, we showed the padres how to open the sardines, remove the spines, put them to dry in the sun. This, they gave away to anyone who asked, having no way to store such bounty, and that was right, and never would have happened, we thought, if the bells still spoke.

On holy day, we left the sardines in peace, went hunting for nests of seabirds that live in the rocks. We passed that day camping on the beach, small groups of us, each with its fire, roasting and eating what we had caught. Friends rested together, gossiping; daughters normally sequestered in the *monjerio* leaned against their mothers contentedly; children ate their fill, slept on the warm sand with bones still tight in their fists. Our souls swam gratefully into dream, whole and unbroken. The padres stood to one side, watched, laughed to see us at such ease.

Mission Bell Guide-Post Marking El Camino Real

Figure 3

Next day, we woke to bells. The voice of the bell is the voice of the padres. We try, but we cannot always obey.

Discipline

Due to their animal-like natures, California Indians often made mistakes or misbehaved even when they had been told the rules. Records left behind tell us how the Indians lied, stole, cheated on their spouses, killed

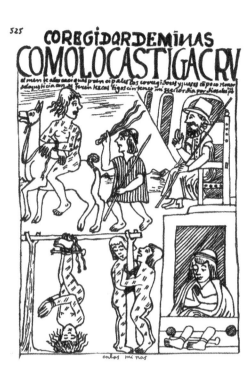

Figure 4

their own babies, ran away from the missions, tried to avoid their work, practiced pagan witchcraft, gambled, or snuck off to gather or hunt extra food for their families without getting permission from the padres first.

Like good fathers everywhere, the padres believed in firm discipline and consequences; usually this meant flogging (another word for "whipping"), but sometimes other kinds of corporal punishment were used as needed. As Padre Lasuén (who took over for Padre Serra as president at San Carlos) wrote sensibly, "It is evident that a nation which is barbarous, ferocious and ignorant requires more frequent punishment than a nation which is cultured, educated and of gentle and moderate customs."

Luckily, the Spaniards had already had experience with taming wild Indians in Mexico and in parts of South America, such as Peru. A very smart Peruvian Indian named Felipe Guaman Poma de Ayala learned how to read and write, and in 1615 he began to write a long letter to the king of Spain.

In fact, it was so long that it took Guaman Poma thirty years to write! Poma used Spanish (although he made many mistakes) and, when he didn't know the Spanish word for something, used Indian dialects written with Spanish letters. He told the king about Peruvian and Andean history, culture, and experiences with Spaniards.

In his letter, Poma provided a little catalog of Spanish punishments for Indians that included flogging (first being tied to a llama or post), hanging upside down, and being put in the stocks. The Peruvian wanted the king to take action against what he felt were unreasonably harsh punishments experienced by Indians who worked in gold and silver mines.

Although Guaman Poma spent most of his life researching and constructing this letter, it was lost for centuries and never reached the king. However, the traditions of firm discipline lived on. Franciscan fathers used these and other disciplinary actions to help civilize California Indians and turn them into good Christians and loyal Spanish subjects. Below are brief explanation of the most commonly practiced punishments in our California missions: flogging, whipping with the cat-o'-nine tails, hobbling with the *corma,* and beating with the cudgel.

Figure 5. Flogging

Flogging

Also known in Spanish as *azotes* (stripes), floggings were usually administered by alcaldes (Indian leaders appointed by priests or, later, voted into office by Indians) or soldiers, and sometimes by the padres personally. Although correspondence between padres and the Crown specified a limit of twenty-five blows per Indian for each broken rule, records from the padres' diaries and other records indicate that some Indians received as many as one hundred twenty-five blows at one time. Those must have been very bad Indians, as the padres did not want to injure the Indians but teach them to behave. It is a common falsehood that any Indian was ever beaten to death by a padre.

Figure 6. Cat-o'-nine tails

Cat-o'-Nine Tails

A whip, usually made of cow or horse hide, with nine knotted lines, invented in and used throughout Europe and by pirates for various crimes. There are stories that steel balls or barbs of wires would be added to the ends of the lines to give them more striking force. The whips might be oiled and wiped clean in between floggings but in that time and place, the Spaniards had no concept of bacteria and germs. They had no way of knowing that the cat-o'-nine tails was a breeding ground for disease and pestilence, or that the sores on Indians' bodies would become badly infected. Honest.

Figure 7. *Corma*

Corma

A hobbling device for misbehaving neophytes. Developed first for use on livestock, such as horses, who required some movement to graze but might run away if left completely unshackled. Steven Hackel, a mission scholar, reports in his book *Children of Coyote*, "The apparatus, which closed around the prisoner's feet, was formed of two pieces of wood hinged together, twenty-four inches long and about ten inches wide. Rags were placed around the prisoner's feet to prevent abrasions and permanent injury . . . the *corma* could be used to punish Indians and allow them to perform simple tasks, such as cleaning wheat or grinding corn . . . [a visitor to the missions] thought the *corma* especially appropriate to chastise Indian women who were guilty of adultery or other serious faults" (no doubt because the *corma* forced the wearer to keep his/her legs together). Similar to the stocks but portable, the *corma* allowed the Indians to continue being productive members of the mission even when having to learn a lesson about obedience.

Cudgel

Wooden club used to strike quickly; alcaldes, soldiers, and sometimes padres carried these with them for spontaneous corrections throughout their day. The alcaldes used these during services in church to remind the Indians to be quiet, to pay attention, and to stay awake. A longer cudgel or cane was useful during Mass because the alcalde could reach far into a crowd without having to move very much.

Figure 8. Cudgel

Figure 9. Carmel Mission, circa 1882

Mission

Massive Conversion Factory centered around a furnace constructed of flesh, bones, blood, grief, and pristine land and watersheds, and dependent on a continuing fresh supply of human beings, specifically Indian, which were in increasingly short supply. Run by a well-meaning European religious order (see PADRE) convinced that they were doing the work of their Supreme Deity, aka God, a mission was meant to suck in Indigenous peoples (see NEOFITO), strip them of religion, language, and culture, and melt them down into generic workers instilled with Catholicism, Spanish values, and freshly overhauled, tuned-up souls. These reconditioned souls (now called "converts") were to be spewed out the back end of the Conversion Factory in about ten years, by which time they would be expected to perform the basic functions of service to both earthly king and Supreme Deity, gladly forsaking their previous lives. However, much as in any religious cult, production of converts involved a radical kind of brainwashing, more euphemistically called reeducation.

Unexpected physical and psychological resistance to conversion (rebellion, murder, self-destructive behaviors, chronic depression, and a catastrophically low birth rate) by Indigenous peoples as well as unforeseen biological reactions to the introduction of European foods, plants and animals, diseases (measles, smallpox, syphilis, tuberculosis, alcoholism, suppressed immune systems) led to extension after extension of the initial deadline. Shoveling in more Indians from distant communities to replace the fallen was only a temporary solution. Result: 80 percent of California Indians dead in a sixty-year period. In the words of anthropologist and historian Robert Heizer, "The Franciscan missions in California were ill-equipped, badly managed places . . . To continue to feed the furnace would have required a [Spanish] military force of much greater power than was available to go further each year into the unconverted interior and bring back the human fuel." Despite Heizer's appraisal, the records of the missions themselves illustrate that even an endless supply of fresh Indians would not have changed the death rate, but merely prolonged the closing down of the factory. The bottom line is that individual missions were successful only for the missionaries, who spent their lives secure in the belief that they served their Supreme Deity faithfully and had done no wrong. Lesson learned: always know the limitations imposed by fuel availability.

Neofito (Neophyte)

1. A religious convert; a newly baptized Indian, or *Indio;* a subhuman, animal-like being from the region where a mission was being established, judged to be desperately in need of Spanish religion and discipline in order to earn a soul, become human, be saved from everlasting damnation. Like very young children, Indians lived by instinct and desire, not knowing what was best for them. Priests regarded themselves *in loco parentis,* fatherly overseers with the responsibility to instruct and guide in both temporal and spiritual matters. This state of childlike existence continued for the life of the *neofita,* who, even should she live to be one hundred years old and have children, grandchildren, and great-grandchildren, was never legally an adult and so could not leave the mission without written permission. Nor could she own land. Officially emancipated in 1836 by Mexico, declared citizens of the United States in 1924, are we grown up yet?

2. *They are born among the mountains and in the ravines like savages, feeding on wild seeds, and are without either agriculture or arts. In their pagan state the Indians . . . mated after the fashion of animals. Their superstitions are as numerous as they are ridiculous and are difficult to understand.*

VI

Habitants de Californie.

Figure 10. "Inhabitants of California"

3. Indigenous human beings who were loved to death by the Franciscan fathers. *The Indians . . . possess in a heroic degree, in eminent fashion, only the virtue of obedience . . . They cease to operate by themselves as if they were a corpse, neither more nor less. It is certain that a gardener, though he knew his business very well, would plant a vegetable in the ground upside down if the father commanded him. When the missionary desires to punish them all that is necessary is to order them to prepare themselves and they receive the strokes. The other virtues they do not know.*

4. *Bestias.* Lazy. Meek. Submissive. Humble. Timid. Docile. Obedient. Superstitious. Stupid. Ignorant. Children.

5. Feliciano María Quittit. Martina Josefa Tutuan. Santiago Ferriol Tocayo Maxya. Cunegunda María Malaxet. Juan Damansceno Yjaschan. María Nicolasa Yaccash. Yginia María Yunisyunis. Fructuoso de Jesús Cholom. Diodora María Mihausom. My ancestors.

Figure 11. Franciscan missionaries

Padre

> *"The neophyte community was like one great family, at the head of which stood the padre . . . To him the Indians looked for everything concerning their bodies as well as their souls. He was their guide and their protector."*
> —*Zephyrin Englehardt*

The padre baptized us, gave us names and godparents; he taught us our catechism, officiated at our first communion, posted our marriage banns, performed our weddings, baptized our babies, administered last rites, listened to our confessions; he punished us when we prayed to the wrong god or tired of our wives or husbands.

He taught us to sing (our own songs were ugly), he taught us to speak (our own languages were nonsensical), he made us wear clothes (our bodies were shameful), he gave us wheat and the plow (our seeds and acorns were fit only for animals).

Yes, that padre, he was everything to us Indians. At the giving end of a whip, he taught us to care for and kill cattle, work fields of wheat and corn and barley, make adobe walls for our own prisons, build the church, the *monjerio,* storerooms—promised it all to us if we would just grow up, pray hard enough, forget enough.

But it all went to Spain, to Rome, to Mexico, into the pockets of merchants, smugglers, priests, dishonest administrators and finally the cruel Americans. Nothing left for the children the padre had worked so hard to civilize, poor savages pulled from the fires of certain Hell. He was our shepherd, we were his beloved and abused flock; now the fields are eaten down to the earth, we claw the earth yet even the roots are withered, and the shepherd has gone away.

But we are pagans no more! Now we are Christian vaqueros, Christian housekeepers, Christian blacksmiths and shoemakers and laundry women and wet nurses and handymen—none of us paid with more than a meal or a shirt or a pair of discarded boots, but Christians. Poor Christians, drunken Christians, meek targets for forty-niners crazed by goldlust or ranchers hungry for land. We are homeless Christians, starving Christians, diseased and landless Christians; we are Christian slaves bought and sold in newspapers, on auction blocks in San Francisco, Los Angeles, one hundred dollars for a likely girl, fifty dollars for an able-bodied boy, free to whoever bails the old men out of jail: every one of us baptized by the padre, our primitive souls snatched from this Hell our bodies cannot escape, we are Christian, we are Catholic, we are saved by the padres and for that, Jesus Christ, we must be grateful.

"Dear Sonora": Writing to a Fourth Grader about Her Project

Starting at only $9.95

Perfect for 4th grade Mission school projects!
Very easy to build. You can paint it, trace it, adjust
size and use any materials you wish.

In 2012, the Ohlone/Costanoan-Esselen Nation received a request from a sharp fourth grader asking about the Native experience in California missions. Here is that letter, and our response.

Dear Ms. Ramirez,

I am a fourth grader and I am doing my report on Mission Nuestra Senora Dolorosisima de la Soledad. I discovered that Coastanoan and Essellen are some of the names of the tribes that went to the Soledad mission, and I was searching for some info on them when I stumbled across your email address on www.ohlonecostanoanesselennation.org. Me and my mom decided that maybe you could help us/me. Anyway, what I was searching for was the opinion of the Coastanoan and Esselen Native Americans. I want to know if the Native Americans liked the mission, which priests were their favorites . . . stuff like that, and I'm hoping you can help me. If you can help me, or even if you can't, thanks a ton!

Sincerely, Sonora

Dear Sonora (what a great name!),

My sister Louise passed your message on to me; she's very busy as Chair, and since I read about and study California missions in my job, she thought I might be able to help you out. I can tell you right away that writing to California tribes on your own is a smart move—many people don't think to ask us, or they think we are all dead. Still here!

You wanted to know the Ohlone/Esselen-Costanoan opinion of the missions. That's a tough question. Some Indian people will tell you that the missions were great, and brought us Catholicism and agriculture; others will tell you that anything that kills about 80 percent of your people can't be good.

California Indians were actually doing fine before the Spanish, Mexicans, and Americans arrived. Our ancestors had everything they needed, including Indian religions, leaders, music, languages, jobs, and education. But because our ancestors' traditions were different from the way Europeans did those things, lots of Spanish people thought Indians needed "civilizing." Of course, Indians were curious about the Spanish, and about their religion, and often helped the Spaniards find food and water, or exchanged things in trade with them, but that did not mean our ancestors wanted to become Spanish. People should be allowed to decide for themselves how they want to live.

Instead, the missionaries made that decision for our ancestors. Sometimes the Spanish priests would "baptize" women and children who came to visit, and then refuse to let them go. The husbands and fathers would come to get them, and were told that they could not see their families unless they, too, allowed themselves to be baptized. Of course, none of the Indians knew what baptism really meant, and when the priests then told them that, once baptized, they could not leave the mission, it was a big surprise. Remember, missionaries and soldiers thought of themselves as "civilized," so they figured THEY must be right and the Indians wrong. Civilized people don't hurt other people for being different, though. Many Indians today do not think the Spanish were very civilized.

The missionaries did a lot of things that hurt Indian people and families. For example, all little girls over the age of seven had to go sleep in the *monjerio*, a small building with no bathroom and small windows way up taller than anyone could reach. These rooms were dark, smelly, and dirty, and the young women and girls kept in there got sick from germs and lack of fresh air. They were also very homesick for their families. They didn't see their parents much, since during the day the parents were forced to work for the missionaries, doing all the work to build, maintain, and farm for the mission. Our ancestors were also forced to attend the Catholic church, learn prayers in a new language, and take new names in Spanish. None of the Indian ways of living—religions, leaders, music, languages, jobs, and education—were allowed by the Spaniards.

Also, I'm sorry to say, Indians at the mission were whipped with a very heavy, painful leather whip if they broke any of the priests' rules— and since Indians didn't know Spanish, and missionaries didn't know Indian languages, there were a lot of misunderstandings about what the rules were. Plus, of course, sometimes the Indians (who had taken very good care of themselves for thousands of years) didn't think Spanish rules made sense in the first place, so they would do things that were against the rules like gather wild food, go hunting, leave the mission to visit their families elsewhere, marry whom they wanted to marry, or other things they considered part of their rights as human beings. Spaniards punished Indians for doing these simple things with whippings or time in the stocks.

Over time, the European livestock and plants that the Spanish had brought with them to California took over the land, and many basic foods that Indians depended on were destroyed, so our ancestors became very dependent on the European foods from the missions. Our bodies sometimes could not handle this change in diet, which made it harder for us to get over small illnesses like colds and flu, and big illnesses like European smallpox, measles, and tuberculosis. So many Indians died in the missions that the padres had to keep sending Spanish soldiers out to capture more Indians to do the work of running cattle, farming, building, weaving, cooking, and doing all the chores a big mission requires.

You might be wondering, why would the Indians put up with all this? I suggest you look up things like "California mission rebellion" or "California mission revolt" on the internet (a better phrase would be "California Mission Wars," but you probably won't find anything using that search term—can you guess why?).

I think everyone, historians and Indians alike, agrees that missionization was a disaster for the Indians: our estimated population numbers went from about one million to fifteen thousand in just under two hundred years. We lost almost all of our land, all of our natural resources (which provided food and shelter); many of us lost our language, religion, and communities. Can you imagine if eight out of every ten people you know died when another group of people showed up and took over your town?

So mostly, the missions were not that much fun for Indians. An Indian baby born in a California mission lived only to be seven or eight years old; some disease or other would kill them before they could grow up. Also, because of a European strain of a disease called syphilis, many Indian men and women could no longer have babies, so there were no new kids to replace the people who died. Every time an old person died, it was like an entire library of knowledge, history, and stories burned down. That's tough to survive!

There were many bad consequences from the California missions for California Indians. Those bad consequences continued on through the Mexican era and into the American era. The hardest consequence was losing our homelands. The Spaniards made us move into the missions, but sixty-five years later when the missions closed down, all of our land had been taken by other non-Indian people. We had nowhere to go, no way to feed ourselves, no food, shelter, or clothing. Mexicans, who governed California after the Spanish, used Indians as free labor on their large ranches. For a meal and a place to sleep, Indians worked almost like slaves for the Mexicans, just to stay alive. Most mission Indian communities were broken up, and it was even harder for tribal members to stay connected than in the missions.

But as bad as that was, after the Mexican government came the American government, with laws that were even worse—American law prevented Indians from owning land, voting, or taking a white person to court for even the worst crimes against Indians. The US Congress passed a law giving millions of dollars to Americans to round up and kill Indians who were "in the way." In my family, we have stories about ancestors who answered a knock at the door, opened the door, and were shot for the bounty money! As late as 1866, Indians could be bought and sold just like slaves in the American South—and thousands were, especially women and children. Even Indians like my great-great-great-great-great grandfather, Fructuoso Cholom Real, who received land in a Mexican land grant after the missions were closed down, ended up losing their land to Americans.

But some of us did survive, and in California our communities are slowly growing and working to recover from those bad consequences. It's hard when many of us, like the Esselen, don't have any land (no reservation, no place to meet). Whenever we have our annual gathering, for example, we have to pay someone to use their land. So we don't have too many gatherings. This is one of the many consequences of the missions that continue into our lives today. Like several other California tribes, the Esselen are petitioning the US government for recognition—that means we would be eligible to get back a small piece of government "surplus" land in our homeland that we could use as a center, apply for educational scholarships that are only available to federally recognized tribes, and receive some basic health benefits.

It's funny, but even though I can prove that my family history was Indian all the way back to 1770, when the Spaniards started keeping paper records, the government still considers me "non-Indian"!

I hope you research hard and learn a lot about the missions and the California Indians who had to live there. It was a crazy time, a hard time, and a sad time. It's a miracle anyone survived at all. California Indians want our ancestors to be proud of us. We know we are here only because a few of them managed to survive, and used up all of their strength so we could live.

Oh—I realize that I didn't actually answer your question about favorite priests. The Spanish priests, and later the Mexican priests, were human beings with the same gifts and flaws as anyone else. So, like most people, some priests were considered "kind" and others were considered "mean." Father Serra, for instance, wrote in his letters about how much he loved the Indians, and how badly he felt when the Spanish soldiers hurt or killed Indians. But as kind as he seemed, Father Serra never questioned whether the missions should be built or maintained. He never thought to ask, as you did, Sonora, what Indians thought of the missions or the priests. He believed that the Spaniard's way of living was the ONLY way of living. So in his view, Indians who lived differently had to be made to change—even if it meant killing them, or spreading disease, or denying them human rights.

This way of thinking is called "colonization." Colonization, or in

California what we call "missionization," is a cruel and unkind way to treat other people. It means, basically, that a colonizer doesn't think Indians or Native people are really human beings. It is a very strange, selfish way of seeing the world.

Good luck with your report,
Deborah A. Miranda

A Few Corrections to My Daughter's Coloring Book

"Clever as they are at lassoing cows and mules, [soldiers] would catch an Indian woman with their lassos to become prey for their unbridled lust. At times some Indian men would try to defend their wives, only to be shot down with bullets . . . even the children who came to the mission were not safe from their baseness."
—Junípero Serra

Note use of passive voice to avoid saying enslaved Indians built it.

San Carlos Borromeo de Carmelo

In 1770, Fr. Serra left San Diego and went north to Monterey to establish his second mission, as planned. He selected a site near the presidio (soldier's quarters), but this proved to be a mistake. The Indians were uncomfortable so close to the Spanish soldiers. In addition, conditions were not good for producing the crops that were so necessary for the mission to survive. Fr. Serra moved his mission to a new site in the beautiful Carmel Valley. He used the Carmel location as headquarters for the entire chain of missions that were to develop. A wooden chapel and the needed buildings were erected in 6 months, but Fr. Serra's dream was to have a beautiful stone church. In 1791, a stone mason was imported for the task. The cornerstone was laid in 1793 and four years later the stone church was dedicated on the same site as the wooden church. After secularization, the church fell to ruin. The roof collapsed in 1851 and the walls stood unprotected from the elements until 1881 when funds were raised to put a shingled roof on the structure. The new roof did not improve the appearance very much, but it did serve the purpose of protecting the church from total ruin. Harry Downie has supervised the restoration of the mission to its present state. Considered to be the most beautiful of the California missions, it boasts a beautiful mountain and sea setting, sandstone walls, Moorish towers, and the famous striking star window above the arched doorway of the front entrance, with its huge hand carved doors. The Carmel site also boasts complete restoration of a mission quadrangle rather than just the church restoration.

Missionized Indians left to starve

Not to mention the missionized Indians abandoned and left homeless

Carved by whom?

But paving over the Indian cemetery and creating multimillion-dollar houses on top of our bones

Meanwhile, "civilized" soldiers and priests survived on "wild" food hunted and gathered for them by "wild Indians."

How about protecting the Indians from total ruin? Money spent on a building, rather than (Indian) human beings without food, shelter, clothing: beginning of California's Mission Mythology!

stolen land

California Indian population before missions: one million. Population after missions: twenty thousand or less.

Usually very poor men from Spain, many of whom were threatened with incarceration if they did not emigrate; mixed-blood Mexican/Spanish men from Baja California with little military training; carriers of syphilis, measles, smallpox; frequent rapists of Indian women

"Here then we have the greatest problem of the missionary: how to transform a savage race such as these into a society that is human, Christian, civil, and industrious." —Fr. Lasuén

Juliana, 1803

In California's Franciscan missions, girls who had passed their eighth year were housed in the monjerio, *in which they were confined under lock and key at night to protect their virtue. The* monjerio *also served as a training school in which girls and widows were confined much of the time.*

The iron lock turns at dusk, our parents on the other side in the mission village, us girls in this dark room. I've hated night for as long as I can remember.

When the padre came to our hut, told my mother I was old enough now, old enough to require the *monjerio*, she told me, "Remember the stars. Remember you'll see them again someday." But I've forgotten—are they silver, or gold? Which direction do they move? Where is the one my mother warned me was sly and mean-spirited? She told me once that blazing stars with long tails were souls on their way to the afterlife. I wonder if the sky burns all night now?

Some of the younger girls still miss their mothers, cry half the night, wet themselves. They keep the rest of us awake. I don't feel sorry for them; I hiss the curses I learned from the *soldados* to frighten them, make them shut up. The *pinche* workday is long enough without losing sleep too. I don't remember being that weak.

True, I had my two older sisters. For years they kept me tucked between them all night; if the door opened in the darkness, if soldiers picked the lock or stole the padre's key, or if the padre himself made one of his "inspections," Dolores pushed me behind her, Ines covered me with her blanket. Till they married those brothers and got out.

Now I lie awake at night, tuck my back into this corner I've claimed and defend when I have to. Smelling some poor woman's shit as she crouches over the trench in the corner, moaning that the posole this morning must've had rotten meat. My own bowels twist and boil, but please God let me make it till morning, and the privacy of a bush or hillside.

And I think about that soldier, Demetrio, the one who came with the San Blas Infantry from someplace called Mexico. The Spanish guards laugh at him, call him "*chulo*," which means, I think, half-breed. They ask him which jail the military pulled him out of, what crime did he commit, has he learned how to shoot an *escopeta*. They make him sound like a little boy. I know he's not.

Yesterday, on the path returning from the *lavanderia*, I hung back, pretended my basket of wet clothes was too heavy. He slipped me a string of dark red beads, my favorite, and said he would speak to the padre soon. Then he pressed against me, knocked my basket into the dirt, spilled all that hard work. He put his hairy mouth on mine. I couldn't move. Clara called my name, and he pushed me away, ducked back into the trees.

Tonight, I can still feel his hands clutching my breasts. I wonder. I wonder what it would be like, to see the stars again.

Dear Vicenta

"Vicenta Gutierrez, sister of 'The Blonde' Gutierrez, when [she was] a girl
went to confession one evening during Lent, and Father Real wanted her,
to grab her over there in the church. And next day there was no trace of the
padre there, and he was never seen again. He probably fled on horseback in
the night. Some said he fled to Spain. He was a Spaniard. He grabbed the girl
and screwed her. The girl went running to her house, saying the padre had
grabbed her."—Isabel Meadows

Dear Vicenta,

I'm sorry, because I don't know what to tell you. I could try to be funny and say, "Hey, guess that priest gave up celibacy for Lent, huh?" Or I could go for the crude wink, "I know what you gave up, honey!" That's how I've learned to deal with it. That's how I talk about what happened to me as a kid. I mean, it happens all the time, right? It's not just that we're women; we're Indian women . . . poor Indian women. The statistics on *that* are predictable. Thirty-four percent of us raped; one in three! And ninety percent of the rapists are non-Indian.

Well, I shouldn't complain. Those are stats from my day and age. For you, it's probably more like 100 percent. I've read the testimonies, the as-told-to stories. Funny thing, that. No one believes what you say. Or cares. Until over a century has passed and the damn guy is dead and buried and safe in his cozy little mission graveyard.

Now it's all legitimate research, figuring out how women survived the missions, how many rapes, how many self-induced abortions, how many infanticides, the Native medicines for birth control, the ravages of syphilis that caused sterility, and worse. Scholars write dissertations, sexual violence against colonized women is a real field of study, and what happened in the dark confessional or between the pews is suddenly outrageous, a weapon of colonization, not a shameful wound.

That Chumash guy, Fernando Librado—the one famous for providing J. P. Harrington with all that old-time information, even how to build a *tomol* from nothing? You can find those directions on the internet now. On websites for children, fourth graders studying the missions, looking for Indian words, how to grind acorns. He's a hero. He saved a culture from amnesia. That's what they tell the kids.

Fernando remembered a whole lot more than recipes, though. Even when no one else listened to him, Harrington wrote it down. The old Indios used to say, "That man would write down the Indian directions for scratching your ass," and it was true! Vicenta, here's what Fernando told:

> The priest had an appointed hour to go there. When he got to the nunnery [*monjerio*] all were in bed in the big dormitory. The priest would pass by the bed of the superior [*maestra*] and tap her on the shoulder, and she would commence singing. All of the girls would join in . . . when the singing was going on, the priest would have time

to select the girl he wanted, carry out his desires . . . in this way the priest had sex with all of them, from the superior all the way down the line . . . the priest's will was law. Indians would lie right down if the priest said so.

Guess we won't be teaching *that* to the fourth graders any time soon. (It happened to me way before fourth grade.)

Vicenta, I keep thinking of how you ran home, telling everyone what had happened. I have to tell you, girl, that was brave. I didn't tell for years and years.

And the priests were gods then, even though by the time that padre came to Carmel, they'd been dumped first by Spain, and then by Mexico. They still had the power. Even if you told, and you did, who would believe you? Who would care? Who would give you justice?

Nobody. Carmel was a ragtag bunch of mixed-blood Indians trying to survive, fighting over food, the very young and the very old the only ones left who hadn't died or gone off to celebrate their "emancipation" by working as maids or vaqueros at the ranchos. What could they do? The priests had all the power. They always did. It seemed as if they always would.

Isabel didn't forget you, though. One hundred years after the padre raped you in the church, Isabel told your story to Harrington. She told it like it happened yesterday. And she was *mad*. She used Spanish and a brutal English to make sure Harrington understood. Vicenta, she used the priest's *name*. "Padre Real."

And she used your name. She made certain we knew which family you belonged to, connected you with your brother.

Isabel told that story like it happened to her, or to her daughter. She told that story like she could bring down the wrath of God just by finding the right words.

Maybe she did, Vicenta. By not following the rules, the rules that said we don't talk about this stuff, we don't name names, we don't tell outsiders. Maybe she figured, "What's left to lose?" Everyone was telling her that extinction was right around the corner, and it sure as hell felt like it. So why not tell the whole story? Why just tell the stuff they can analyze in a monograph, simplify for their children when they learn about the exotic animals that used to live here?

"If we're going out," she might've thought, "we're going out with some guts!"

Isabel says Padre Real was gone the next morning. Maybe even gone back to Spain. That was wishful thinking. He left Carmel, all right, but he didn't go very far. Right around that time, historical records say, Father Real moved his home base from Carmel Mission to the chapel in Monterey, and from there to Mission Santa Cruz, where he tried to sell the church's land illegally as the Americans came flooding into the country. And then—he just vanishes from the record. Poof. Nothing.

Erasure is a bitch, isn't it?

Vicenta, I don't know if the fact that your story survives, that Isabel's angry words fight for your dignity and honor, really brings any kind of justice to you. Not the kind of hands-on justice I'd like, anyhow. When the Indians at Mission Santa Cruz killed their priest—a man known for his use of metal-tipped whips and thumbscrews—they made sure to rip off his testicles, too.

Now, those were some Indians who listened to the "eye for an eye" part of the Bible pretty good.

But the scribblings of an obsessed white man trying to record the memories of an aging Indian woman attempting to tell the story of an Indian girl's rape one hundred years before—can *this* change the world?

Maybe nothing can bring you justice after all this time, Vicenta. That's probably too much to ask. I hope for the basics: I hope someone was there for you when you ran home. Someone to hold you. Someone to help you clean yourself up. Someone who comforted you after the nightmares. I hope nobody told you it was your fault. I hope some old lady cussed out Father Real in front of the gossips.

And if no one did any of that for you, I hold onto this: Isabel remembered your story, and she told it to Harrington, and he told it to me, and I'm telling it to everyone I can find.

You told first.

Maybe that's why Isabel felt, of all the stories she knew about violation and invasion and loss, *your story* was the one to tell Harrington. She was proud of you. She respected you for refusing to shut up. She liked that you weren't a good Mission Indian. Maybe she even thought future Indian women could learn from you.

That 34 percent hasn't gone away since I started this letter.

Vicenta. If that was your name, the padre should have been more careful about giving it to you. Even in Spanish, it means "conquers."

Not conquered.

Nimasianexelpasaleki.

Isabel Meadows

Isabel Meadows in Washington, DC, circa 1934

The daughter of Loreta, granddaughter of María Ygnacia, great-grand-daughter of Lupicina Francisca Unegte, great-great-granddaughter of Celedonia Josefa Usari was born in Carmel Valley in July 1846, the same month that the American flag was raised over Monterey's Custom House. A child of a former whaler from England, James Meadows, and Loreta Onésimo, a member of a local Indian family, Isabel was a speaker of Rumsien Ohlone and Esselen, both languages of the Monterey coastal region. In the 1930s, Isabel became "a primary informant" of Smithsonian ethnologist J. P. Harrington. In her eighties, she accompanied Harrington to Washington, DC, for five years to continue their work on Carmel/Monterey/Big Sur cultures and languages; she died there in 1939.

Isabel never married and did not leave behind any direct descendants. We are related by marriage: Jacinto, one of her half-brothers through her mother's first marriage, married my great-great-great-grandmother Sacramento Cantua. Isabel also vouched for the Indian blood of many of my relatives on their 1928 BIA applications, using her thumbprint as "mark," or signature.

Witnesses to Mark	Signature of Witnesses
	Isabelle Meadows Mark
	Augustine Soto
Subscribed and sworn to before me this **21st**	da/ o
July, 19 **30**.	*Fred A Baker*
My commission expires	Examiner of Inheritance.

Meadows knew she was a valuable resource to Harrington; he returned to her again and again, pleaded with her to work with no one else, snapped up the bits and pieces of cultural information and language she fed him. But in between the language lessons and Coyote stories Harrington was after, Isabel snuck in the stories *she* wanted to salvage: her own private project, a memorial, and a charmstone of hope for future generations.

I see Vicenta's story as a precursor to modern Native Literature, a stepping-stone between oral literacy and written literature. The women of her community heard and remembered her story, but how could it survive beyond their lifetimes? Isabel seemed to understand that in a perilous time, Vicenta's narrative had to enter into that written realm, leave the community of Indian women in order to return to us someday—as it turns out, almost two hundred years after it happened. To me, this means that Isabel herself knew the power of story, and believed in our survival—in the future, there would be Indian women who would need this story! I regard the field notes that J. P. Harrington took while working with Isabel Meadows as her body of work: her engagement in the creative use of words, literacy, and empowerment on behalf of her community.

Isabel's story also serves as a teaching device for contemporary California Indian women—for me, my sisters, our daughters. Isabel and

Vicenta's story passed down through California Indian women to California Indian women is as potent as any coming-of-age ceremony, as medicinal as any gathering of women's herbs, as healing as any grandmother's caress of a fevered forehead. Through the vehicle of this field note we are engaged in a very Indigenous practice: that of storytelling as education, as thought-experiment, as community action to right a wrong, as resistance to representation as victim. Isabel preserves and praises Vicenta's brave act and exhorts women of her generation, and the women who will one day read Harrington's notes, to claim that kind of self-awareness. We are valuable human beings, she tells other Native women: our bodies are sacred, and we *have a right* to speak out against violence and violation.

The People Before

a found poem from the stories of Isabel Meadows

The people from before,
they were so old
they grew like mountains.

* * *

The people before didn't cure
themselves with doctors.
They cured themselves
only with herbs
from the countryside
and with songs.

* * *

There were wild strawberries
on the Carmel River banks,
lots of them. Sweeter
than tame strawberries.

* * *

Omecía knew the names
of the constellations. She knew
the Siete Cabrillas,
and told which ones
come out in the summer.

* * *

The people here
did not say Don, Señor,
but always Tio, Tia,
or some relationship
name, though they were not
relations. Even to the Americans,
they applied such terms.

* * *

At El Monte del Diablo,
Fortunato beat the devil
out of all the Indians
gambling there
and at San Antonio.
When dancing, he used
to make a big toad
come hopping out
of the fire.

* * *

And they made *cayucos*,
canoes, before. Of tules.
There used to be a big lake
just this side of the Carmelo mission
in the time of Junípero,
and the padre used to like
to go out to ride
en el cayuco, on that lake
on Sundays. The Indian boys
would take him out.
The *cayuco* was woven
of tules, I don't know how.

* * *

When they hung her son,
Santiago Tíkes,
from an oak that still
stands, Omecía threw down
her *azadón*
where she was hoeing
and cried, *They tear it,*
they eat it,
they swallow our flesh,
the Americans.

* * *

A deer will attack
a person   bringing both
front feet down
upon him,
and they cut.

* * *

Arnicio Tiquez once killed
an elk at El Peñón
and had it hanging up
at his house. We looked
on it with fear;
I remember seeing it
as if in a dream.
My brother later found
the skeleton of an elk
in the hills. I think
it must have been
the compañero of the last elk
that was killed at Monterey.

* * *

My mother knew how
to say a prayer
for the repose of the soul
of him that buried
a treasure—
that's the way that one
should do.

* * *

My mother told me
that the Indians,
when they went out to work,
took a little stick
and when the shadow
of it was very straight,
it was midday,
and they ate where they were
in the *potrero*.

              * * *

Ignacia Cornelio,
my grandmother, was the one
that cooked *pozole*
at the mission, carried
their *lonche of trigo*,
maiz, *chicharo*,
or *garbancillo*.
The indios sat on the ground,
ate using clam shells
as spoons.

              * * *

If I had known how to write,
I would have written up the life
of those Indians.

              * * *

If they had not all died,
the Indians here,
the country would be full
of them, telling stories.

Notes, Isabel Meadows speaking to Smithsonian ethnologist J. P. Harrington, 1935, about my great-great-great-great-great aunt Estéfana Real's son Victor, born March 1846

Isabel [consultant]

Mar. 1934

Estéfana Real had many husbands. Her children had many fathers—they were *joteras*, the old ladies before.

Isabel

Mar. [19]37

understands "*joteras*" above to mean that the old women were very macho. But no, the real reason Isabel used "*jotera*" in 34 was because Estéfana had a son, Victor Acedo, who was a *joto*. The old lady Estéfana never said nothing, or she didn't know, maybe, that her son, Victor, was a *joto*. This was why in '34 Isabel spoke of Estéfana as very macho, she had a son who was a *joto*.

Harrington R73:282 B

Cousins

(for Victor)

We dressed in skirts of tule or deerskin, worked hard, side by side with our sisters: gathering and pounding acorns with pestles into the bedrock slabs, weaving tight baskets and caring for the sick child or wandering toddler. We shared secrets about men, stories about lovers, remedies for broken hearts.

Our sisters opened the way for the next generation, gave birth to the tribe's future with each squalling, hungry voice; it was dangerous work, but they had charms of creation inscribed in their spirits and flesh. We midwifed the dead, carried each body tenderly from this world to the next without risking contamination; always in two worlds at once, poised between, we kept our balance on those slippery paths between life and death.

Then the soldiers came, the priests came, christened us *joyas,* jewels, laughing at how our tribes treated us—sodomites, *nefando pecados, mujerados*—as treasures. Treasures? They called us monsters. *Joya* was a joke. But we had other names before that: *aqi, coia, cuit, uluqui*, endearments only the ancestors remember.

In the missions, we were stripped bare, whipped, made to sweep the plaza for days, pointed at, cursed. "In the south, we fed your kind to our dogs," soldiers grinned, and stroked the heads of their mastiffs.

Worst of all, threatened with beatings, our own husbands disowned us, children grew to fear us, and our sisters, oh, our sisters turned us away.

Some of us fled into the mountains, died alone. Some found new homes in bands not yet captured by soldiers or starvation, tried to forget the violations. Some of us, unable to escape the missions, hid amongst the men, passed as *just* men, tried to whisper our knowledge to a few survivors, pass on the negotiations with death which life requires.

We weren't trying to save ourselves. We were trying to save the world.

But we disappeared, murdered or heartbroken, and the end of the world came anyway.

When all of the burying baskets and digging sticks were burnt, when only the shame remained with its stench of fear, we became *jotos.* When our names were forgotten, our responsibilities forgotten, when we lost the gift of swimming in that liquid space between life and death, we became *jotos*. Our families despised us, old women gossiped about us. If our mothers fought to protect us, they were called *joteras*. If our names were recorded by history, it was only to reiterate our sins. If our bodies survived, our spirits were poisoned by ignorance and grief.

How strange it is, now, to hear young voices calling to us. Calling out names we have not heard since the baptismal font in the mission yard, names like *Coutesi, Liuixucat, Yautaya*, recorded alongside *armafrodita, joya, amugereado*. Who remembers us? Who pulls us, forgotten, from beneath melted adobe and groomed golf courses and asphalted freeways, asks for our help, rekindles the work of our lives? Who takes up the task of weaving soul to body, carrying the dead from one world to the next, who bears the two halves of spirit in the whole vessel of one body?

Where have you been? Why have you waited so long? How did you ever find us, buried under words like *joto,* like *joya,* under whips and lies? And what do you call us now?

Never mind, little ones. Never mind. You are here now, at last. Come close. Listen. We have so much work to do.

In this photograph, undated but marked "Monterey natives," two Indian men stand side by side, identified as Victor Acedo and "Kitus Cantu." Victor (born "Nestor Bitoreano Antonio") was baptized on March 4, 1846, as an infant. He was the son of my 4x great-aunt, Estefana Real, and her second husband, José Acedo. Estefana's sister, Teodosia, married Ventura Cantua, cantor at Mission San Carlos. Isabel Meadows tells us that "the son of Ventura & of Teodosia was nicknamed Quitos, his real name was José Antonio" (72:261A). "Kitus Cantu," then, is most likely José Antonio Cantua, baptized January 19, 1849, at about a month old. Isabel noted that around Monterey, however, it was known that Ventura was not Quitos's biological father.

The Genealogy of Violence, Part II

My little brother loses a tooth during a rough wrestling session with our forty-five-year-old bear of a father. Blood spills out of Little Al's round mouth, a lower tooth hangs, comes out in his hand when he reaches up. He is frightened by the sudden hole in his gums, the bright warning color of his spit, the sudden jolt that reverberates from lower jaw through his small body.

Parents love their children extremely. They seek every kind of way to feed them. They would rather suffer want themselves than to see their children in need.—Mission San Diego

---

Our father scoffs, pushes his small four-year-old son, says, "Aw, it's just a damn tooth, come on, no crying." I'm sitting at the kitchen table, trying to finish a report on Pearl Harbor for my eighth grade social studies class. I'm totally absorbed in proving the stunning (to me) fact that Franklin Roosevelt knew about and in fact encouraged American vulnerability to Japanese "sneak" attacks, but something in the tone of my brother's voice snakes into my gut and wakes me out of my academic fog. Our father's voice is harsher now, making fun of the tears. "Ay, little baby, only babies cry! Are you a baby?"

When it concerns the children . . . their parents love them to such an extent that we might say they are their little idols.
—Mission San Gabriel

There is a chasm between these two male Mirandas, a chasm that shouldn't be there—both so brown, so Indian, so dear to me. I rise from the kitchen table where I am working, rise so fast that my chair, with its torn plastic covering and raw metal feet, tips over behind me, crashes to the linoleum floor of our trailer. "No, Daddy, no!" Little Al sobs, "I sorry, I sorry," and there is the horrifying sound of a belt buckle being flipped open, the clinks of metal on metal, the dull *ziiiiipp!* of a leather belt being pulled angrily through the hard denim loops of my father's Levis.

Toward their children they show an extravagant love whom they do not chastise. Nor have they ever chastised them but allow them to do whatever they please. We know now, however, that some are beginning to chastise and educate them due to the instructions they are receiving.—Mission San Miguel

"You want something to cry about? You want the belt?" our father yells, embarrassed by his cowardly son, this son he waited half a lifetime to have, this son who carries on the family name as none of his seven sisters can, this son whose tears break every rule my father ever learned about surviving in this world. Before I can take the ten steps from kitchen to living room, my father has seized my little brother by his plump arm, swung him around across the lap that should be comfort, should be home, should be refuge, and is swinging the doubled belt with such force that the air protests; the arc of my father's arm is following a trajectory I know too well, the arc of leather, sharp edges of cured hide, instrument of punishment coming from two hundred years out of the past in a movement so ancient, so much a part of our family history that it has touched every single one of us in an unbroken chain from the first padre or the first *soldado* at the mission to the bared back of the first Indian neophyte, heathen, pagan, savage, who displeased or offended the Spanish Crown's representatives.

They likewise love their children; in fact, it can be said that this love is so excessive that it is a vice, for the majority lack the courage to punish their children's wrongdoings and knavery.—Mission San Antonio

Flogging. Whipping. Belt. Whatever you call it, this beating, this punishment, is as much a part of our inheritance, our legacy, our culture, as any bowl of acorn mush, any wild salmon fillet, *pilillis* fried and dipped in cinnamon and sugar, cactus fruit in a basket. More than anything else we brought with us out of the missions, we carry the violence we were given along with baptism, confession, last rites. More than our black hair, brown eyes, various hues of brown skin flecked with black beauty marks, our short stubby fingers, our wide feet and palms, our sweet voices and tendency to sing, to dance, to make music and tell stories.

In this trailer in the woods, just outside a small town called Kent in Washington State, hundreds of miles from California, where the three of us were each born, my father's arm rises and falls in an old, savage rhythm learned from strangers who came with whips and attack dogs, taught us how to raise our children.

Some parents who are a little better instructed punish their children as they deserve while others denounce them to the missionary fathers or to the alcaldes.—Mission San Antonio

---

Bridges: Post-Secularization
1836–1900

Lies My Ancestors Told for Me

Riddle: when is a lie the truth?
when is the truth a lie?
When a lie saves your life,
that's truth; when a lie saves the lives
of your children, grandchildren
and five generations forward,
that's truth in a form so pure
it can't be anything
but a story.

After the mission broke
up, it was better to lie
like a dog about blood,
say you are Mexican
Mexican Mexican Mexican
put it on the birth certificates
put it on the death certificates
tell it to the census takers
tell it to the self-appointed
bounty hunters who appear
at your door looking for
Indians Indians Indians
and when you tell that lie
tell it in Spanish.

Give your children Spanish
names—Tranquilino, María Ignacia,
Dolores, Faustino—
lies that deflect genocide,
so tell them loudly
at the baptismal font in the Old Mission,
to the Indian Agent collecting bodies
for the Boarding School at Riverside;
broadcast the names in the street
like wheat when you call

your Mexican children in at dusk
for a bite of acorn mush
and cactus apple.

Grandmothers, dress like a poor white
woman—in other words, like a Mexican.
Wear their heavy aprons, high-necked
muslin dresses, and shoes
shoes shoes shoes.
Shame your grandchildren
when they run around
barefoot, what are you,
an Indian? and stand
silent, approving, when *Digger*
becomes their favorite
slur to hurl at the youngest,
the awkward, the slow,
the dark. Don't tell them
you still speak Chumash
with their mother. That's a lie
your descendants will hate you for
but lie anyway,
so they'll be alive
to complain.

Grandfathers, lie
about where you're going
when you slip out at night,
retrieve your dancing clothes
from the hiding place,
drive up unlit roads
to a rancheria in the hills
where clappers and rattles
whisper the truth
and bare Indian feet
beat against the earth
beat beat beat like children begging
to be let back inside.

Don't teach old songs
to your grandchildren,
don't make the regalia
in front of them, don't
dance where young eyes
might see. Sing the *alabada*
when the priests can hear;
hum the Deer Song when they can't.
Drag your feet in the dust;
buy a tie for Sundays.
Tell the lies now and maybe later
your descendants will dig
for the truth in libraries,
field notes, museums,
wax cylinder recordings,
newspaper reports of massacres
and relocations, clues you left behind
when you forgot
to lie
lie lie lie.

Ularia's Curse

"Pero la maldición de la Ularia cayó en la familia de los Sarchens."

—Isabel Meadows to J. P. Harrington

Isabel says it was Ularia's curse that killed Sargent. The American ran Estéfana and her children off the land at Rancho El Potrero—that same land awarded to Estéfana's parents, Fructuoso Cholom and Yginia María Yunisyunis, by the Mexican Governor Alvarado after the mission was shut down; the very land where Echilat, the village of Fructuoso's mother, his maternal grandparents, and his great-grandmother, had existed long before the mission was a gleam in Padre Serra's eye. The American told Estéfana, "Those signatures are no good anymore; Indians can't own land."

Estéfana and the other displaced Indians she had taken into her home carried their few belongings to the banks of the Carmelo River. They camped there a few days, paralyzed by grief and anger, wept themselves hollow with frustration. "And then," Isabel says, "they dispersed."

Ten years later, Sargent fell into the Carmelo River while herding his cattle across during a storm. He became ill, and a few days later, he died.

Isabel says what happened was Ularia had cursed Sargent that day ten years before, sitting there on the banks of the river, her worn skirts heavy and wet with rain and mud, her hair burnt short in mourning. She didn't have much left to work with—no bundles of mugwort, no roots, no cocoon rattle, not even a clapperstick. She was just an old Indian woman, beaten by soldiers, chastised by priests, her last grown child hung from the big oak as a horse thief by the Americans. She was cast off, discarded. She wanted to abandon her old woman's body, even if the Spaniards *had* killed all the two-spirited *joyas* and left not one to carry her past the dangerous male and female gods that guarded the path to the Ancestors.

But out of habit, Ularia leaned down, her spine crackling with age, and scooped a handful of Carmel's clear water in her palm, brought it to her lips, drank it down. She tasted the cold roots of mountains off to the north. She felt the sharp grit of river sand in her worn molars, sparkle of a stray flake of gold, scales of a little fish on her tongue. And Ularia remembered: the river would be here long after she was gone.

"Will you miss us, River?" she wondered. "Will you miss our feet on your riverbed, our twined fishing nets combing your waters, our sacrifice of the first salmon every year?"

Isabel says the river must have said yes, because where else would Ularia have gotten the idea? She reached down, plucked a smooth round stone from beneath the water, spoke to it in the old language. She gathered salt from the estuary to the west, a gritty sand mixed with ocean and fresh-water spirits. She added charcoal from that last fire built on the river's banks by the refugees, great oaks reduced to ashes. She smudged the curse in the scent of toasted chia seeds made for the journey away, the scorched redbud of the basket that held them. Ularia made that curse of mud, the decomposing body of our mother black and thick enough to trip even a strong stock horse; she made that curse from slick water weeds that can tangle a man's legs, pull him down beneath the surface; she made that curse out of a rainstorm's rage, conjured waves ten years hence into heavy walls that would fall like the stones of a church in an earthquake.

The Americans say Ularia cursed the river. But Isabel says no; Ularia wouldn't do that. Isabel says Ularia gave the river the idea to curse Sargent. But rivers tell time differently than people, and so it took ten years before the river finished what Ularia had begun. Ularia was long since dust on the day the river took Sargent, took his life from him like that, drank him down, and cleansed itself of his greed.

Isabel says wherever they are, she's sure Ularia's bones are laughing.

"The Diggers"

Oscar Penn Fitzgerald (1829–1911), a Southern Methodist minister, was sent from North Carolina to California as a missionary by his denomination in 1855. He stayed for more than twenty years and was appointed state superintendent of public education in 1867 despite the pro-Southern position he had taken during the Civil War. Returning to the East in the late 1870s, Fitzgerald edited the *Nashville Christian Advocate* for twelve years and was appointed a Southern Methodist bishop. *California Sketches*, first published in 1878, offers brief anecdotes about Fitzgerald's experiences in the mid-1850s as a pastor of churches in the gold mining town of Sonora and in Santa Rosa and Santa Clara, and as editor of the *Pacific Methodist Advocate* in San Francisco.

Excerpt from *California Sketches,* by O. P. Fitzgerald

The Digger Indian holds a low place in the scale of humanity. He is not intelligent; he is not handsome; he is not very brave. He stands near the foot of his class, and I fear he is not likely to go up any higher. It is more likely that the places that know him now will soon know him no more, for the reason that he seems readier to adopt the bad white man's whisky and diseases than the good white man's morals and religion. Ethnologically he has given rise to much conflicting speculation, with which I will not trouble the gentle reader. He has been in California a long time, and he does not know that he was ever anywhere else. His pedigree does not trouble him; he is more concerned about getting something to eat. It is not because he is an agriculturist that he is called a Digger, but because he grabbles for wild roots, and has a general fondness for dirt. I said he was not handsome, and when we consider his rusty, dark-brown color, his heavy features, fishy black eyes, coarse black hair, and clumsy gait, nobody will dispute the statement. But one Digger is uglier than another, and an old squaw caps the climax.

"Digger Belles"

"My dad called us Mission Indians," my father told me. "He hated being called Mexican. Mission Indians—but at school, out on the street, sometimes they called us Diggers—like nigger."

What is a Digger Indian, exactly? The term comes up over and over again in newspaper articles and government documents from the gold rush and the late nineteenth century, in the Riverside Indian School records, and in stories told by old-timers like my grandfather Tom.

I came across this image, "A Digger Belle," in *The Argonauts of 'Forty-nine* by David Rohrer Leeper (1832–1900). Leeper left Indiana for California, traveling overland, in 1849. His memoir details his journey and his experiences prospecting at Redding's Diggings, Hangtown, and the

From *The Argonauts of 'Forty-nine* (1894)

Trinity River and lumbering in northwest California. He illustrated the book with sketches of "Digger Indians" in tribal garb from his personal collection.

This "Digger Indian" woman's portrait, drawn from a photograph, tells a story, and tells it with devastating strokes. At first glance, the woman's hair seems to be a prophetic look forward to the punk do's of the 1980s, with their spiky crowns and elaborate, tiny, decorated braids. But this wasn't a traditional California Indian style; even as my initial smile fades, I realize with horror that this woman had probably cut or burnt her hair close sometime in the recent past, the most likely reason being a traditional act of mourning. Her full breasts indicate she is a young woman in the prime of life, perhaps even a young mother (if so, where is her baby?). A typical skirt woven of tule or grasses sits at her waist, and her hands are clasped in front of her in a pose that seems to me both passive and resistant. Her gaze meets the eye of the camera lens head on, her eyebrows slightly drawn, her lips firmly closed.

The nature of photography silences in a peculiar way, crowding out all senses but the visual. Yet I do not see the classic "stoic" Indian in this face; I see deep grief, and desperation, and the burning of the kind of strength that emerges when all else fails.

The term "Digger" (never an actual tribe, but often used as such by government officials and in the vernacular of the day) referred mostly to Northern California Indians, peoples who had not been missionized by the Franciscans but instead endured the gold rush. (Indians from the San Francisco area knew both edges of the sword.) If this woman was in or near the goldfields in '49, she was in the middle of one of the bloodiest genocides ever documented, one approved and funded by the United States government.

In 1851 and 1852, Congress appropriated and paid out over one million dollars in bounties to white men who harvested Indian scalps from the California goldfields—scalps taken from men, women, and children by men eager to make easy money. April Moore, a Nisenan Maidu and educator, says of that time period:

> And at one point it was something in the neighborhood of $25 for a
> male body part, whether it was a scalp, a hand, or the whole body;
> and then $5 for a child or a woman. In many cases, they only had to
> bring in the scalp. And in other cases, the whole body was brought in

to prove that they had this individual, they'd killed this person, and receive their reward.

And it was well after 1900 when the law was repealed, that bounty hunting, or whatever you may want to call it, on the California Indians was repealed. It was shortly after the discovery of Ishi that the nation, or I should say the state, became aware of the fact that it was still legal to kill Indians—so that the law had to be changed.

More patient bounty hunters had other uses for women and orphaned children; they sold them as slaves—yes, true slavery existed in California, and persisted until after the end of the Civil War. In fact, most white households throughout the state had at least one Indian slave, and often several. Many Indians had been enslaved to work in the gold rush camps of whites, including the infamous John Sutter of Sutter's Mill. In 1844 Pierson Reading, one of John Sutter's managers, wrote, "The Indians of California make as obedient and humble slaves as the Negro in the south. For a mere trifle you can secure their services for life." Young girls, of course, were bought up by single men, for about a hundred dollars apiece.

In 1857 the California State Legislature issued bonds for $410,000 for the "suppression of Indian hostilities," a euphemism for continuing the bounty system. Ultimately, California approved over $1 million in such bounties.

Involuntary labor by Indians was a crucial, endemic part of California's Anglo-American economy. In his book *Indians of California: The Changing Image,* James Rawls writes that "although forced recruitment and Indian peonage were part of life at the missions and ranchos, the actual buying and selling of California Indians was an American innovation." Indians were "free," but must be employed full-time; thus, California's 1850 "Act for the Government and Protection of the Indians" allowed any white person bailing out an Indian (jailed for vagrancy) to compel that Indian to work for him. In 1860 this law was expanded so that anyone who wanted an Indian child could simply appear before a judge with a list of names and have the judge sign it. "The main markets for Indian children, other than in the northern counties themselves, were in the counties of the Sacramento Valley and the San Francisco Bay Area," Rawls notes; these children worked as domestic servants in white households or in white-owned businesses. They were not paid, and in many cases endured severe abuse. In 1862 this law was repealed, but as the *California Police Gazette* noted in 1865, Indians were still being held "as slaves were held in the South; those owning them use them as they please, beat them with clubs and shoot them down like dogs." In 1866 a special investigator for the commissioner of Indian Affairs found that Indian slavery was "not uncommon" in California.

Slavery and murder were bad enough, but thousands more Indians simply starved to death as their food resources were devoured by miners or trashed by gold mining techniques that reduced ecosystems to poisoned mud and rock.

So when I see this woman's image, see the title "Digger Belle," I am stunned by what she has survived, and I wince at her probable fate. Was she paid to sit for the photograph, or simply forced? Paid in money, or food? Released afterwards, or returned to her owner? And if released, what home, what homeland, what community, did she have to return to?

Her fierceness—her face a mask of hardness and suspicion—burns through the photographer's lens and artist's hands.

The term "belle," with its connotations of civilization and domesticated females with the sole purpose of serving as objects for male enjoyment, seems to have been a widespread joke in California—sarcasm, irony, mean-spirited derision of Indian women.

Here is another example, titled "The Belles of San Luis Rey"—three elderly Indigenous women seated in the ruins of Mission San Luis Rey.

When I searched the internet for more information about the elders featured in this photograph, I found an original for sale with the following blurb:

WAITE, C. B. The Belles of San Luis Rey. All over 100 yrs old. Indian Women, ca. 1895, gelatin silver print, 20.4 x 12.3 cm, on mount. Photograph no 140. Slightly faded. Offered for EUR 81.75 = appr. US $129.08 by: KRUL Antiquarian Books - Book number: 27715.

Exorbitant amounts of money are made from the ruins of Native lives, and that angers me. Somehow, I doubt if any of the women pictured here received even a fraction of that price for the taking of their images.

I also found that this image had been marketed as a popular hand-tinted postcard in the early 1900s. One copy, which was not for sale, carried a message written by "Harvey," scribbled around the edges: "This is a joke on the Mission bells so much talked of out here." How easy it is to recast human beings as objects, and mythologized objects at that! The Camino Real, or King's Highway, that connects the chain of twenty-one missions is marked throughout the state with identical "mission bells" on hooked poles; they alert tourists to nearby spectacles and mission activities and remind all who travel that road that they tread the paths of truly

admirable and historic men. If a "Mission Bell" is an icon of touristic pleasure, then to be a "Mission Belle" is to also be marked as a commodity,
female (thought not human): marketable, a product for brief enjoyment.

"The Three Belles of San Luis Rey" photograph also turns up in
Oceanside: Where Life Is Worth Living, one of those local histories sponsored by chamber of commerce committees. Oceanside is the town now
located near Mission San Luis Rey. I contacted Kristi Hawthorne, author
of this book, who generously shared with me a newspaper article she'd
uncovered. The photograph of the three elders was featured above the
article, with the caption "Rosaria, Tomása, Vaselia."

DAILY NEWS

OCEANSIDE BLADE

The Belles of San Luis Rey

At the time the photograph was taken, the
combined ages of the trio exceeded 300 years.
So far as we can learn, no one knows just how
old they were. Rosaria came from the Santa
Margarita and for years lived at San Luis Rey
until her death last year. Tomása is known
to be more than a hundred years old and is
put by some above 130. She claims that she
packed "dobes" when the mission was built,
and, as its construction was begun the first
decade of the present century, there is little
ground for doubting that she is, at least, in her
second century teens. She was the mother of a
large progeny, some of whom lived to be very
old, she surviving them all, as is the case with
Rosaria and Vaselia. At the present time she is
totally blind and has been for several years.
Vaselia is the youngest. They live by themselves
at the rancheria on the north side of the river
near San Luis Rey mission, and subsist chiefly
by begging, being quite able to get about, in
fact, are still so strong that the loads of wood
they will carry on their backs would stagger an
ordinary man not used to heavy burdens.

Ms. Hawthorne shared that this photograph, still very well known in the San Luis Rey area, came up as a difficult topic in her interview with Luiseño elder and keeper of culture Louise Munoa Foussat, who died in 2005. Foussat had always been offended by the newspaper's use of the word "beggars" to describe the three women, she told Hawthorne, asserting instead that in exchange for spare change, the women would tell stories to visitors and pose for pictures—not begging at all, but a straight-forward, above-board business transaction. In fact, if anyone came up short in that exchange, it was Tomasa, Rosaria, and Vaselia. When writing her book, Ms. Hawthorne stated, she wanted to honor Foussat's percep-tive retelling of an inaccurate history, so she substituted "tour guides" for "beggars" when writing about the photograph.

I wrote back, thanking her for making that choice, even though her euphemism was not entirely true either; the complications of mission-ization are not so easily unknotted, and such rhetorical changes cannot entirely discredit destructive mythologies. But the beginning of aware-ness is good to see.

This image of these three women about whom we have such limited information—their first names (baptismal, not Indigenous), a fragment of their story—intrigues me, breaks my heart, haunts me. I have so many questions. What kind of housing did the "Three Belles" have on the ran-cheria? How many tribal members shared that land with them? How did they earn money during the rainy season, when no tourists visited? What were their last names, were they ever married, what happened to their children, do they have any living descendants?

One of the stories I read in the "Digger Belle's" face, in the faces of Tomasa, Rosaria, and Vaselia, is bottom-of-the-barrel, end-of-the-line, tenacious survival. If not of the land, or tribe, or language, or soul, then at least—oh God at least—survival of the body. For just a little while longer, survival.

Sometimes all you can do is sell what you've got. Your face. Your breasts. Your Otherness. Your frailty. Your story.

Or the story people with money want to hear.

Burning the Digger I (Newspaper Article)

In *Five Views: An Ethnic History Site Survey for California*, Dwight Dutschke writes, "In April 1922, the Miwok Indians of the Jackson Valley held a 'Big Time,' which is a gathering of all Indian people in the area for social or ceremonial reasons. This particular Big Time attracted many Indians from the surrounding region, especially from the Ione, Tuolumne, and Jackson areas. On April 20, a dummy, made of old clothes and stuffed with straw, was burned as an effigy for the name "Digger." Prior to the burning of the Digger, the Miwok Indians, also called Mewuk and Mewok, had been named Digger Indians by the federal government."

Indians Score Victory after Government Eliminates Name Digger from Official Use

After the "Burning of the Digger," as this event was called, the Commissioner of Indian Affairs issued a statement that appeared in the *California Indian Herald:*

Hereafter the term "Digger" as representing the name of a tribe of Indians in the Sacramento jurisdiction, and appearing in the records of this Bureau, will be discontinued, objections having come from others that this term is one of contempt and regarded by the Indians as humiliating and opprobrious. It will, therefore, be replaced by the name "Mewuk" which, upon accepted ethnological authority, is the true tribal designation of these Indians.

The name change resulted from an appeal made by the Indian Board of Co-operation and nine of its delegates. As Dutschke further explains, "Today, the Place Where They Burnt the Digger is important to the Miwok [because] it represents official recognition of the Miwok Indians and their cultural tradition."

Burning the Digger II

Strike
the match,
yellow-blue
flame
cupped
in your callused
hand.
Let it eat air—
hungry, unfulfilled.
Touch it
to dirty straw feet,
dry as hatred.
Watch flames
sizzle up lazy legs,
smoke seep out
of filthy pants. Burn
poverty
of that cotton,
pop lice
like delusions.
Burn
gluttony, thirst
for alcohol,
lust for white women.
Burn that spineless
body, burn
those ape-like arms,
burn that beastly
face. Oh
let black
smoke rise
above our heads
like a smudge,
wrap around
our limbs,

bless us.
Lean in.
Let heat singe
your hair. Wail
lost names, but
do not cry.
You know
this death has been
a long time
coming.
You know
this death
is a good one.

Ishi at Large

A found poem from the article "Strange-Voiced Whale at Large in the Ocean" (Reuters, December 8, 2004)

A lone whale,
with a voice unlike any other,
has been wandering

the Pacific for the past
twelve years,
singing at a frequency

of around 25 hertz. Its calls
do not match those of any
known species of whale,

which usually sing
at frequencies of between
15 and 20 hertz.

The mammal does not follow
migration patterns
of any other species either.

The calls of the whale,
which roams the ocean
every autumn and winter,

have deepened slightly
as a result of aging,
but are still

recognizable.

Old News

It is difficult
to get the news from poems
yet men die miserably every day
for lack
of what is found there.

—William Carlos Williams, "Asphodel, That Greeny Flower"

1.
Sacramento Union, November 14, 1851

A disturbance
took place at Los Angeles
on the evening of the 25th.

Indians got into a quarrel
over a bottle of liquor
and attacking the guard,
drove them off
the ground.

Sepulveda, the Marshal,
finding that he could not
contend with the Indians
and that they appeared determined
to burn the house
came to town
for assistance
and returned with
seven Americans.

How many of the Indians
were killed is perhaps not
positively known but
eight bodies were piled up
before Ivarra's house.

The verdict
of the Coroner's jury
was "that the deceased
came to their deaths
while resisting a sheriff's posse
and that the killing
was justifiable."

Among the killed
was the Indian Coyote.
He is represented
to have fought
with great desperation.

2.
Sacramento Daily Democratic State Journal, Sept. 1, 1855

A white man bargained
with an Indian

to give the latter a horse
for a squaw.

The Indian,
not being able to suit

him from the stock of squaws
under his control,

went over and stole
a squaw from the Applegate Tribe.

Big Tom,
the white man,

was so well pleased
with the stolen squaw

that he would not give her up
to her people

when required, notwithstanding
he was urged thereto

by his partner
and the other whites.

The consequence was
the massacre of all the whites

by the Indians
and to mark

their particular animosity
against Big Tom

they cut him up
into a thousand pieces

refraining
at the same time

from mutilating
the others.

3.
San Francisco Bulletin, January 7, 1858

Our readers will remember an advertisement
that appeared in our paper last spring,
stating that Bill Farr would fight a grizzly
bear, single-handed, on the 4th of July

at Tehama. His life seemed to be of no
consequence to him. We have frequently

heard him remark that he would as soon
be killed as not, and upon one occasion

we actually knew of his standing up
very coolly with a person as reckless
as himself, each taking a shot at the other's
hat, a distance of fifty steps, as it remained

on his head. The result was that Bill's
hat was shot through, and a small bunch
of hair cut away, while the skin on the other
man's cranium was laid bare for three

or four inches by Bill's half-ounce ball.
Bill was a terror to the Indians, having killed
a great many in his time; some of whom,
as he said himself, he shot to see them

fall.

4.

San Francisco Bulletin, January 6, 1859

On Thursday or Friday last
two volunteers, Messrs. Hyslop and Olvany,
were looking for horses
about four miles from the camp
near Mad river
when they saw six Indians
and about the same number of squaws.
As they were without rifles
and mounted
they adopted Light Dragoon tactics
and charged upon the Indians
wounding some—
one mortally—
and took the squaws
prisoners.

The same day,
three men from the camp at Angel's
came upon a party
of ten Indians
and had a bout with them—
killed one Indian,
wounded several—
two so badly
that they may almost be called
"good Indians."

5.
San Francisco Bulletin, May 12, 1859

An old Indian and his squaw
were engaged in the harmless occupation
of gathering clover

on the land of a Mr. Grigsby
when a man
named Frank Hamilton

set Grigsby's dogs upon them
(which, by the way, are three
very ferocious ones,)

and before the dogs were taken off
of the Indians, they tore
and mangled the body

of the squaw
in such a manner that she died
shortly after. It is said

the dogs
tore her breasts off her.
The Digger man

escaped without any serious
injury, although bitten
severely. Of course

it was the dogs' fault
although Hamilton had lived with Grigsby
over a year and knew full well

the character of the dogs
for this is not the first
instance of their biting persons.

But he only set them on
for fun
and they were

only Diggers.
There is talk of having Hamilton
arrested but no doubt

it is all talk.

Jacinta's Medicine

Jacinta Gonzalez worked at the
restaurant Robert Louis Stevenson
frequented in Monterey and nursed
him during one of his severe illnesses
in 1879. She recorded gambling
songs and a coyote myth for Alfred
Kroeber in 1902. She passed away in
the influenza epidemic of 1917.

It was the same old story:
witless white man gets lost, plants
himself face-first in the Carmel hills, dreamy head
translating scent of oak into black words.
But mean spirits hunt the soft breath
of lonely men like that, take what's left.

They pierce the body like knives, leave
a man swollen with poisonous stories.
Now he lies abed, fevered, breath
rattling his throat like a dried-up plant.
They call for me: Jacinta, you know words.
Come lay your hands on his forehead.

But what I know are medicines from heads
much older than mine; crushed leaves
gathered from windswept hills, not words
so much as roots, not roots so much as story.
I made a plaster for his chest, planted
a mugwort bundle under his pillow. *Breathe,*

I hummed into his glittering eyes, *breathe.*
Heard the dark buzzing inside his head,
knew the spirits wanted to supplant
his soul. Between his fingers I left
the sticky cobwebs of a story.
The only cure for ghost words

is salty cleansing waves of words.
Sail oceans, I said, *dream islands, give breath
to your own cure. Make up a story,
scare the poison out of your head;
I'll catch it in my hand when it leaves,
strangle it, burn it, plant*

the ashes under a redwood. I planned
to sit up all night. He muttered words
in his sleep: *pirate, treasure, shore leave.*
When the sun rose, his breath
turned easy, his pale creased forehead
cooled. Just one more hard-luck story.

My plants gave him back his breath.
Together, we dreamt words to clear his head,
ordered poison to leave. The rest is history.

tsa'a kakalu / uncle crow

for Ventura

I want to know if the sound of your
voice, singing, lives on after you left us;
if your songs still reverberate in earth,

in breeze, in bone. I study sound energy
and molecular vibration, waveform
and resonation. But the answer is no:

kinetic patterns ultimately fade away.
This doesn't explain why, in the indigo
moment before dawn, when Venus flares

in the eastern sky and the first bird
raises a note of pure faith, I hear all
the songs you ever sang: the Gregorian

chant of Kyrie, Salve Regina, the Bear
Song, songs for gambling, songs about
drinking and loving and loss. And awe.

Bridges

This drawing might as well be titled "Mission Mythology of Happy Indians Working at Productive and Useful Chores Instead of Lolling about the Undeveloped and Wasted Paradise of California." Published in *Harper's Weekly* on October 20, 1877, forty years after secularization, the drawing and accompanying article show how quickly, how deeply embedded this mythology became in American history. And, of course, this mythology continued to affect the descendants of the Indians in this drawing, including my great-grandfather Tomás Santos Miranda.

MISSION INDIANS OF SOUTHERN CALIFORNIA MAKING BASKETS AND HAIR ROPES.—[Drawn by Frenzeny.]

Caption: "Mission Indians of Southern California Making Baskets and Hair Ropes"

He was born in 1877, the same year the article was published. When Tomás was growing up, the only way Americans knew how to conceptualize California "Mission" Indians was the way they are depicted in this *Harper's Weekly* article: obedient, hardworking, unambitious mission drones whom the Spanish and Mexican padres had painstakingly trained to do some of the lowest, most labor-intensive chores of the era. As early as 1792, the traveler Navarete had visited Carmel and noted that the

Natives there were "the most stupid as well as the ugliest and filthiest of the natives of America."

What do I know about Tomás Santos? It's a short list:

Tomás's father, Tranquilino Miranda, had been born in Mexico in 1837, the oldest of ten siblings, and had traveled to Carmel with his parents, Cruz and Cristina Miranda, around 1850. Cruz and Cristina were both Indigenous Mexicans, most likely missionized long before, perhaps drafted for the journey up the mission trail as part of a larger party traveling between missions. California had just become a state in 1850, and stories of gold abounded—Cruz Miranda, listed as forty-six years old in the 1860 census, may have thought there was some chance for his family to strike it rich, or perhaps he was simply fleeing the postwar chaos in Mexico. The fact that Cruz ended up at Carmel Mission, family in tow, and was listed as a "laborer," immediately becoming a member of that community, indicates a scenario dictated more by church connections than by gold.

If there was a connection to the mission system, though, it would have been a tenuous one at best. The Carmel Mission was in a sad state even before the Mirandas arrived. Steven Hackel writes in *Children of Coyote* that:

> By 1833, only about 220 Indians lived at San Carlos. The most skilled and independent had left or died. An untold number had never been born because of the sterility of many San Carlos residents [due to endemic syphilis]. Of those at the mission, nearly half were under age twenty and a third were over forty, leaving just about two dozen men between the ages of twenty and thirty-nine. Too small to be an economically productive community, the mission had become a decaying congregation of families and dependents, an increasingly dilapidated place where people often competed with one another for food.

So, by the time Cruz and Cristina had their first California-born child, Cruz Miranda Jr., in 1856, the mission was long since abandoned except for late-night parties held by its survivors, the ransacking of its adobe, timbers, and roof tiles for the makeshift homes of its survivors, and a few loyal *neofitos* who tried to keep an eye on things in case the padres ever came back. Just one year after Cruz Jr.'s birth, it finally became illegal to buy and sell California Indians as slaves. Cruz's older brother, my great-great-grandfather Tranquilino, was nineteen years old.

In 1871, at the age of twenty-two, Tranquilino married Severiana Ramírez, age eighteen, a "Carmeleño" woman, an Esselen Indian from the local area. Her parents had been residents of the mission in its final days; born in 1836, her mother, Sacramento, was of the generation immediately post-secularization. Severiana was, in fact, the only one of her mother's twenty children (all born during the final two decades of the Mission era) to survive, but was marked by disfigurement of her hands—only three fingers on each—a mutation most likely due to the chronic syphilis that plagued California Indians, a "legacy" of soldiers that also decimated Indian women's fertility.

Six years later, Severiana and Tranquilino's son Tomás Santos was born in nearby Monterey.

Around this time, Father Angelo Casanova, appointed in 1863 to the parish of San Carlos Church in Monterey, was working to raise interest in the small community in renovating the mission, whose walls had been literally melting away since opportunists, builders, and time spirited away the church roof and tiles. In 1879, as part of his efforts, Fr. Casanova held Mass in the ruins of the Carmel Mission on the feast day of San Carlos Borromeo, as depicted in a drawing by Joseph Strong, who accompanied his friend Robert Louis Stevenson to the occasion. Stevenson, then living in Monterey, wrote of this Mass, and the essay was included in his 1892 book *Across the Plains*:

> The padre drives over the hill from Monterey; the little sacristy, which is the only covered portion of the church, is filled with seats and decorated for the service; the Indians troop together, their bright dresses contrasting with their dark and melancholy faces; and there, among a crowd of somewhat unsympathetic holiday makers, you may hear God served with perhaps more touching circumstances than in any other temple under heaven. An Indian, stone blind and about eighty years of age, conducts the singing; other Indians compose their choir; yet they have the Gregorian music at their finger ends and pronounce the Latin so correctly that I could follow the meaning as they sang. . . . I have never seen faces more vividly lit up with joy than the faces of these Indian singers.

When Stevenson wrote these nostalgic words, my great-grandfather Tomás Santos was two years old and had, in fact, been baptized by Fr. Casanova, as the Monterey Book of Baptisms attests.

Fr. Casanova's Mass at Carmel, 1879, by Joseph Strong; Loreta and James Meadows are to the left of Casanova, and the Indian "Ventura" is to his right.

His parents, Tranquilino and Severiana, living the reality—not the nostalgic fantasy—of missionization's consequences, may even have gone to that San Carlos Feast Day Mass. Maybe they sang that Gregorian plainsong—his father would have learned the same Latin words in his

Mission register, baptism of Tomás Santos Miranda

Mexican mission, and his mother had grown up at Carmel. James and Loreta Meadows—parents of Isabel Meadows, who would later tell ethnologist/linguist J. P. Harrington many of our stories and much genealogical gossip—were there, identified by name in Joseph Strong's sketch. (In fact, Isabel's half-brother Jacinto from Loreta's first marriage was married to Severiana's mother, Sacramento, later in life, a second marriage for both parties.) I've often wondered if the blind Indian singer of Stevenson's story—"Old Ventura"—was the Ventura Quittit in our family married to my great-great-great-great-aunt Teodosia Real. Isabel told Harrington that Ventura "was *cantor de la iglesia,* & knew how to read & to read Latin, and . . . was one of the] singers of Carmel Church." He'd been blinded when Teodosia threw hot coals at him in a fit of pure rage.

One of Tomás's mother's relatives, Jacinta Gonzales, would soon be called to nurse Robert Louis Stevenson through a severe health breakdown, saving his life and thus enabling him to go on and write some of the most famous novels of his times and ours—*Treasure Island, The Strange Case of Dr. Jekyll and Mr. Hyde.*

Years later, Jacinta and her aunt Viviana Soto Mucjai would sing Esselen songs into a contraption that recorded their voices (and their laughter, when they botched a line) onto wax cylinders for anthropologist Alfred Kroeber.

I heard those songs and that delicious giggling many years later, after the songs had been copied onto cassette tapes, playing on my car's stereo. By then, over one hundred years since Tomás Santos Miranda's birth, the Carmel Mission had long been a glorious, painstakingly restored, active church complete with cobalt blue Mexican tiles in the fountain, recreated Indian-designed painted décor, adobe walls, clay roof tiles, and fragrant, colorful gardens. By then, Carmel Mission was the biggest tourist destination in Monterey County.

That was all just Fr. Casanova's pipe dream in 1879. Meanwhile, Tomás Santos grew up.

Like his father, Tomás married a Carmeleño Indian woman, my great-grandmother María Inés García. It was in the spring of 1901, in Monterey County. Witnesses were Laura and Alfonso Ramírez—both consultants for Harrington and related to Tomás by marriage (Alfonso was also Tomás's godfather). In the years to come, their children would all be baptized in Monterey. Thus it is through Carmel Esselen women that my

María Inés García, probably on her wedding day

official "United States Approved" Indian blood comes. The Indigenous Mexican blood doesn't count, according to the government, even though California had just stopped being Mexico when Tranquilino and Cristina "arrived" (the 1860 census lists Cruz Miranda's birthplace as "lower California"). My father's mother's Chumash blood is, as yet, undocumented.

The young couple Tomás and Inés were counted in the 1905-06 Kelsey census in Sur, along with two children: my grandfather Thomas Anthony Miranda and his sister Carmen. The Mirandas were noted as "Indians without land."

The Kelsey census is a long story. Suffice it to say that without it, my family would not have been officially Indian, but with all its incomplete, inept, careless record-keeping, the Kelsey census obliterated the Esselen people. Its inaccurate "count" of Esselen people encouraged Alfred Kroeber's 1925 pronouncement that Esselen people and culture were extinct, thus making it easier for Sacramento Bureau of Indian Affairs Superintendent Lafayette A. Dorrington to drop us off the list of landless tribes who would benefit from a reservation. (Actually, Dorrington dropped 135 other tribes, and completely left Esselen off either list— but we were promptly designated "terminated" anyway when that little loophole was uncovered.) We have been fighting for recognition as a California tribe for many years; even though Kroeber corrected his own mistake in 1955, arguing and demonstrating to the BIA and the Justice Department the existence of Esselen tribal families, you will still find "Esselen" cheerfully recorded as the first tribe in California to be declared extinct, and the US government still does not recognize our existence as tribal people.

Tomás Santos Miranda died in 1943. He was sixty-six years old. Inés lived to be eighty-five, passing away in 1966, five years after I was born. It is one of my greatest regrets that I never met her.

In the tapes that Tomás Santos's son Thomas Anthony Miranda made in 1978 and 1979, he says little about his father: that he was a hard man to work for; that he demanded absolute obedience and dedication from those who worked with him, including his sons. Thomas Anthony left home at fourteen. Looking at Tomás Santos's face, remembering my own father's fierce work ethic, I can understand why.

In notes taken by someone—I think his second wife's daughter, Bella—Thomas Anthony sketches out a less scarred, early memory of his father. The note reads:

Rabbits—7 years

1907 Father built big home. Had never seen little rabbits. Finished [house] by xmas eve. Father had saw and ax. Took Tom clear across hill to brush between Pacific Grove and Presidio. Dad stopped and looked at tree. Dad cut down tree and gave Tom ax and saw to carry home. Dad working for PI Co then. Dancing—party. Indians and Portuguese. Women wore big skirts. Couple weeks later Dad built rabbit pens. Dad went to work and Tom wandered out to pens and saw five or six tiny ones in nest. He ran to mother—hollering—She came running—just baby rabbits!

Father went to school. Spoke good English.

These notes are written in blue ink on the back of a form letter from AARP. Both the story and the form letter are undated. A little map at the top of the page shows where the house was located in reference to Pacific Grove and Presidio. This was in Monterey, I think; Tomás and family must have moved back from Sur. This bare-bones story, together with marriage and death certificates, a single photograph, is all the information I have on Tomás Santos. But my son, my brother, and my father are all darkly handsome, and as little boys they all shared the same Miranda face; it's easy to imagine my grandfather as a small boy running to Inés, his mother, hollering about these weird little animals that had suddenly appeared in the cage.

Where had these creatures come from? How had they gotten *into* the pens, and *why*, when the pens so clearly were meant to keep rabbits from escaping? *What* were they? Oh, I can just hear Tommy's relentless questions, and imagine his mother's anxious rush to the pens to see what was happening. "They're just baby rabbits!" she must have laughed.

The image of Tomás and Tommy going to cut down a Christmas tree is unexpected and surprises me for some reason. My own knowledge of and experiences with the Catholic Church have embittered me; I am forced to remember that many of my relatives grew to accept it, practice it, and believe in it. I'm glad Tom remembered this ritual and the part he played. I'll bet he felt important, carrying the ax and saw all by himself, at age five or six. I wonder how they decorated the tree. I wonder what else they did to celebrate Christmas.

And oh, those parties. How I would love to have been a fly on the wall! What music did they play? What dances did they dance? Who was there? How grand that must have all seemed to a little boy—the music playing (perhaps guitar or accordion, as in the group photo?) late into the night, the laughter of adults, the swirling skirts, the stomping feet. Maybe as a young man Tomás Santos knew how to play as hard as he worked.

And exactly where was this "big home"? And how big was it? (Remember, children often think small places are huge.) And what happened to it, did they lose it, did they sell?

Thomas Anthony said his father had gone to school, "spoke good English." Which school? How long? What else would he have spoken besides English? Old Carmel Spanish? Indian? Scraps of various Indian dialects?

I think about these questions as I look at the photograph of my great-grandfather, the only one we have.

Tomás kneels, one knee on the ground, resting his left arm on the other, long white sleeves buttoned around his wrists. He is staring—no, glaring—into the eye of the camera. Into my eyes. Seeing that he is dressed in clean denim overalls and a white shirt, I imagine this is a dressy day for him; the swoop of a watch chain runs like a wing from a buttonhole at the top of the overall to what I imagine is his watch, tucked in a shirt pocket—his arm obscures it, but what else could it be? The cuffs of the overalls are carefully folded up about two inches. I think my great-grandfather is meticulous about his appearance, even if he is just dressed for working or a cookout. It reminds me of how my grandfather Thomas Anthony was known for his sharp dressing and precisely ironed creases, how my own father trained me to iron his work shirts, even press

Tomás Santos Miranda, circa 1930s

his jeans. How he insisted I do the same for my little brother, his Mini-Me! I remember scorching those sharp creases in Little Al's small jeans, patched knees and all.

I never met Tomás, but I'd know that face anywhere. Ay, his face. There's too much of my own father in that face; it scares me, makes me wonder what the hell I did wrong this time, makes me want to turn tail and run for the hills. The dark skin, the wide nose, the scowl, the thin lips set in an almost straight line—yes, I know Tomás, though he died long before I was born.

Tomás bears the look of a man who has seen the worst life can throw at him, yet refuses to give up. But he's not fighting back with faith or tenderness or even a sense of protecting his family. No, this man fights back out of bitterness, out of sheer cussedness, out of a bent and misshapen pride. He fights back because violence is the only way he's ever known anyone to get what he needs. He fights back with his fists and feet, his bear body, his biting wolf teeth, his human eyes.

You don't mess with this man. He's created a space around himself that few dare to breach, a kind of glow, like a smoldering ember, that makes you want to go out of your way to maintain a safe distance.

Even in this family portrait around a campfire, twelve of the other fourteen people gathered seem huddled together on the left, their bodies held away from Tomás. It's hard to believe this is the man who took his son out to find and bring home a Christmas tree, who danced at a party of Indians and Portuguese laborers. Of course, that was when Tomás was still young—twenty-nine or thirty. He didn't know then that he was already halfway through his life. He was tough then, but this man in the photograph is dangerous. Not because he's bad or mean or evil. But because he has seen too much pain, witnessed too many of his loved ones killed, known too much injustice to even imagine that justice might exist somewhere.

This man is dangerous not because of what he believes in, but because of all he does not believe in. He has no faith in God, in religion (Indian or white), in goodness or tenderness that goes unpunished. Everything he's ever loved or hoped for has let him down, betrayed him, or abandoned him to this solitary place on the edge of the family, poised on one knee, ready to lunge upward if necessary, ready to strike without asking questions. Doubt is one problem that doesn't plague this man. He knows his truth well: Don't trust this world.

His hands—or rather, the one hand I can see, his left hand, is huge. Like my father's. Big square palms with thick strong brown fingers, callused knuckles. He's worked all his life, from the moment he could hold a basket or hammer or grab hold of a stick. These are not the slender graceful hands that some Esselen ancestor left on the cave walls, hands immortalized by Robinson Jeffers, the poet laureate of Big Sur. These hands are not the hands of a peaceful or content soul.

These hands are hungry. These hands have had too many things slip out of their grasp. These hands can't be gentle; gentle means dead. And while these hands may be deadly, they are very much alive, and intend to stay that way as long as possible, by any means possible. Desperate hands. Ruthless hands. Frightened hands. Frightening hands.

This is my great-grandfather, my grandfather's father, my father's grandfather. This is the bridge between missionization and post-secularization.

In 1877, Tomás Santos's birth year, Crazy Horse was killed, Sitting Bull escaped (temporarily) to Canada, and Chief Joseph surrendered after his amazing journey. In that same year, Rutherford B. Hayes became president of the United States, beating out his opponent by one electoral vote; Thomas Edison patented the phonograph; Reconstruction came to an end in the Old South; Queen Victoria was proclaimed empress of India; and the first Easter Egg Roll was held on the White House lawn. In California, 1877 was the year that Hubert H. Bancroft recorded the testimony of Lorenzo Asisara of Mission Santa Cruz; Asisara's recitation of punishment by padres, violence between Indians, attempts on the padres' lives by desperate Indians, and theft of the little land awarded to Indians during secularization is American history at its lowest.

In 1877 it had been 107 years since Junípero Serra founded San Carlos Borromeo del río Carmelo. From a pre-missionization population estimated as high as one million, California Indians now numbered about twenty thousand. Few Indians, if any, owned land. Most of those who did would eventually lose it to American squatters, outright theft, taxes. Indians from San Carlos Mission lived in and around Carmel, Monterey, Big Sur, in whatever housing or refuge they could find—or they left, traveled far away, and did not return.

Into this world, Tomás Santos Miranda was born to an Esselen Indian woman named María Severiana Ramírez Miranda and her husband, Tranquilino Miranda, near the ruins of Mission San Carlos Borromeo del río Carmelo and—somehow—lived.

"I am the result of the love of thousands," Linda Hogan, herself a survivor of genocide, wrote. And sometimes we are the result of the bitter survival of thousands, as well. Sometimes we get here any way we can.

Sometimes our bodies are the bridges over which our descendants cross, spanning unimaginable landscapes of loss.

The Light from the Carrisa Plains: Reinvention
1900–1961

Tom's Stories

I inherited a bagful of cassette tapes featuring my paternal grandfather, Tom Miranda (1903–1988), a twentieth-century descendant of the Carmel Mission Indians born just sixty-nine years after the missions were secularized (although it took another ten to fifteen years for the missions to completely close down), and just one generation removed from legal slavery. Tom traveled all over the West Coast from the age of fourteen, curious and observant. He was born in the Monterey/Carmel area, close to the Carmel Mission, but these tapes tell of journeys as far north as Seattle and back down into Mexico, even into the Midwest. He also traveled extensively through the infinite varieties of California terrain in search of work, good times, relatives, and often, I think, something he could not name.

His life story is not just about being Californian, but being California Indian after a great holocaust: out of an estimated one million Indigenous inhabitants, only twenty thousand survived the missionization era. Even though his parents were Esselen (with Indigenous Mexican from his dad's side), Tom defies stereotypes of "Indian" in many ways: working as a lumberjack, cowboy, pipelayer, truck driver, racetrack money runner—doing any kind of labor to feed himself and his growing family. At other times (as in the following stories "Davy Jacks" and "Grandfathers") he clearly has a deep attachment to the lands of his childhood, and he feels the loss of those lands sharply. He talks, especially, about his love/hate interactions with technology, which sometimes literally swept him off his feet ("He Told Me") and yet fascinated him no end.

I never met my grandfather Tom, except as a baby. He came to my baptism in 1961—showing up, typically of him, at my parents' apartment early in the morning while my mom and dad were still in bed. My father told the story in a tone of astonishment; apparently Tom had not come to any of his other grandchildren's baptisms, but he was there with bells on for mine, and my parents scrambled to "get decent" and answer his loud knocking. But by the time I was three, my father was in prison and my parents had divorced; by the age of five, I had moved out of state, and I never saw Tom again, though a thread of contact remained through a complex chain of relatives and, eventually, my father.

Tom died when I was twenty-seven or so; some of the tapes are at least thirty years old, others older. I feel as though they are his legacy to many—not just me, but California Indians as a community—and also that his voice and his stories are gifts that bring him back to me. Listening, I'm awed that he survived; I'm amazed by how hard he works, how multitalented he is, how naive he is, how he masks his tenderness and affection for loved ones, the history he lives through, his perceptions about the US government and, as he calls them, "Americans." (Warning: Tom also used racial designations common to his time and place: "Dago," "Jap," and so on. I did not edit these out.) His stories about his parents and their parents before them remind me with painful but enlightening clarity how it is that California Indians lost so much culture, language, land, identity—and yet still have an identity and community, albeit often fragmented and/or reinvented.

Tom's stories also help me understand another California Indian who has remained mostly a mystery to me, despite much more intimate contact: my father, Alfred Miranda. If Tom was no saint (as "When I Woke Up" hints), Al in his heyday was still more contentious, prone to violence and heavy drinking and hurtful relationships. It has helped me to know what he came out of, how he was raised, and the world that shaped him as a child and young adult. Along with an inheritance of loss and damage, my father also passes on to me his creative urge, love of rich colors, the restorative power of language, a talent for construction (whether it be with wood or paper), and a love of and visceral need for close proximity to forest and water. Recent work by Eduardo and Bonnie Duran (*Native American Postcolonial Psychology*) suggests that the survivors of genocide manifest symptoms of post-traumatic stress disorder many generations past the original violence. This seems so useful in understanding the dynamics and dysfunctions of my own family!

The tapes I inherited were made in the midst of life: dinners, family gatherings, odd moments when someone would think to turn on the recorder and ask Tom questions. Sometimes I hear my father's voice prompting Tom; other times, it is his late wife's daughter, or one of my sisters; even my little brother's voice is sometimes present, along with the panting, barks, and occasional scuffles of Tom's beloved dogs. It was during one of these storytelling sessions that a picture of three generations of Miranda males was taken.

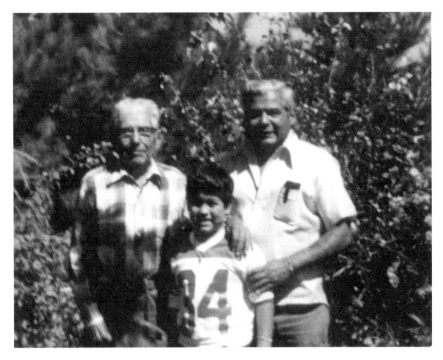

Tom Miranda Sr., Al Miranda Sr., and Al Miranda Jr., circa 1981

I want Tom's voice to come through, his stories to chronicle and give Indian testimonio to part of California's past that has been erased or subsumed under that catchall "assimilation." I offer them with all the pleasure of sharing good family stories with those I love.

Grandfathers

After a good many years they were married, my grandmother and this man. And the old man went into business making medicine. They said he was good. Every kind of weed, root, whatever he got—he cooked it some way, put it together. He was known as Dr. Tarango. Oh I guess he's been dead years and years. Everybody said, something go wrong, "Let's go see Tarango." I was up there when the pumpkins came in bloom one time.

But Faustino Garcia, that was my grandfather. Him and my grandmother, I guess they separated. The old man, he had a nice place way back up there, the other side of the mission. On the other side of the river. I think he spent all his life there. He had a little place about ten acres. And he used to dry salmon, when they speared salmon. He got some pieces of wood and he used to dry 'em, then cut the skin off the fish. Salmon this big, you know? He put it up in this tray-like, and he charged money too. He said it cost him money to buy salt. I remember him well.

Old Tarango, he was ornery, he didn't want nobody. I stayed with my grandfather up there two or three different times. I was very small but I remember—he used to treat me nice.

This story is like the rolling waves of the Pacific—just the surface of what is really going on.

Beneath Tom's wistful words about his grandfather Faustino, I hear the voice of a small boy whose experience with tenderness, with gentle adults, with a respectful and loving relationship to the land, is brief but potent. He must have feasted his eyes on those rich yellow pumpkin blossoms to remember them so well in his old age. I hear Faustino's quiet efforts to live out his life close to what remained of the mission where he'd spent his life, going back to the survival skills that had served his ancestors well. I hear a longing in Tom's voice, a longing for the warm welcome of his grandfather, for a place to belong.

Also beneath the surface of this story: Tarango, who married Tom's grandmother. Tarango's name turns up in some of Harrington's field notes, as does his daughter (probably from a previous marriage); he did indeed have a reputation as someone who knew his way around cures, curses, and supernatural matters. This would have been around 1913; quite late for such Indigenous knowledge to be practiced by California Indians—according to ethnologists and anthropologists. Tarango was one of many whose work went on in the background, where few whites would notice, where only the Indigenous people could see.

And hidden, except for this story: Faustino Garcia's tender care of a young boy whose family probably couldn't afford to feed him; the retention of Indigenous fishing and preservation practices; and the future loss of that land my grandfather speaks of with a homesickness his descendants still feel.

* * *

Davy Jacks

Then when I was about nine years old we moved, first to Metz, and worked for Charley Tibbits. But my dad didn't like Metz, it was too lonesome. I didn't like the school, either; it was way out by the railroad tracks. So that's when we got on at Davy Jacks's, got on there where there was a lot of action.

At that time they must have had two or three hundred men working with them horses. White guys, Spanish, and Indian—oh I don't know, about thirty or forty thousand acres of land that they was leveling. In those days they just had ol' scrapers and two or three mules. That was old Davy Jacks's—they owned all the way from Sempular to Greenfield, a distance of about twenty-three, twenty-five miles I guess, and width of three to five or six miles. All Davy Jacks's. His parents, I guess they came from the East way back a good many years. I guess they said, "This is mine and I'm going to stay on it." Spreckels had a lot of land that way too. But Davy Jacks, his was clear up to Greenfield from this side of Gonzales . . . everything was Davy Jacks's. They just said, when they came to this country, "We'll take this." Old Davy Jacks himself, the old man, I might've seen him but I don't remember. Yeah, he knocked all the Indians and poor people out of there and said, "This is mine."

That was in 1909 when my father stopped down there. Third or fourth ranch this side of Greenfield. It's still known as Davy Jacks's ranch. But new fellows came in. I knew one of them, Charlie, he was a hell of a—he said, "I'm going to get what's mine." And he did, and a lot of fellows like him. And they did. Davy Jacks died and everything went boom boom.

Well, he stole it from the Indians, and those new fellows, they took it away from him.

David Jacks appears frequently in California history books. Apparently Jacks found ways—both legal and illegal—to acquire more than sixty thousand acres. He set up land auctions in which he was the only bidder and bought off lawyers who sought to reverse decisions made in his favor; my grandfather's impression of Jacks as a man who "gets what's mine" was dead-on. Kathleen Thompson Hill, author of Monterey and Carmel: Eden by the Sea, *writes that despite his well-known reputation for gobbling up land that wasn't his, Jacks "never could understand why he was disliked." She adds, "Not many cried when David Jacks lost a bundle in the short-lived Monterey and Salinas Valley Railroad." Even as a child, my grandfather had a clear understanding of injustices going on all around him—and relished payback.*

* * *

Guadalupe Robles

Guadalupe Robles was a great big man, about two hundred pounds; he had blue eyes and his hair was as white as this wall. He was my girl's grandfather. Lived there in Santa Barbara—oh, there was a big family of them Robles; I bet there was five hundred Robles in Santa Barbara at one time. I remember visiting Keta. I said, "I'm going to take your grandfather for a walk."

I told him, "You can't walk very fast, eh?"

"No," he says. He's a big man. I took him down the road. He wanted to show me a tree. "This one tree," he told me . . . Tomás," he says, "when I was a young man just down from the border—I was sixteen, seventeen years old—this was a little tree. The fishing boats used to drive clear up to it and the Indians would tie their boats to it. *Mira,* look now, the ocean is about a mile from here. There was a beach and the highway and the railroad. See how much different the ocean is now? It was a good mile from that tree over there to the beach. *Agua* over here," he said.

Guadalupe, he was a white man, his eyes were blue and his skin was just as white as any white person, and of course, since he was old, his hair was just snow white. And I used to look at him and say, "*Mucho pelo, eh?*" He'd say, "*No, poquito now, muchacho.*" But he had a lot of hair. It was white all his life.

He wouldn't let none of his relations take him walking 'cause "*muy malo,*" he said. Oh, he hated drunks. *Cochinos,* he called them. He asked me, "You don't drink, do you?"

"No," I said. *Cochinos.*

I took him a couple times down the highway about a half-mile, exercising. He wouldn't let anyone touch his cane either; he had a long cane, and it was about this big around from the top, and that thing was the hardest piece of wood I ever saw. "Papa Guadalupe," I said, "where did you get your cane?"

"*Oh, muchos años,*" a good many years ago. He got it when he was a young man down on the border somewhere, I guess. He might've been sent to Mexico to be raised by family there, since he was illegitimate. We don't know. Boy, that cane was the prettiest piece of wood I ever saw; it shined just like it had varnish.

Poor old Guadalupe Robles. I guess he's been dead now for seventy years, sixty anyway. But he said he was no Indian. He said the Indians "*muy prietos.*" And he was white as snow; his father must have come from Spain. That's what I figured. He couldn't speak English: "*Nada,*" he said, "*nada.*" He said probably the mission had been there fifty years before he came.

The old man—Guadalupe was his name. I remember they called him Papa Guadalupe. There was no Mexican down there that was like him.

Guadalupe Robles remained a mystery for my mother, the genealogy sleuth. She searched for his birth certificate for years, finally tracking down a death certificate that contained very little information about his origins. My mother's best genealogical guess was that Guadalupe may have been the son of Nicolás Robles, from Branciforte, Santa Cruz, who was in turn the son of José Antonio Robles and Gertrudis Merlopes, both immigrants from Guadalajara, Mexico, who did very well in Alta California. Nicolás and his brothers were known as hombres malos *(bad boys), according to Leon Rowland in* Santa Cruz: The Early Years: *frequently in trouble with the law, mostly for stealing horses, drinking, and carousing, all the while dressed in velveteen breeches with silver filigree trimmings, satin jackets, earrings, and silk sashes.*

Guadalupe and José Robles, circa 1879

Guadalupe was most likely a mixed-blood, as there is no record of his father, Nicolás, being married to Guadalupe's mother, Louisa Domingues (coincidentally, born at the Carmel mission in 1846 and, perhaps, Esselen).

Tom's impression that some of Guadalupe's recent ancestors had been Spanish makes some sense, given this background. After my mother's death, while sorting through her boxes of research, I found a photo of a photo that someone had shared with her; the names "Guadalupe & José Robles" appear in her handwriting underneath the image. Both men have big bushy mustaches and look very dark, contrary to Tom's impression of Guadalupe late in life, although it is difficult to tell if that is the lighting or their complexion. José Robles was a half-brother of Guadalupe, another of Nicolás's sons. I don't know where my mother found the photo, or who has the original. I don't know how she identified these two men, nor do I know which one might be Guadalupe, and which one José. A good guess is that she wrote the names down left to right; perhaps her source said the men are posed in that order. My mother did a lot of research in California, attended many family gatherings, celebrations, visited many

José Robles, circa 1879

libraries; in this photo of a photo it looks like the original was posted on a board, perhaps as part of a display.

Recently, while searching through the UC Berkeley photograph database, I found a strange connection to that photo: a picture of someone I recognized instantly: José Robles! José (if the names are, indeed, in order from left to right) stands in profile in the same stiff pose, same place, same clothes—obviously this photo was taken at the same time. At the bottom of the photo is a shadow whose hat and shoulders match up perfectly with Guadalupe. The photo was part of C. Hart Merriam's collection, but nothing was noted about identity, time, or place. Perhaps they were consultants, or friends, of his.

* * *

The Light from the Carrisa Plains

I wanted to get away. I'll tell you what made me leave there: I could see a light from the Carrisa Plains every night, and I said, I wonder where the hell that light is? You could see it from the Carrisa Plains as soon as it got dark every single night. None of the guys knew what it was. It was that light that they had over here on Mt. Diablo. You could see it that far, about three hundred miles. You could see it that far. We never could make out just what it was. You couldn't see the mountain in the daytime but as soon as it got dark, we could see the light. If the days were hot or there were fires, we didn't see the light for two or three weeks at a time. When the earth would clear up and the air was clean, we could; we used to sit out there and we were wondering, especially me. I didn't know how big the world was, anyway. I used to sit out there and look at the damn light. There was a Missourian there and he said, "That's a big light, it's a long way from here." We were told that it was three hundred miles; we could see that light going around just like that. It looked like it wouldn't ever stop.

I left the Carrisa Plains in 1914. I went to Santa Maria and that didn't work; shoot, go around with a bunch of kids? I was a big man, fourteen years old, so I said, "I'm going to get the hell out of here, I'm going to see the country, see the world." What I wanted to see was where the hell that light was coming from.

I went to work down in the valley over here by Merced, worked there two or three months, came over here to San Joaquin and thought, "Where am I going to work now? I was standing around an office one evening about four p.m. and a white man came out, looked around and said, "Hey kid, you want to go to work?"

I said, "Oh yeah."

"You ever tend cows?"

"I sure have."

"Where?"

"In the Carrisa Plains."

"For Christ's sake, where the hell is the Carrisa Plains?"

I was a regular tramp, I had my roll of clothes with me, and that's how I met Mr. Shonck and all his little Shoncks. Mr. Shonck said to me, "I don't know how long this job's going to last. Your name's Tommy? Job might last two or three weeks or a month or so, Tommy."

I stayed four or five years.

I stayed even after him and his wife separated. All that time he kept asking me, he says, "Tommy, I'd like to know where's those plains. I've heard of them, where are they?"

I said, "Well, up in the hills. You ever been to Bakersfield?"

"No," he said.

"Well then, I can't tell you very well. If you get into Bakersfield, you just follow the sunset and you get right into the Carrisa Plains."

He'd say, "I've heard of them. You ever work around Tulare Lake? I never been to Tulare Lake, but someday I'm going to get a farm at Tulare Lake. By golly, one of these days we're gonna go," he says.

Ah, we never got there. Poor old Al died . . .

* * *

Thomas Anthony Miranda (right) as a young man,
circa 1916

My First Drink

I never even tasted any liquor until I got about forty. But I got to working with drunks and I started drinking too. Dagos and Mexicans and an
Indian or two. I took my first drink when I lived in King City. Well, I had
to—gosh almighty, working with all those Dagos, and I was boarding in
a Dago place, Roselli's.

The second year I was up there at the lumber camp, a fellow got killed. I was driving two horses and a sled, hauling lumber from where the guys chopped it. Sometimes it was half a mile or so from the yard. That's what they burned—wood—for the yarder to make steam, to run the engine that pulled the cables; they didn't have no gas, no coal up there in the mountains.

This one morning about 9 or 9:30, I had these two horses, wonderful horses, and I was going over to get some lumber for the yarder. We had to go up over a hill and a lot of flat rock; the horses were panting, so I stopped to give them a rest. I saw this two-inch cable moving on the ground. They had it tied up to a stump as big around as this roof is high—a great big thing, eight foot around, twenty or twenty-five feet long. I guess I was six or seven hundred foot from it when I saw Shorty, this little Dago. He was going to ride behind the log. They call them "road runners" or something like that. That cable, it was coming tight. You can hear the yarder a half a mile from there just pumping, and I mean those things *pulled,* not like a old truck or a train, they *pull.* And I saw that cable straighten up stiff as anything, pretty soon, and the stump started to move down the hill. All at once there was another big stump—from a tree they had chopped down a year before—and it snagged on the stump Shorty was following. The yarder down below there, it faltered—it stuck a little bit, and the operator, he give it a big pump.

They say there is nothing stronger than steam boilers, and when he pumped it, that cable broke. A piece of iron with wheels on it kicked back and chopped that little Dago's head right off.

I saw it all. I seen it all, and I like to go crazy. George came running and said, "What happened, Tommy?"

I says, "Look, Shorty's dead."

And he says, "Jesus Christ, what are we going to do?"

I said, "I know what I'm going to do!" I took my two horses back and I quit. I said, "I don't want to see anything like that again." I was sick for six months. I quit right there.

* * *

He Told Me, "Have You Ever Been in a Plane?"

I said, "Never."

Anyway, there were two brothers, they was both bachelors and they had both been in the war and they had planes. They were Americans, Germans I think.

When we got through working about 2:30 or 3 in the afternoon, another Indian fellow that had worked with me, Vic Caravajel, he told me through the summertime him and these guys flew back and forth every day. "I heard you've never been in one," he says.

"Who the hell told you that?" See, that paisano, that Indian, what the hell was his name, Vic tells those brothers I've never been up, and one of them says to me, "I'm going to be the first one to give you a ride."

"Like hell you are," I says. "I got a truck to drive." I had a big Dodge truck there. It was about twenty-five miles to town.

"The hell with the Dodge, let Vic drive it."

I said, "No, Charlie will give me hell if Vic wrecks it," but I couldn't get out of it. "I want to be the first one to give you a ride." People in those days got a kick out of taking people up for the first time. Anyway, we got through work, put all the tools away, I told Vic, "Now, be careful, there's a downgrade for about fifteen miles, lot of curves. Don't bust everybody with that truck." I knew Vic was a good driver when he was sober.

Anyway, they took off, Vic in the truck with a couple of guys, and we went over to the hangar where they had a couple of planes. Beautiful planes, service planes they bought after the war. He said to me, "Which way do you want to go today, Tom?"

I looked at him. "I don't know," I says, "I think I'll take the car."

We rolled the plane out a little bit, he started the thing and let it run for five or six minutes while he looked it over. He said, "Tom, are you ready to go? Where do you want to ride, in the front seat or the back? You sit in the front so you can see better."

I wasn't about to see anything. I was kinda leery of it, kinda shaky, you know? I says, "How high can you go?"

He says, "How high do you want to go?"

The runway, oh it was a long one, about a mile, and there were big oak trees for eight or nine hundred acres. It was good rain country. I got in the front, fastened the belt; felt like that old propeller was right in my face.

"Okay, here we go," he says. We was off the ground and I didn't even know it! I could see the oak trees going by just like that. It didn't look to me like the plane was moving, the oak trees were just going by backwards, and pretty soon I couldn't see no oak trees, just blue.

He says, "How are you, Tom?"

I says, "Where the hell are we at, where's the trees?"

"Look over there towards the bottom, right down there about a thousand feet."

You know, that scared me then. We got up there so quick I never even noticed it. I could see the Salinas Valley for a long, long way and the ridge of the mountains across the valley.

He said, "See King City?"

I said, "Where the hell's King City? I can't see it."

"He said, "Look down there." There was a little spot and he circled it four or five times. He got down pretty low, I guess four or five hundred feet. He says, "There's your little house over there."

"That little thing?!"

He said, "Yeah, that's where you live."

Then the wind came up and he had to make three trips around the airport before he could land. Charlie Reagan, my boss, was out there waiting, and he was scared, afraid we wasn't gonna make it. When we hit that big slab there I thought the damn thing had broke. We went on about a mile before he turned around and went back.

I says, "I will never get in another one."

Charlie was laughing, he had never been on. "How did you like it, pal?" he asks me.

I says, "Now, brother, do you want to try?"

He said, "Hell no, I don't want to die yet."

Honest to God, I was shaking. I used to go out and play cards all the time, but I didn't go no place that night. I didn't want anyone to see me. I said, "I'll never get into another damn plane with nobody." It frightened me. It stayed with me. My heart was beating so hard for about a week, I couldn't even drink my whiskey!

* * *

When I Woke Up, It Was Daylight

She had all her clothes on and I did too. We had a big bottle of whiskey between us. I looked at her and she was a beautiful woman, well dressed and clean. I guess we got tired of dancing and went to bed. We must have been pretty well soused. When I woke up I was over on the left side, and I said, "How did you get in here?" I guess she didn't know either. And I saw the bottle of whiskey and it wasn't even open. I sneaked around and washed my face and combed my hair, went downstairs. I'll bet when she woke up she was surprised!

It must have been about 6:30. I looked out and saw a streetcar going east, and I asked the conductor when I got on, "Where can I get a beer?"

We go down there about two or three blocks. "You look pretty bad, you must've hit the damn stairs last night."

I said, "I only want one beer." I walked into the bar and heard the man walking around just a-whistling, nobody but this one man behind the bar. I says, "Give me a drink of whiskey, I'm sick."

He says, "You sure do look it."

I says, "I went dancing someplace . . . "

He says, "What nationality are you?" (I knew the minute I saw him he was a Slav.) "You're not a Slav, are you?"

I said, "No, I'm a California Mission Indian."

"You come all the way from California?"

I says yes.

"What, they got no whiskey in California? You mean you come all the way to Kansas to get a drink of whiskey? You must be crazy."

About nineteen hundred miles. He just couldn't get over it.

I says, "You're Slavonian, aren't you?"

He says, "Yes, I come from the old country."

"Good," I says, "I'm glad to see you." (Why is it I always work for Slavonians?) I had one more beer and then some soda water.

He said, "You're not drinking any more?"

I said, "I gotta get home, I've been here two weeks and I've spent two thousand dollars."

"Jesus Christ," he says, "I wish you'd come over here and spent it."

This was about three miles from where all the dancing was. I don't know how I got there . . . Well anyway, I woke up, I saw this woman at my side, well dressed and all nice, clean, you know. I wondered, "Where she come from, did I bring her over here?"

I never said a word. I just sneaked out.

* * *

Tom Miranda, dandy, circa 1955

War

I rented from a German, George. He came from the old country when he was a little boy, he said. You know, he married one of those Cholon Indians; her name was Maggy.

One morning George came up to the house. It was when they had that big blowout at the Hawaiian Islands with the Japs. George came by one morning when an Indian boy, Bill, from Seattle was staying with me—he was working the same place as I was, working for Charlie Reagan. "Already everybody get up, we're at war! The Japs bombed Pearl Harbor!"

I said, "Bill, did you hear that?"

Bill said, "Yeah, somebody's drunk." Bill didn't drink—that's the first Indian that didn't drink! So we didn't pay any attention.

George came by another time and he says, "Pearl Harbor has been bombed by the Japs." I'd never heard of Pearl Harbor, didn't know where it was. By that time it was almost seven a.m., we were still in bed. George yelled, "Get up, you guys, we need help today. They's putting men across the bridge there with rifles and guns."

"What the hell's wrong, George?" I ask.

"Pearl Harbor has been bombed by the Japs!"

I said, "Who the hell cares?"

"Jesus Christ, Tom, get up, we have a war!"

"Where the hell is this war?" I asked.

Bill said, "What's the matter, George, you going crazy?"

"Oh no, the Japs have just bombed Pearl Harbor," George said.

"I wonder what's wrong with George," Bill says.

"Ai, he's nuts. He's drunk."

But George never took a drink in his life that I know. You shoulda seen the clothes in his getup; a pair of old overalls that looked like the dog had got them, and he had an old shotgun. We was right on the bridge, our place was right on the end of the bridge there, a damn long bridge too, about a mile long. Jesus Christ, there I looked out at the bridge and goddamn, there was about eight or ten men there with rifles and guns and everything. I said, "Jesus Christ, has everyone gone mad, Bill? I guess they have! Have you heard any bombs of war, George?"

And he said, "No, we never heard nothing," but they closed the bridge right up, you couldn't use it anymore.

I thought, "All these bastards have gone crazy." Around 9:30 or 10 I said to George, "Where the hell is the war? I don't see anybody shooting!" even though all those guys on the bridge had pistols in their hands, rifles and shotguns and everything.

George said, "We're stoppin' the Japs."

"Well, goddamn," I said, "there's no Japs around here, I never saw one yet!"

He says, "Well, there's gonna be some comin', we gotta kill them, hold them back, you know."

Well, I went out that day and you know, they wouldn't let me cross that bridge until about two in the afternoon. I wanted to go see my boss, Charlie Reagan, see what he's doing. I went over there finally—Bill wouldn't go. I asked Charlie, "What the hell's going on?"

And he said, "Ah, people has gone crazy. Somebody shot a ship over there in the islands."

I said, "What islands?" I had never heard of those islands. So I went back home, I asked my landlord, George, "What the hell is this with the islands, what the hell have we got to do with this? Let 'em shoot each other!"

It was the Hawaiian Islands. They caught the US asleep, all right. Why wasn't this country prepared for something like this? I never knew anything about it till George woke me up. We didn't go to work for three or four days; they wouldn't let us cross the bridge. It seems to me if the Americans had those battleships in the Hawaiian Islands, wouldn't they expect anything? What the hell, was we asleep or not?

Yeah, the big war, I guess it was. They sunk one of the biggest battleships the US had. Boy, the Americans picked up those Japs right out of bed and took and put 'em in camps. There were a lot of Japs around Salinas Valley; I bet the population was about two thousand. They took every goddamn one of them. They kept them prisoner for two or three years.

Well, until that time those Japs hadn't even done anything yet. They put them up there in Northern California in prison there for three or four years until everything got quiet, and then they turned them out. There is something to me that doesn't fit. Who the hell was our president then? Seems it was a setup. It was a put-up job.

The government can do some funny things. See, what they did after all that, they took ships down to the South Pacific, to the Marianas; I know, 'cause one of my boys was down there, Tom, and Alfred too, he was in Japan right after that.

I asked Alfred. He said, "We never done a goddamn thing, Dad. We sat in them caves in those islands a month at a time, never heard a shot." What the hell were they doing? And Tom was down on the Mariana

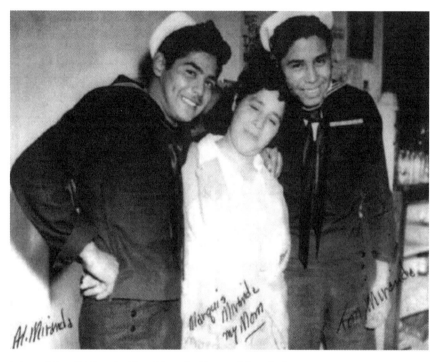

Left to right: Al Miranda, Keta Miranda, Tommy Miranda Jr.

Islands, by the Philippines. He said, "All we did was run all around on that ship; finally we got hit." And Tom damn near died, but he got over it. He was never in no hospital, just the one on the ship. Guess he got over it in three or four months.

"And that's all the war I ever saw," Alfred said. "I never heard anything, Dad. They had I don't know how many sailors there, locked up in the islands in tunnels. Never heard a shot, just passing ammunition to someone else, we don't know who it was—might've been the Japs!"

Box after box, that's all they did on them islands, pass those boxes on.

"Every once in a while they'd bring us a bottle of whiskey. That's where I learned to drink, Dad."

Those boys never knew what whiskey was. They was there about eighteen months in those caves, right off the coast.

And then the war was over. The whole thing was a matter of money. This country and the Japs—how could it get so big? Yeah. I think there was a lot of dirty work there, dirty work.

"BAD" INDIAN GOES ON RAMPAGE AT SANTA YNEZ.

SANTA BARBARA, Aug. 2.—[Exclusive Dispatch.] Juan Miranda, a bad Indian on the reservation at Santa Ynez, got on a rampage today, thanks to some fire water, and Constable Knight and Game Warden Crabb went over to reconnoiter. As the two officers approached Miranda's cabin the Indian came out of the door with a 44-caliber Winchester, which he leveled at them. Next there emerged from the cabin the Indian's daughter with a six-shooter. She was followed by the man's wife, who had chosen a double-barreled shotgun for hers.

Constable Knight, undaunted, ordered Miranda to drop his gun. The Indian refused to do so. Knight walked toward him, and as he got close the Indian deflected the barrel of his rifle. Quick as a flash Knight hit Miranda on the head with his revolver. After several hard blows from the butt of the six-shooter the bad Indian was subdued and arrested.

A cholo whose name the officers have not determined, but whose attitude at the Indian's cabin was offensive, was also arrested. Both are now in jail at Santa Ynez.

A third cholo leaped through the cabin window during the excitement and escaped through the bushes. The Indian's militant family was not arrested with the "brave."

Los Angeles Times, August 3, 1909

Novena to Bad Indians

"The only good Indians I ever knew were dead."
—General Philip Sheridan

Day 1.

Indian outlaws, banditos, renegades, rebels, lazy Indians, sinful Indians, you gamblers who squatted out behind the church instead of assuming the missionary position behind the plow; oh, lusty Indians who tied bones to sheets thrown out of the women's *monjerio,* climbed up that swaying skeleton of salvation and made unsanctified love all night; oh, women who tossed down those sheets: hear my prayer.

Day 2.

Hail troublemakers, horse thieves, fornicators, I implore you, polygamists, Deer Dancers, idol worshippers, chasers of loose women, heathens who caroused in the hills, stole wine from the sacristy, graffiti'd Indian designs on the church wall, told Coyote stories instead of practicing catechism, torched mission wheat fields, set fire to tule roofs, ran away, were captured, flogged, put in stocks or irons, ran away again: help me, suffer me, in this hour of loss.

Day 3.

I ask for your grace, you dirty Indians, you stupid Indians who wouldn't learn Spanish or English, lazy bastards who mumbled *"no quiero"* when asked to load wagons with tons of stinking skins, who chased the bottle instead of cattle, who were late for Mass, confessed everything and regretted nothing, took the whip thick as a fist, laughing; you who loved soapstone charms, glass beads, eagle feathers but wouldn't learn proper usage of land or gold: have mercy on my weakness.

Day 4.

Queens of earth, you women who sold yourselves for a tortilla, a hand-ful of beans, the dog's meat; sons of incorrigible cattle thieves like Juan Nepomuceno, who could no longer find elk or deer or salmon; *cabecillas*, ringleaders like Hilario, who endured the *novenario* for throwing a stone at a missionary—twenty-five lashes on nine separate days and then, on nine consecutive Sundays, forty more: oh my martyrs, grant me strength, grant me courage in my desperation.

Day 5.

Oh magnificent Aniceto, who refused to name thieves of money, choco-late, shoes, string, knives from the presidio—thirteen years old, you took a flogging in silence; oh renowned Yozcolo, alcalde from Mission Santa Clara who raided mission stores, freed two hundred women from the *monjerio;* dear Atanasio, found guilty of stealing from the *comisario,* shot dead by a firing squad at seventeen years of age, begging for your life as you knelt in the estuary at Monterey: guide me out of the stone walls of this cell.

Day 6.

Accept my praisesong, you women who aborted pregnancies conceived in rape by soldier or priest, attend me, barren Indian woman, stripped and prodded, who refused to let Father Ramon Olbes examine your geni-tals or test your fertility—you, who bit him, suffered fifty lashes, shackles, imprisonment, a shaven head, were forced to carry a wooden false baby for nine days; blessed Apolinaria, midwife, *curandera,* dancer, keeper of potent medicines: heal me.

Day 7.

Ever full of faith, Pomponio, who cut off your heel with your own knife to slip out of leg irons; terrible heart of Toypurina, shaman revolutionary who dared raise your gods against Spain's; blessed Chumash woman who heard the earth goddess Chupa tell you to rebaptize neophytes in the tears of the sun; Licquisamne, most merciless Estanislao, telling the padre, "We are rising in revolt . . . we have no fear of the soldiers": make me unrepentant.

Day 8.

Oh valiant Venancio, Julián, Donato, Antonio, Lino, Vicente, Miguel, Andrés, Emiliana, María Tata, who suffocated Father Andrés Quintana at Santa Cruz before he could test his new wire-tipped whip; oh Nazario, personal cook to Fr. Panto at San Diego, who slipped "yerba," powdered *cuchasquelaai*, into the padre's soup after enduring 124 lashes (you said, "I could find no other way to revenge myself"): I beseech your tenderness.

Day 9.

Oh unholy pagans who refused to convert, oh pagans who converted, oh pagans who recanted, oh converts who survived, hear our supplication: make us in your image, grant us your pride. Ancestors, illuminate the dark civilization we endure. Teach us to love untamed, inspire us to break rules, remind us of your brutal wisdom learned so dearly: Even dead Indians are never good enough.

In the Catholic Church, a novena is a nine-day period of private or public prayer to obtain special graces, to implore special favors, or to make special petitions. The novena has always had a sense of urgency and immediacy.

Gonaway Tribe: Field Notes

Arrived here amidst mud and rain. There are twenty-one Indians left. Very few of them are old and wise!

The ones I have found are living with the younger Indians near town. This is bad because the young Indians tell the old ones to ask for more money, but I get around that by telling them that I am to pay a certain price and no more.

The old woman, Sadie, says that I am fortunate in coming here in the wintertime because it is against the law of her people to tell these stories she told me in the summertime. She says if she told a story like this in the summer a rattlesnake would bite her. (But I bet with a dollar bill or two flashing in her face, she would forget her law.)

These Indians realize they are the last of their tribe and they ask a frightful price. But I have managed to jew them down to half of what they ask or less.

These Indians are altogether too civilized. They would not have me around this week at all, said they were "too busy, it is Christmas and we do not want to be bothered." Also, they keep saying that I should come back when the sun is out, that I mess up their houses and track mud in.

Every day means another Indian gone! Our work is probably and secretly the most important in the Indian line, because in the years to come people will always be finding Indian relics, but they can't find talk no matter how deep they dig. Once it is gone, it is gone for good.

Mrs. Simpson is dead. Her son and Susie are alive, though. I have arranged to talk to them this afternoon—that is, Susie is going to talk. Petie Simpson says he doesn't speak much Indian language. He says that he was brought up around white people and only speaks a very little Indian. I don't know how much of this is true but I will go to work on him.

Isn't it a shame that Mrs. Simpson has died? Another valuable specimen gone! Susie says that white people do not pay enough but I told her that there is no work to this, all she would have to do is talk. Petie hates the government, says that they are not doing a thing for the Indians, says all the whites are moving in around here; that there are more whites than Indians on the reservation.

He swore and cursed the government all the time I was there this morning. Susie says the government has robbed her people ever since the start. She hates white people. I told her that I consider no Indian below my class and that I like Indians very much and that I felt just as she does about the whites coming in and taking the country away from her people. After I made friends with them and made them believe I felt the same as they did, they finally consented to talk—Susie is going to tell in Indian what she thinks about the government.

My, how the Petie Simpsons hate white people—they could not use too many words in telling me. It is a good thing they don't know that this research is for the Smithsonian.

When I go to bed at night, it makes me happy to look back over the day and know that I am getting the language before the last of them that speak it are gone.

Juan Justo's Bones

From letters by A. P. Ousdal, Doctor of Osteopathy in Santa Barbara, to J. P. Harrington. On December 9, 1930, Ousdal was issued US Pat. No. 1,784,382, for an apparatus for utilizing solar radiations for therapeutic purposes.

1.

I took it upon myself to take care of this Indian as he has been very sorely neglected. I found him sick with gangrene of the leg. I immediately began to photograph and X-ray him in order to get some records for comparative studies before he should die. However, the ulcer, approximately eight inches in diameter, is healing and the man is feeling so very much better that I am in hopes of making more of a personal study of him. I am trying to make several sets of X-rays, not neglecting any bone whatever (realizing that one set can be lost or destroyed, and in being handled will receive a certain amount of abuse, as they are not everlasting). When I get the sets completed, I will certainly cooperate with the Smithsonian Institution, making an interesting exhibition and a small booklet of my study. I hope to raise enough money from this booklet to pay for a granite monument, full size, of our friend Juan Justo. So far I have taken care of all expenses myself, which is only my contribution, tribute to the race that once was.

2.

Enclosed: measurements of the bumps on the Indian's head:

Horizontal—16 cm

Breadth—15.25 cm

Depth—18.75 cm

Temple—13 cm

Circumference—17 ¼ inches

Social—2%

Idealism—8%

Combatative—6%

Ear Formation—10% (Almost perfect ear)

Width of nostril—4.25 cm

Width of cheekbone—12.25 cm

Depth of face—16 cm

Round prominent chin,

cataract over right eye:

Color—Peculiar agate brown

I am also taking Juan's heart rate today by the Electrocardiograph, which will make an interesting record.

3.

The ulcer on Juan's leg has healed up a couple of inches, looks much better. It is of a varicose nature. I think with a little care the old boy might outlive any of us. It seems that a touch of soap and water, with a few rays from the sun, go a long way with him. There are two burial mounds near the city that we ought to excavate; I believe that they are rich in deposits of bones and skulls . . . I am anxious to compare those skeletons with Juan's—they are of the same tribe. He is improving but with a gunnysack in the window and a leaky roof. During the rainy season his palace on the dump is not any too inviting. He had to move his bed to the far corner of the shack the other day; to protect himself he has an empty cement bag which he slips over his feet at night beside his regular bed clothes, and this in spite of all our organizations for charity.

4.

Our Juan has been sick this last week from absorption of poison from his leg. I was hoping to have his picture in the nude soon. Once I have that, with the headdress you are making up, and your manuscript, my book will be ready for publication. I am hoping that when he wanders with the spirit of his fathers and has no use for his old bones, that they may become the property of the Smithsonian Institution. That has been my aim since I knew the man, so as to not lose track of the data, and I pray that I will be able to accomplish it. In the meantime our X-ray work will have to do. It is a good idea to let the public know that Juan Justo is Smithsonian property. Somehow I like that idea.

J. P. Harrington: A Collage

You and I are nothing, we'll both of us soon be dust. If we can grab these dying languages before the old-timers completely die off, we will be doing one of the FEW things valuable to the people of the REMOTE future. You know that.

Power beings are capricious, unpredictable, amoral; they may manifest themselves for or against man's benefit.

Coyote's positive traits include humor and sometimes cleverness. His negative traits are usually greed or desire, recklessness, impulsiveness, and jealousy.

He would bring things, he would send gifts, he would give my mother gifts towards the end. And so it was kind of nice to see him. I always knew I might get a couple of dollars or something to get lost. And it worked!

Coyote often plays the role of trickster, god of tricks, although in some stories he is a buffoon and the butt of jokes and in a few is outright evil.

. . . It's fitting that people who made stone bowls instead of clay pots, and made a canoe with planks sewn together instead of digging one out, would attract a complex man for kind of a complex people.

Tears come to my eyes as I think of you the way you used to be and the way I used to be. I never made it back. The best we can do is to do the best we can do at this late day.

What we found in his notes was that my great-grandmother burned acorns, it was the ashes of the acorn that she put on her face, at the death of her son.

. . . Haven't I gone back even two weeks later to find them DEAD and the language FOREVER DEAD?

Coyote possesses great powers of creation and regeneration; at the same time, his propensity for destruction and clumsiness in relationships often dooms him to repeat his mistakes.

In some stories Coyote seems oblivious to his own faults; in others, what others may perceive as faults become powerful tools for his ultimate success.

It's like what the basket people talk about, that baskets are all around us, we just have to go gather them together. And it takes a long time to do this; it takes a long time to make a basket. That's how I feel with Harrington's work, I have to go out gathering all the materials to come together, and it will be a pretty good picture at the end.

If it were not for him, all of you would not have your publications, and your stories, and your dictionaries or lexicons, and your theses, and whatever else you've done out there, were it not for this crazy man. Crazy like a fox.

In many myths Coyote meets his come-an-uppence due to his enormous appetite. He wants everything, all the time, hates to share, tries to keep his caches secret, inviolate. As a rule, Coyote hoards and lusts and covets.

The time will come and SOON when there won't be an Indian language left in California, all the languages developed for thousands of years will be ASHES, the house is AFIRE, it is BURNING!

John Peabody Harrington, April 29, 1884–October 21, 1961. They called you by so many names. Glutton. Savior, cheat, outlaw. Clown. Creator. Pragmatist. Who were you, J. P.? Wanderer, champion, prince? Angry god? Bringer of Fire?

J. P., you died the day before I was born; you left this world just a few miles and a few hours away from the place where I emerged. I often wonder: did our spirits nod as they passed above Southern California that late October day? Did you reach out and tag me, say, "You're it!" as you headed for the stars? Or did you laugh, keeping all your secret treasures to yourself, knowing what a long, tangled trail you'd left behind for me to follow? Could you even imagine that the descendants of Isabel, Laura, Maria, and so many others would track your every syllable as you'd tracked theirs?

In your wildest dreams, did you ever think that we would survive you?

Teheyapami Achiska: Home
1961–Present

Silver

I. Forge

It's my earliest memory. A man presses a woman into a stucco wall, holds a knife to her throat. A small child in a white cotton dress and white leather shoes sits in a corner and cries. She needs to be picked up. Maybe she's wet or hungry or tired. There is a fourth presence in the room. It's fear.

The man is my father, the woman is my mother. I am the screaming child. The knife—a kitchen knife, silver and bright—is my fear.

I remember a little more. Now I'm three years old. We are still living in the barrio, my mother, father, and me; we are like Stone Age people giving way to Bronze. My father will soon be sent to prison. My mother, always on the edge of some bottomless place, will disappear for almost a year. But for this little time we are a family. Daddy builds L.A.'s skyscrapers, coming home to shower, slicking back his black hair with Tres Flores, face and tattooed arms almost black against his clean T-shirt and chinos. Mama tends our little apartment, watering the avocado tree crucified on toothpicks and suspended in the water of a highball glass, speaking broken Spanish to neighborhood women when she hangs out our laundry on the communal clothesline in back. And me, in sunsuit and sandals, short "pixie" haircut, darting in and out of the ground-floor apartment from coolness to perpetual summer.

On this day I am playing with a boy from another apartment—his name might be Tony—who offends me deeply. To prove how seriously I take this—whatever it is—I run into our apartment to ask my mother for a butter knife. I know, of course, that she'd never give me a sharp knife, but I use butter knives in my play often enough that it isn't an unusual request. Prying rocks from the hard earth, making mud pies, chopping up spiky yucca leaves for my doll's dinner . . .

I find my mother in the kitchen. Slender, her skin luminous in the dark air, she is humming with that inner peace she sometimes attains when the delicate details of shopping, housekeeping, and errands have gone smoothly. Her hair is in pin curls, crisscrossed all over her head, under a gold silky scarf that hangs down her back. She smells bright, like cold purple wine in a clean glass. Her eyes are deep blue and have a familiar faraway focus. She hands me the knife absentmindedly; she is doing dishes, cooking. Maybe my father will be home from work soon.

Maybe the apartment smells of tomatoes soaking into fried onions, green peppers; rice grains slowly swelling into plumpness. Maybe, like the other mamas, my mother has a pile of tortillas, made early that morning, wrapped in a damp clean dish towel and warming in the small gas oven, while chops or hamburgers grill on the stove.

I take the shiny silver blade and walk outside into the sun, to the boy in white T-shirt and shorts. I back him up to the cream-colored wall of the apartment building, with its sharp nubbly swirls of texture, and I hold the knife to the boy's thin brown throat. I tell him, "Don't say that again!"

I remember his eyes, dark as mine, wide and defiant, but beginning to be scared. Maybe he hollers. Maybe my mother follows me out to see what use I have for the butter knife. "What's going on?" she cries, "What are you doing?"

Maybe he called me a name, said I was white, or worse, Indian. Maybe he was repeating something the barrio women said about my pale mother. I don't know for certain, but I still remember the long cool butter knife in my hand: hard, smooth, a kind of silver that will last.

It stays there, hidden in the shadows of my hair as it grows. Every once in a while I test the edge—every year, the blade cuts a little deeper. I break crayons, smash soft wax into the imperfect letters of my name. I kick my way through the crowd of older kids at the playground who say I can't use the swings. My father says I should hit those kids. I see how he fights for what he wants; how his fists work for him. I hear my mother crying that she's leaving for good. I am afraid, afraid of what I might do with this anger against people who don't understand that my whole body feels as if it is wrapped around a bright and soulless blade.

II. Sheath

By the time I am six I have a reputation. Not what you think: I am not a bully. Too much has happened to me for that easy solution. My father has disappeared. My mother has disappeared and come back; remarried. We are in Washington State now. Instead of an apartment, we live in a trailer, in a trailer court tucked into the wet, rural lands of south Puget Sound. On Sundays when we visit my stepfather's relatives, I hide behind Mama's chair.

The aunts think I'm adorable, try to bribe me out of the corner with

Rice Krispie squares and kind voices. One of them tells me, "I wish I had a permanent tan like yours." The uncles don't know I exist, and I don't, not in the rec room world, feet propped up, a game on television, TV trays loaded with chips and sandwiches and beer in short fat brown bottles. It's all new to me: thick gray and red wool socks, bright orange hunting caps, plaid shirts, boots heavy with mud tracking across Aunt Carole's clean kitchen floor while she yells at the men, "Get out, out!"

I stay close to Mama, watch the cousins slam in and out of the house grabbing handfuls of chips to eat outdoors, where their domain begins and the adult world ends.

For a long time I am too shy to explore. But I guess kids are attracted to kids; it's normal to want to play blind man's bluff and sing B-I-N-G-O. For a moment I forget that I'm not normal. When Pete darts inside the house, my aunt grabs her son, nudges him toward me, prods him to ask, "You wanna play, too?" I can hear voices chanting a familiar rhyme in the front yard. I slide from behind the chair, follow Pete through the door.

Outside CeeCee and Betty exchange looks. Pete mutters, "My mom made me ask her." The way he says "her" sets me apart, makes it okay for the cousins to trip me during a game of tag. I play anyway. I'll show them I'm not a baby. They know I won't complain: they wallop my skinny chest with interlocked arms when we play red rover out on the asphalt streets of their subdivision, or snatch an ice cream bar out of my hand.

What they don't know is how sharp I am inside. I can stand there without tears, watch one of them lick my Creamsicle down to the clean wooden stick, and not say a word. I can stand there because inside I am slashing them to ribbons.

"Say you're ugly," Pete demands, holding my ice cream above CeeCee's wide-open mouth. "Say you look like an old brown piece of dog turd."

My lips are pressed so tightly together, they sting.

CeeCee lunges up at the now-dripping orange and vanilla ice cream slab, and misses. Pete hoists it higher, his small blue-gray eyes easily estimating the distance. "I'm gonna let Cee have it, Mexican. Come on, Brownie, just say it. Say, "I'm ugly . . ."

"Geez, Pete," Betty is whining, chin sticky with her own ice cream, "It's melting, it's gonna fall off the stick. Hurry up! Give it to us!"

I feel the scratchy branches of my aunt's huge juniper bushes at the back of my knees, smell their unmistakable heat stench rising up behind me. Pete leans closer and I have to step back. I don't want to, but his milky face looms up.

For a second our eyes click level. Pete sees my usual scared-of-her-own-shadow self; I see deep into his happy lust. How glad he is that I am terrified! But up close, his pleasure strikes me like a flint, and he sees something unexpected—defiance—spark in me. He narrows his eyes.

"Take your stupid ice cream," he sneers, slams the wet gooey mess into my face, laughs as I gasp, fall backward into the junipers, into the stinking warm green branches that break under me and release still more acrid oil. Then I cry.

My cousins think I'm not tough; but Mama strokes my hair and says to Aunt Carole, "If she has Al's blood, she can take care of herself. You just wait." I wonder if she knows. I'm so careful not to let it show; clench my jaw, my tongue pressed into the roof of my mouth. If she knows the bad things I think, she might leave again. Or I might be the one to disappear. At night I grind my teeth. Nobody says anything about the sharp hungry part of me.

III. Whetstone

Except Buddy. Buddy must know. He's a friend of my mama's. I'm seven years old now. My stepfather isn't home much, drives trucks to places with names like Tiger Mountain, Woodinville, North Bend. Buddy, who lives close to our neighborhood, is at our little trailer almost every day, bringing beer, cigarettes, candy. There's always something for everyone, and a few minutes of that special attention, that tenderness human beings crave and do not get. I want some of it, too. I like the way he listens when I read out loud, how he says I'm the smartest girl he knows; I take the candy and the hugs eagerly, guiltily.

But Buddy kisses my mama in a way that I don't like. I glare at him. Mama laughs and tells Buddy, "Let's go for a ride."

"What about . . . ?" Buddy asks, nodding at me.

"Bring her," Mama says, Pall Mall in one hand, beer in the other. She slurs words in the way that makes my stomach knot. "Put her in the backseat and drive around for a while. She'll drift off."

She always tells people what a good traveler I am. It's true. I can't fight the dark sky, the warmth of the heater coming on, tires against the asphalt. I am betrayed by my mother's intimate knowledge of me. Even as I see my mother's shadow sliding across the front seat closer to Buddy, I fall asleep.

It doesn't take long for Buddy to get me, and Hannah, too. Hannah is a year younger than me, but we are best friends. Hannah is a redheaded, freckle-faced white girl, but when we stand together in our matching green dresses, matching socks and shoes, we think we are twins. I'm better at reading, she's better at math, so we help each other with homework. But I'm older, I watch out for Hannah on the playground or at the park. I let her play with my special doll, the one that has a real horsetail for hair. Buddy teaches us to braid it, and it's glossy, thick. There's a lake where Hannah and I love to swim. He takes us for the whole day, and we have fun; but I don't like spending what seems like an hour changing into my swimming suit because Buddy won't stop peeking. And there's an orchard near his house where we can pick apples for free, if we spend the night. His wife loves kids, he says. Our mothers say it's okay.

But Buddy's wife sleeps hard, goes shopping the next day. It is here, in his house that night, and in the orchard next morning, that Buddy finally rapes me. I don't know this is rape; I do know I can't tell. Does he say that to me, "Don't tell"? No, he doesn't need threats. I can't tell because at seven years old I don't have words to describe the pain thrusting into my vagina—a hand around my throat—sound of a man's ragged breath next to my ear. I can't tell because I never said "no" to anything Buddy ever gave me. I can't tell because I didn't stop him when he did it to Hannah, too. Most of all, I can't tell because there is nobody who wants to hear.

There are some things I can never do without thinking of Buddy. Braid my hair. Put on a swimming suit. See apple orchards, hear the buzz of bees and yellowjackets when the fruit falls to the earth, bruised. And after my family moves away, I never have a best friend again. I hate that he is still in me, that cells in my brain hold his image. Some people forget being molested. Some people don't even know it happened to them. My problem is that I can't forget. Instead of growing dull and faint, my anger gets sharper and sharper. Like a knife. Like a big silver knife.

IV. Unsheathed

I am fifteen years old. We are in yet another trailer, this time on an isolated five acres of land. My stepfather has left us; my father has returned. He brought a son with him, conceived the moment he stepped out of San Quentin. Little Al is five years old now, and I have raised him for the past two years, losing my heart to the dark skin, arched eyebrows, brown eyes wide with curiosity, pain, life. He is the first person I have ever met who looks like me. He is my only family. Little Al is sleeping at this moment, exhausted, on his stomach, in the next room. He can't sleep on his back because of the welts left by our father's belt.

I am standing over my father as he lies passed out on his bed. I don't know where my mother is. The smell of spilt beer and sweat is strong on the sheets, the pillowcases, in the thick curtains of the window above his husky, muscular form. It's very late at night, or else early in the morning, and all around our tin trailer one-hundred-foot pines sway shaggy and green in the winter rain. There are no stars, no moon. There are no lights anywhere but in this room, the overhead light striking what is in my hand, reflecting a false silver aura to the walls, furniture, linoleum.

I am holding the little handgun my father keeps in the trailer. It is gray metal, with a black handle. I want to put it to my father's temple and pull the trigger.

Yes, it's loaded. Yes, here is the safety, here is the way he taught me to take the safety off. My hand is not even trembling. My teeth are clenched. I list the reasons: he would never hit Little Al again; he would never cause Mom to drink, cry, ask me to call in sick for her again; he would never read my journals, break into my locked file cabinet, my secrets, again.

I try to think of consequences. Blood. Police. Remann Hall, where they send the bad kids, the place I have been threatened with forever, by grown-ups, by the whispers of schoolmates.

What if it doesn't kill him, what if he wakes up? Am I more afraid of failure than success? What about Little Al? What about his life, tortured by this man? Can't I do it for him?

Maybe this is a movie. Someone else's movie. If this moment were captured on time machine film and examined frame by frame, would I see dozens upon dozens of angels flitting in and out of the picture, holding my hand down? Keeping my hand from lifting the gun to my father's head, to my own head?

The gun butt hefts in my hand. Why do I think it feels like a big butcher knife? Why do I feel as though I have stood here before with this weapon in my hands? I put it back on the shelf. I go to bed, cold. The rains come down all night without stopping.

V. Cutting Edge

I'm a grown woman. I'm married. I met my husband a year after the night I held that gun in my hand; he was a thirty-two-year-old married man with two small children. He said he loved me. He told me I was brilliant. He wrote poems for me, slipped them to me in books as I stood at his desk in the classroom. We used to meet in the woods behind my house, or at the school track. He was my teacher. My first lover. My only lover. We married when I was nineteen.

Twelve years later, we have two children, two years apart. Sometimes, when they have been sick a lot, or up all night for too many nights, or both, I scream at my children, enraged over dirty clothes, writing on walls, toys never put away. For a long time, I can hold in these explosions, clean the house or eat instead. Then I begin to write again. It is the first time I have considered being a writer since I was fifteen. The writing seems to help at first; it's a relief to capture my daughter's temper tantrum in a poem, create something whole from the destruction of a day. The deeper I go, the less patience I have. My life—carefully constructed to include husband, children, solid old house—is no longer moving forward in time. The more I write, the further backward my words take me. I don't go easily or willingly. But I need to write too much to let it take the blame for my mood swings. It's easier to blame the kids.

Around the summer my daughter turns seven years old, I begin to have bad dreams. Knives. Bees. Screams that are unheard. I feel something coming unwrapped, coming loose, unleashed inside me. My children have never seen me so uncontrolled; they laugh. In order to be taken seriously, I begin to throw things. At them. One day I take my daughter by the wrists and squeeze. I, who have only ever swatted behinds gently, spank hard. I scream into their faces. My son, the one with my little brother's face, is terrified, learns to hide when he hears me lose my temper, come stomping up the stairs. He promises me he'll "be good." My daughter is defiant, without apology. She screams right back. This happens several times a week, then several times a day. I know I am losing her. My husband asks what's wrong. I don't have words to tell him. He doesn't really want to know. He's as afraid of me as I am.

I confide in two friends what is happening. These women live two thousand miles away, and the written words we exchange are safe. These women are partners, lovers, lesbians. I am secretly in love with one of them. Maybe what I'm in love with is the fact that they love each other. They share with me their own stories of lost families, abuse, and healing. Yet even on paper I am ashamed of many things: the rape, my silence, my anger. Slowly, our letters to each other draw me out of my shell. Finally I write a poem about my being raped at seven years old. I cannot show it to my husband. I send it to my friends, apologize for anything that might upset them. What happens next saves me.

One woman writes back, "Your letter and poem make me want to cry with rage." The second woman tells me not to apologize for the ugliness of what I've written. She says, "Let it out."

I can see there has been no forgetting of the events—only the emotions. Terror, loneliness, terrible anger. Anger is cutting a way out of layers of scar tissue, slashing a path through anything standing too close to me—even my daughter, my son. It is a knife that has been sheathed too long, never disposed of properly, left out where a child could find it. I decide I won't let that happen. I must tell. I give the poem to my husband.

When he reads it, we both cry.

But he never looks at me the same way again. He begins to ask to see the letters from my friends.

Other poems follow this one, written in safe moments at the beach, in the sun, while cleaning the house. I cry a lot; this scares me. I want to stop hiding from these emotions, but I want to survive them, too. One night I dream that I take a knife—a kitchen knife—from my house, ride through town on my bike. I hold the knife pressed between my right hand and the handlebar as I pedal through dusk, blade pointing out. This is dangerous; I could accidentally stab someone. I must get rid of the knife. But where? The streets are crowded, full of after-work shoppers and pre-dinner strollers. Finally I drop the knife into a dishpan full of dirty silverware at an outdoor café and ride on into a cool evening, full of relief and pleasure at finding a solution. No one will ever look there; and the café will quickly absorb the extra blade as part of its inventory. Out of my reach, it will not harm anyone.

VI. Crucible

Getting rid of the blade is not so easy. I try to hide it by plunging the damn thing, hilt and all, into my own chest.

I hide in an early morning, almost dawn, as I sit in my study. I want the door I installed by myself to be closed. I want the cedar paneling on the walls and ceiling to glow warm, almost cinnamon. Hanging here and there should be paintings, presents from friends, announcements for poetry publications. There should be a desk, a file cabinet that stands unlocked. And I want a white cat stretching out on the braided rug, while my husband and two children sleep upstairs, peacefully.

In my fantasy, my daughter awakens first, comes drifting downstairs with her brown hair flopped to one side, rubbing her eyes, heading for my lap. She whispers, "Will you braid my hair for school?" Behind her question crowd years of frustrating tangles, slippery baby-hair fiascoes. I have never been able to braid her hair. My fingers don't know the right moves, somehow; or, I tell myself, Miranda didn't inherit the thick Indian hair that falls to my waist. We've kept her hair short for a long time. But in my fantasy I say, "I think we can manage a little braid today," and that sharpness between us is gone. What remains is like old silver, smooth and warm, just a little bit polished by time. "Like most pure metals," the last sentence of this scene should say, "it gives to the touch."

But that's not true. I write this story by waking up each morning and writing until I feel myself begin to change the truth. Then I walk away from the work till I can face reality again.

I walk away from this story for nearly a decade; walk away with its false ending: the warm old house, the husband, the fiction of a healing that doesn't cost, but doesn't transform. I fight transformation tooth and nail. At last, I recognize change as my old friend Truth. I stand still, and I embrace her.

VII. Reforged

Trees in my neighborhood dance in quiet wee hours. Cedars take turns waiting for the wind to come, lift their limbs in green ceremony. The oaks still have their leaves, pines drop dry cones onto the wet earth. Each species moves in her own favorite sway. I listen and watch, eyelids made heavy, heart blessedly silent.

I left the marriage house with almost no belongings, re-possessed myself from yard sales, thrift stores, the generosity of friends. Now, towels or silverware match only by chance. Inside myself is an entire houseful of furnishings. All the dreams, actions, words I've kept locked up in the attic of my soul. This morning, my children sleep two blocks away in their father's house. Next week, they'll sleep down the hall.

My mother, whose name means "dove," tells me Indian languages originate from the gleaming throats of birds. A friend whose father is mentally ill won't do the automatic writing that feeds her art; the gush of it frightens her. She thinks her own words can lock her up. I think of both these things while I wait for morning to arrive out on my small porch, writing words that might have the power to take away my children permanently.

The sun rises, breaches heavy clouds. We call this sapphire light "dawn," but what do we know? Where is the foggy edge between *then* and *now?* Maybe it is the difference between inner and outer worlds. I'm remembering the day my anger transformed like molten silver into a blinding nova that I learned to call desire.

> She surprises me with Shoshone Falls. Directs me, "Turn left here." Says, "Let's take this exit." The road is suddenly a crevasse: opens jagged in this flat earth, slants fast down to the river. A gift. She saved this moment to please me. The Indian at the gate takes our user fee and grins as if she'd called ahead to conspire. "I'm bringing a woman to the Falls this afternoon," she might have confided. "Make sure they roar real good." The waters are wide as my hopes. Out on the boat dock, our bare feet in cold current, she kisses me: lips pursed, trembling, inexperienced for all her boasts. It's what I want, though. Innocence; the almost virginal state before passion. The love of children who plan to marry each other when they've grown up. Later we can teach each other about desire. Today I want Shoshone Falls, our brown feet in frothy waters, even the blue truck of good old boys

who back their boat-trailer down to the ramp, interrupt us, cause us to stand up and move on—two brown women traveling through a place where no maps exist, where every turn takes us home, but no place takes us in.

Robins and house sparrows flit between the dark lines of houses, between what is dormant, what awakens. I loved a woman; I will love other women. Never like this first time—I'm grateful for that!—but always with the same truth. Just before the smallest cry of sun is a crack where peace emerges, heated and still gleaming from the fire. I write these words down with the tip of a pen forged out of grief and violence. I'll send these stories out where other women are waiting, slashed by nightmares and fear. Cutting themselves, their children.

Sometimes security is a knife that slits your own wrists. Nothing in my life or world prepared me to suspect such a thing. I kept trying to play by the rules I'd learned: the cure for poverty and loss is property and surety. The remedy for violence and alcoholism is control and cold rationality. The way to fill the gaping hole left by abandonment is to never leave; not even to save your own life. The balm for self-hatred is to marry white skin; or to desire skin so much like your own that scars arise of their own accord out of shared histories left unresolved.

It's none of that.

I thought perhaps the cure was telling. Then I thought the cure was telling the truth. Now, in the cool of dawn, I think to myself, maybe it's each woman telling her truth in a language forged from every knife ever held to her throat, or wielded in self-defense. It's not about destruction or forgetting, but transformation. The crucible is love.

Transplant

I was born on Tongva land, not far from my father's homelands of Carmel, Monterey, and Santa Barbara, where our Esselen and Chumash ancestors had lived forever. Those places—some of the most beautiful in the world—hadn't met me yet. My mother's parents were from a tiny town in Nebraska, and before that, those French and English ancestors had traipsed from their landing in New York across the continent, east to west, until they smacked up against the Pacific Ocean. None of those ancestral places knew me, either.

Yes, continents collided when my parents met in East L.A., dancing in a bar—my father, born on the Tuolumne Rancheria in 1927, my mother born in a small cottage in what was not, quite yet, Beverly Hills, 1935. I emerged inside the aftermath of that explosion, a world awash in both colonized and settler trauma, manifested in alcohol abuse and hair-trigger temperaments.

For a few years after my birth, we lived in a series of Los Angeles apartments with faux-adobe walls; Tongva land, yes, but my feet rarely touched it. My mother and I walked on cement sidewalks and streets, caught a bus to go to the doctor or the grocery store; my father bused or carpooled downtown to build skyscrapers. For me, a child of L.A., the natural world happened in those small, sprinkler-fed green swatches of apartment complexes, where pigeons nested by the dozens in palm trees, and small lizards scuttled across landscaped lava rock. Inside, cockroaches popped out of a roll of socks; black widows lurked in damp bathrooms. Occasional trips to the beach meant crowds, "sandbugs" in my swimsuit, watching Daddy plunge under the waves and pop up like a seal in the distance. Sometimes, nature happened in the backyards of relatives where giant bushes with fuchsia blossoms my elderly relatives called "dancing ladies" were reverently tended, bougainvillea vines covered chain link fences, and orange trees loomed like lords.

Heaven was a trip to my grandparents' cabin in the Tehachapi mountains, a place where gophers, horny toads, rabbits, chipmunks, deer might be seen. The mountains around my grandparents' cabin were dotted with sagebrush and the occasional manzanita tree; shade was rare. Once, I thought I'd solved that problem by camping out beneath the outside staircase; in the cool gray light, I had made up some game or other with the sand, twigs, and carved wooden animals. The bites of dozens of ants drove me back indoors and taught me deep respect for such tiny creatures. Sometimes, I'd go into my grandfather's garage where he had a small shop, and watch him make "jewelry trees" from manzanita branches. The twisted, deep red branches and trunks reminded me of my father's sinewy arms and legs. Early in the morning, I often accompanied my grandmother while she watered her tiny flower garden; green leaves bowed beneath the spray of water from a hose, and ruby-throated hummingbirds came to sip at the pink, white, and purple blossoms of flowers never meant for the desert. When I walked outside on the porch at night, every star in the universe sang a silvery lullaby, and the heated scent of chaparral and sage cleansed the day. This was Kitanemuk land, and I was loved there.

But when I was three years old, the State of California sentenced my father to eight years in San Quentin. My mother suffered a breakdown and disappeared for a year; Aunt Sally and Uncle Pat took me into their home nearby. Their daughter, a year younger than me, was unhappy about sharing her parents' affections. That was the least of my worries. Eventually, my mother returned, temporarily rehabbed as per my aunt's demands. With my mother's new husband Tom driving, we headed north to western Washington State where he had a sister, and job prospects.

I was a shy transplant on Muckleshoot territory, but also the only Indian child (a half-breed, at that) in the all-white trailer park (*mobile home* was a phrase not yet invented). The only dark-skinned child in each of the four elementary schools I attended between first and third grade, I stayed a transplant as we continued to move from one trailer to another, burning candles when there was no money to pay the electric bill, often a step ahead of the landlord. In the summer, parents boosted their kids up on top of metal trailers with a hose to spray water over scorching roofs; few trees existed within the trailer park itself. In the long winters, endless rain filled potholes and soaked shoes on the way to the bus stop.

While we lived in one of those trailer parks, a man raped me. I was seven years old. Buddy was a classic pedophile: he befriended my mother and stepfather to get close to me, brought cartons of cigarettes and cases of beer to the trailer, candy in his pockets and generous attentions to neglected little girls. I didn't tell anyone. Not too long after this incident, we moved again—to another trailer. It could have been the same old thing all over again. It was not: my mother's parents had loaned their daughter money to make a down payment.

And this trailer came with land.

That is how I arrived—traumatized, fearful, neglected—on the 3.5 acres that would shelter me. Located on East Hill just above the wide Kent valley and the small town of the same name, the only structures on this land were an old single-wide trailer and a little red three-stall horse barn; we used to joke that the barn was in better shape than the trailer, but it wasn't really a joke.

For a brief time in the 1870s, Kent had been famous for its hops and other agriculture; before that, countless ancestors of the Duwamish and Upper Puyallup tribes had flourished in this part of the state, enjoying the fruits of a dark, rich soil left behind by flooding rivers and a prehistoric mudflow from a volcano the Indians called Tahoma, which I grew up calling Mt. Rainier. When we moved there in 1968, the Indians lived on the Muckleshoot reservation the next town over (though I wouldn't know that until I was thirteen and my father returned; he'd head straight for those familiar faces). Our land was surrounded by large tracts of other wooded properties and fallow farmland, with tall pines and a creek along our western and northern boundaries, and open fields to our south and east. My home for the next ten years, this land offered a protection and healing I had never known before.

I was still a transplant, but now I had earth that succored my bare roots. And it had come at a crucial time.

It sounds like a cliché to say that the land mothered me during these roughest of years, but the truth will out. Inside our trailer, my mother smoked, drank, cried, fought with the men in her life, and made of herself a silent, isolated island. Even sober, she kept herself apart from me, buried in a book or simply going about her day without speaking more than necessary. Inside the trailer, strangers passed through in varying degrees of intoxication or high on drugs. One day, a man crawled from a bedroom into the living room, banging his head on the linoleum, over and over; I kept trying to slide a pillow under his head. I was no more than ten years old. It was all I could think of to do. The smell of weed, cigarettes, vomit, unwashed bodies often permeated the trailer, and I slept with the small slat windows in my bedroom cranked open. My lungs protested the smoke all winter long, to the point that my doctor asked me accusingly, "Are you smoking, young lady?"—in the fifth grade, I had a chronic smoker's cough.

So that first spring, the woods drew me away from our small trailer, that thick atmosphere of despair. I doubt my explorations took me more than a mile or two away in any direction, all forest with deer paths through the trees or open pasture. But it wasn't about distance; it was about my body's deep dive into this place, and how this place received me. Our dogs kept me company, taught me how to smell this, dig that, run here, trot there, taste this, lie in the sun, play in the creek's cold shallows. If I had to pee, I moved off the trail and squatted. Hungry? I'd find berries, in season, or chew on sourweed to satisfy my mouth with lemony flavors. Never any hurry. Creek mud on stinging nettle blisters, my shirt a quick basket to carry stones for dam-making or berries for lunch. Was this freedom, or neglect? Was I adrift, or taken in? I never asked.

Old cedar fence posts strung with barbed wire appeared occasionally in my ramblings; I didn't think twice about climbing deftly in between the wires to get into the blackberry patches on nearby parcels of land, and my arms and legs bore more than a few scratches; but it was understood that berries were first come, first served. Sometimes, my mother joined me—we'd pick early in the mornings before the heat came up, when the spiderwebs were bejeweled with dew and the mosquitoes still a little sleepy. Now I learned something new about my mother: she knew how to make an amazing blackberry pie. And she taught me other new things: how to bathe the berries in the kitchen sink (pick out the overripe and hard red-green berries that snuck in, wash away the most obvious bugs), how to stir in sugar, simmer over a low heat, dip out a bit of the dark juice and mix it with cornstarch, then slowly stir it back into the pot. While that flowery, thorny, sweet mix cooled, my mother taught me how to mix the ingredients for a crust that would melt in our mouths (a little vinegar was her secret to smooth, elastic dough), roll it into a circle, and settle that into the bottom of pie tins; she taught me how to pour in the blackberries, cover with a smooth sheet of dough, prick it with a fork in a starburst pattern. Then she taught me how to sit quietly, reading, as the purple, tangy scent of August filled our trailer. Later, we ate these slices of the land sitting at the small kitchen table together, took those berries into our mouths, and felt lit from within. I will never forget that sincere, lingering sacrament.

Our closest neighbor, old Mr. Franklin, gave me permission to roam the steep slope of his even older orchard. Pretty soon I had my favorite apple trees staked out: the best eating-out-of-hand tree, the best pie apples, the best snack tree for another neighbor's horses. I braved the tall unmown grass with its leggy, surprising insect inhabitants, buzzing yellowjackets and bees who came to feast on fallen fruit, and the clusters of birds seeking sweetness. Now my mother made apple pies, filled the big freezer my stepfather had bartered for and kept in the barn. Later in the fall, I discovered two fat hazelnut bushes tucked away in one corner of the orchard, heavy with clusters of nuts in scratchy green husks flared like skirts. Squeezing close to the base, I learned that the ripe honey-colored nuts popped right out into my hand. Trial and error also taught me to find a nice flat rock—or a stray cinder block!—and fit another stone comfortably in my hand to strike the hard shell. The slightly sweet nutmeat crunched between my molars, rich and satisfying. My body relished the fat and protein—especially after my mother threw my wayward stepfather out, and we were on our own. To my relief, she told me, *we* weren't going anywhere.

That land was in my mother's name.

She applied for food stamps and welfare; she applied for financial aid and began attending a local community college. Now she studied at the kitchen table after dinner, and all weekend long. Pot after pot of black coffee slowly replaced cases of beer, although the drinking would come and go for years, returning full force when my father reappeared in a few years. But we got by—just.

I remember:

The beautiful bright rust-red of a crumbling old-growth cedar nurse log, home to glossy black beetles, bright black-and-yellow millipedes swirling through the bright dust.

Deer paths carpeted with fallen cedar and pine needles that softened my steps, perfumed the air, heated by sun into an incense like medicine, a smudge created by the earth and the day to bless me and protect me, to cleanse my body of loneliness and fear.

The creek, a musical voice who murmured all spring and summer, froze into richly patterned layers in the winter. On her banks, I found the tracks of raccoons, deer, porcupines, skunks; made twig and leaf boats; soaked legs scratched by thorns or blistered by nettles. I remember the clarity of that water, the spongy mosses that colonized the banks, the deeper pools where I shed my clothes, slid in like a salamander.

No one ever formally explained anything to me about how to live where we lived. Yet I was not untaught. I listened when adults talked about what was edible, what was not, and when to say, "I don't know." But the landscape, the weather, the geography—they, too, educated me about harvests of change and beauty. And maybe I have never put this into words before, but I often think now, I needed a green forest in which to hide; only a place without human beings could salvage my humanity.

My mother—a voracious reader raising another voracious reader— took me to the small downtown Kent library once a week. We arrived with paper grocery bags to carry home our loot. I found books that provided names for the riches surrounding me. Field guides, children's encyclopedias. I started with birds, their songs the first thing I heard each morning. Crows I knew, along with robins and blue jays, but now woodpeckers were much more than a cartoon character, and now I could name cedar waxwings singing in a towering grove of salmonberries, their olive bodies and bright red seals flitting among the fruit. Chickadees, goldfinches like flying flames (though my mother insisted they were "wild canaries," and I liked that name better), hummingbirds, red-tailed hawks; a great horned owl on the road one night, lifting over the windshield of our car; barn swallows over the fields at dusk; nuthatches, wrens, song sparrows, pine siskins, juncos, warblers, tanagers.

The more names I could put to a creature, the richer my loneliness became. I could not name the dysfunction around me—I didn't have words for alcoholism, depression, trauma—but I learned the language of naming to make sense of what I could.

Oh, salmonberries: translucent orange lanterns, heavy and sweet in the rain. Lady fern, sword fern, deer fern, salal with its exquisite white bells blushing pink. Skunk cabbage bursting out of creek mud like bright yellow heads, fireweed crowning ancient stumps, buttercups all leggy around the old horse trough, pollen smearing my hands when I picked them. And carpets of pristine trilliums (mostly white, some mysteriously purple), bleeding hearts in sweeping colonies with their lacy leaves, twinflower, tiny wild strawberries, horsetail ferns like prehistoric remnants, wild roses twined with bindweed (my mother called these white trumpets by the prettier name "morning glories").

Above me, trees: red cedar, vine maple, bigleaf maple, alder, willow, fir, pines that swayed during winter storms like old grandmothers swishing their skirts, raining down cones I'd find covering the edges of pastures. I saw deer stepping delicately through snow, held a raccoon stunned by an encounter with a car; the dogs came home one morning, their muzzles studded with porcupine quills (that required an expensive trip to the vet!). I heard coyotes yip at night, but never saw one up close. Squirrels whistled and chittered from the tops of pine trees, the ground beneath littered with pine-cone scales. One strange furry creature standing outside a burrow dug into the embankment of our dirt road required a teacher's help to name: mountain beaver. I encountered and studied garter snakes, pond turtles, tree frogs, toads, ladybugs, grasshoppers, potato bugs, spit bugs, a multitude of spiders; observed methodical banana slugs and their small gray or rust-colored relatives with delicate, alien tentacles.

Once, at the edge of a pasture, I came upon a castle of intricately patterned dried pine needles, raised up over a foot high by red-and-black ants—thatching ants, I later learned. The number of pine needles required for this kind of construction boggled my mind. Crouching off to the side, I marveled at the energy and cooperation between these thousands of ants. But when I mentioned the castle to my mother's boyfriend, Frank, he was not as impressed. Too close to the trailer, he said. They'll bite. He took a can of gasoline out to the cone-shaped nest, poured it over the anthill, and set it on fire.

I learned, again, when to keep my mouth shut.

Outside, in the woods, in the fields, along the dirt road, down by the creek, I was still wounded, still lonely. But here was respite. The summer sun and winter rains lavished themselves on my skin. So did mosquitoes and stinging nettles, blackberry thorns and pine sap. I waded in the creek, wallowed in the deeper hollows making up stories about fish and alligators, dried myself off walking through the underbrush. Beautiful greens of infinite variety surrounded me, and the scent of all those growing things cleansed my lungs, moistened my eyes, drenched my hair.

It is true that my mother did not know how to mother me. Perhaps she was too unmothered herself; it would be years before I began to understand her story. For now—by accident, by luck—I ended up in a place where the land gave me what I needed to keep my spirit alive.

I was still a transplant, a seedling whose roots would eventually call me home to California, to those ancestral places where relatives—human and nonhuman—waited to welcome me, teach me, ask me for my contribution. But this land—oh, this land was home, too; it held me, fed me, nurtured my curiosity, educated me in its own ways. It could not actually save me; that task lay ahead for me, a long journey that I am still walking through.

On this Muckleshoot land, I learned about love, gratitude, and respect from my oldest relative of all.

Petroglyphs

All my life, I knew I would disappear. I knew my presence here on earth was so tentative that I was in constant danger of being devoured, absorbed, vanished.

So from the time I could hold a crayon, I scribbled. I scrawled. My hand grew cramped and tired, calluses formed on my fingers from holding a pen, a pencil. I gripped my writing utensil with four fingers instead of three, used my pinky to support the others. Gripped so hard my fingers hurt but couldn't stop. Couldn't stop, because if I did, I would disappear. Everyone I loved had disappeared. I knew I was next.

But if I could keep marking my presence on the earth, on tables, on scrap paper, if I could keep telling the story, if I could keep making words on the page tell the story, then maybe I could hang on.

It wasn't that my world was full of emptiness and nothingness. No, my world wasn't barren. That might have almost been a relief. My world was too full—of violence, abandonment, a mother who didn't come home, fathers who kept disappearing, siblings who were there one day, gone the next. Homes disappeared. Neighborhoods, friends, schools, teachers, friends. Everything in my life disappeared all the time. Why should I be any different? Why had I not disappeared? It was only a matter of time. I knew it.

I remember the first word I ever wrote. On a brown paper bag, with a red crayon. **D E B Y.** I sat at my grandmother's kitchen counter in a red cabin with white trim, high in the Tehachapi Mountains. How can I put this into words you'll understand? Armageddon had already happened. I was three years old. My father had been incarcerated at San Quentin, serving a sentence of eight years. My mother had run away. My two older siblings were put into foster care. I had been taken from the apartment we lived in, and I never saw it again. I never saw my babysitter again. I never saw our furniture, our dishes, our silverware, our blankets, our *life* again. Every single familiar thing in the world had disappeared.

(Except for my grandmother, my grandfather, and this little red cabin up in the mountains. And even that, my bedrock, my haven, would soon be taken away when I was sent to live with my aunt and uncle. I didn't know until I was thirty years old that although my grandmother wanted to keep me, my grandfather said no. Even at thirty, I learned: there are many ways for people to disappear.)

I held the paper bag out to my grandmother, who was at the sink washing up. We had probably just had lunch; I was allowed to eat sandwiches at the counter, but dinner was always at the table. Tepa wasn't there; maybe outside working on the boat, or the trailer, or the garage, or his fishing gear. It was safe in Mommer's kitchen. The pine paneling, the sunshine streaming in, the mountains all around us, holding us. It seemed I'd always known this place: as a sixth-month-old baby, I'd contracted a severe case of chicken pox; my mother and siblings were miserable with the disease, but I was listless, thin, and needed special care. My father had brought me here, left me so he could go to work. My grandmother bathed me in that stainless steel sink with cool baking-soda water, held me in her hands, far away from chaos and calamity.

So now, years later, I showed her my name, written in big shaky proud letters. **D E B Y.** That was how my mother had spelled it, how everyone spelled it. That was how I'd learned it. Little red sticks and a few shaky curves, lined up in the right combination, in the correct direction, each one performing a necessary task.

I'm sure my grandmother was proud of me. I'm sure she praised me. I'm sure I'd been practicing. But that moment: that's when I made a transformative leap in my understanding of being. It was as if, when I wrote those letters, made a written record of my self, my name, my existence, those letters grew roots and plowed down through that Formica countertop, into the wooden floor, beams, and concrete foundation of the cabin, deep into the heart of the Tehachapi Mountains themselves.

I had staked myself to this world. I had created a space for myself. I had claimed my fierce life in four little letters. **D E B Y.**

And the potency of those letters was that even when I was far away from this peaceful place—highways and stop signs and backseats and long hot naps away from these mountains—the waxy strokes of those letters, my name, the ability to muscle my way into reality, into existence, came with me. Always connected me to that mountain, that cabin, the pungent sage on the mountainsides, the sandy earth, dry heated winds, scorching sun, cold blue nights pierced by silver stars.

From that day on, every time I put pencil to paper, I recreated that moment when I came into being. I learned how to carry myself in the world even when nobody else could. It was powerful magic for a little girl. It could have carried me off. Under other circumstances, to touch such power might have burnt me up. But I needed this magic. I needed every single ounce in order to survive what had already happened, what was to come.

In that cusp of time on the mountain, I had to learn fast. The world outside the mountain was a tar pit, a black hole, and my entire family had been swallowed up in it; right down to the last black bobby pin on my mother's head. I was the sole survivor. And although I didn't understand why, and although I grieved silently for all that I had lost, I did not want to follow. I wanted to live.

I have always been drawn back to that mountain, to that brown, stony land. I have dreams in which I simply stand on the porch, look up into the black mass of mountain that stood behind the cabin, and above that shadow, the piercing white constellations of summer.

There is a kind of physical strength that comes to people in moments of extraordinary need—the ability to lift a car off a child, push aside obstacles, pull someone back from a cliff. Fueled by adrenaline, desire, need, often the sudden surge of strength is gone, never to return again, as soon as the emergency is over. I think writing came to me like that. Power came to me in those mountains. Power was visited on me. Power was given to me. And at the same time, I called it. I reached out to it. I found it. Because I was searching. Because I was desperate. Because I knew that black hole was oozing up behind me, lapping at my heels, coming to swallow me up, too. Unlike physical "hysterical strength," however, writing never left me.

D E B Y. When I lifted my red crayon from the paper bag, I had earned the magic. I didn't understand it, I hadn't mastered it, but I had touched it, tasted it. And it was good. I could breathe again. I knew where I was. I knew how to keep myself there. I knew how to beat back Disappear.

That red crayon: my wand, my staff, my paint, my ocher, the material that made it possible for my voice to materialize outside of my body. I knew how to say, "I am here." I knew that as long as I kept writing, I would stay here.

This magic has worked for over forty years now. I have a big green plastic footlocker padlocked shut, filled with words, testimony, glyphs, chronicles of those years. I have hauled that footlocker, in various forms, back and forth across the North American continent several times, up and down the West Coast, needed those journals for something, some validation of my continued survival. Along the way I have married, borne children, buried both grandparents and mother, then father, divorced, been in love, found sisters, battled the disease of disappearance at every turn. If I'm not a good wife, I'll disappear. If I'm not a good mother, I'll disappear. If I'm not a good daughter, I'll disappear. If she doesn't love me, I'll disappear.

I journaled my way through it all, and I still do. This essay started in a journal.

But recently, I realized that I am ready to let go of those old journals now. They are just words. No matter how I try to preserve them, the words will fade. Lead markings will soften, ink will lighten. Paper will crumble. Water will seep in, soak apart wood fibers, bleed colors. Like the ancient petroglyphs of my Esselen and Chumash ancestors, my journals are subject to wildfires, floods, lightning strikes, vandalism, time.

I am no longer dependent on making a mark on a piece of paper to know that I am alive, not disappearing, not swallowed up by the horrific unknown that once pursued me. It was good power that I learnt, but there are other ways to use it than to just hold on. It kept me alive, but now . . .

Now I am what is *behind* the markings on paper. I paint my sunburst on the thin wall of a rock shelter, transfer my power from my body to a symbol. Create a thing from no thing.

And then I release it, walk away, leave it there for you to find—a bright handprint, or faded shadow, or just the hint of spirit animal. I'll wear away, too. Rock faces flake and chip, mosses dissolve pigment, rain releases minerals that streak and stain. I'll return to the elements that created me. But through this mark you will know I was here, and I know you are coming after me. We have stories to exchange about this difficult gift, life, and those stories will never disappear.

Mestiza Nation: A Future History of My Tribe

The original acts of colonization and violence broke the world, broke our hearts, broke the connection between soul and flesh. For many of us, this trauma happens again in each generation, to children too young and too untrained to try to cope with dysfunction that ravages even adults. Gloria Anzaldua knew this. Paula Gunn Allen knew this. Chicana, Indian, these women knew that the formation of a Mestiza Nation was as much about healing from our childhoods as healing from larger histories.

I am of the seventh generation since my great-great-great-great-great-great-grand-parents Fructuoso Cholom and Yginia Yunisyunis emerged from Mission San Carlos de Borromeo in Carmel, California, in the mid-1830s. I am half white, half Indian, mixed with Mexican and Jewish tribes. When I look at all that has passed since Fructuoso Cholom and Yginia Yunisyunis were emancipated, I wonder if they dreamed that their descendants would still be struggling to free ourselves, seven generations later.

When I look toward the next seven generations, I imagine this is the kind of story that my descendants will tell, seven generations from now, in the future mythology of the Mestiza Nation.

Once there was a girl without a mother.

She'd never had a mother, even though she called the woman who gave birth to her "Mama." This woman kept leaving her daughter behind at relatives' homes or forgetting her in stores. It wasn't entirely Mama's fault; often when she thought her arms were full of little girl, or that the little girl was safely clutching Mama's hand, it was really the ghost of a daughter Mama had lost years ago.

So when Mama felt the weight of a child heavy against her hip or tugging at her arm, she didn't know it was actually the pull of persistent sorrow distracting her from the real child. Sometimes the real little girl caught sight of her dead sister, hungrily wrapping her chubby arms around Mama's neck as they went out the door together, leaving the little girl once again. Sometimes the little girl's father followed them.

Her father was why the little girl was different from her older sister and brother. They were light-skinned, with clear blue eyes and hair the color of cornflakes. But the girl without a mother was cinnamon-colored, with thick dark hair, vivid against her family. When the girl without a mother held hands with her brother or sister to cross the street, their long slender fingers seemed to tangle up with her wide flat palms and short fingers. At the park, no one listened to the little girl when she claimed her brother and sister, not even when the big sister yelled at the bullies trying to push her off the swing.

The girl without a mother began to understand that she was invisible. She wondered if this was why her Ghost Sister had become a ghost in the first place; if she herself were becoming less and less real, too.

Eventually the woman who gave birth to the little girl went away and didn't come back. Secretly, the girl thought perhaps her mother was looking for the girl's father, who had been missing for some time now. The big sister didn't tell anyone, but bathed her little brother and sister each night, fed them cereal each morning, sent the boy off to school, dropped the little girl off at a babysitter's. The big sister brushed the little girl's hair and helped the little brother with his homework, but one day the food ran out, and the big sister had to call a grown-up. The big sister and brother were taken to a foster home, a place for children without parents. But the home only had space for older children. "Bring the little one back in the fall," said the people in charge. "We might have room then."

That is how the girl without a mother came to stay with her mother's parents for one short season.

* * *

Her mother's parents were light-skinned and blue-eyed as well, but in those days it was common for such people to settle in the very land from which the little girl's father and his people had emerged. The girl loved her grandmother's house in the dry Tehachapi Mountains; she spent the summer playing with lizards and horned toads, sleeping between cool cotton sheets, watching the glimmer of hummingbirds come to her grandmother's feeder very early in the morning. Her dark eyes feasted on the sagebrush dotting the brown hills, and she spoke regularly with a black bird perched in the manzanita behind the house. She ran barefoot all day, her feet finding joy in the dust. Once, she sat down on some ants who were busy with their own matters, and was badly bitten. Later, after apologizing to the ants, the little girl watched them work for hours, at a distance.

Every evening the grandmother bathed the girl in a deep shiny white tub, but no matter how the woman scrubbed, the colors wrought by soil and sun would not be cleansed from the girl's knees and cheeks.

"More like that man every day," the grandfather muttered to himself, shaking his head. "The sooner they have room for her at Mrs. Samm's, the better."

But the grandmother saw her own lost daughter in this little girl's movements and wished for a chance to correct her mistakes as a mother. The grandmother let the girl without a mother sow corn in the small fenced flower garden, where the green stalks were watered generously each evening along with the morning glories, petunias, pansies, tall daisies, and brilliant orange poppies.

When the corn reached the girl's waist, the foster family called: they still had no room for the girl without a mother. The grandfather silenced the grandmother's look with a curt "No." The grandmother turned away.

No one asked the girl where she would like to live. She would have chosen to stay and see the corn grow past her head. But one day before the sun was up, her grandmother came to wake her for a trip to yet another place.

* * *

The girl without a mother stood on the steps of her grandmother's house. Behind her rose a mountain, dark and seemingly still. Before her rose the sky, arched black and brilliant with stars, and the cleft of a long valley. The air was dry, cool, gently opening.

From her grandmother's garden came the smooth slippery surge of petunias, snapdragons, poppies. The happy leaves of the corn plants shivered with pleasure as they grew upwards in their slow spiral. The girl without a mother stood alone, huddled in a soft sweater, wearing only a sundress underneath because it would be hot later. Inside the house, her grandmother packed sandwiches and thermoses of coffee and milk. The grandmother cried as she tightened the lids of containers.

No person saw this; only the grandmother's heart knew this grief that she would not speak of until she was a very old woman, many thousands of miles away from this place, dying, and asking forgiveness. In the garage, the grandfather loaded up the truck that would take the girl without a mother home. He would start the motor any minute.

But for one moment before dawn the world was humming with quiet power, and the girl without a mother heard a funny sound.

Thump and pause. *Thump* and pause. Scraps of a song wandered in between the sounds. It almost seemed to be asking a question, a question the girl couldn't quite hear all the words to, but that she wanted to answer. *Thump*, pause. *Thump*, pause, *song*.

The girl went quickly down the wooden steps and around the back of the house, stepping carefully around the gopher traps she'd watched her grandfather set. *Thump*, pause. *Song, song, song*. The girl wandered into a dry streambed, followed the stones. The rocks were washed and smooth and she could see where to put her feet better and more easily the longer she climbed; the sun was following behind her.

She climbed and climbed. When the girl without a mother got tired, a woman came to meet her and took her through the side of the mountain. "Come here, this way," the woman said; she picked up her grinding stone and basket, pushed aside a curtain of dried grasses and sticks. "We are little rabbits looking for our nest," she smiled, "we are fawns, called to our mother's side in the warm grass." And the girl without a mother followed the song of the woman who came out of a mountain.

Inside the opening was a cool, sandy tunnel. The darkness seemed soft, like a light blanket, not frightening at all. After only a few steps, the two came out into another place, a land with a stream full of big silver fish swimming lazily in from the sea, seemingly straight into the nets and hands of laughing men; oak trees covered thick green hills. Under the heavy branches, families with baskets gathered acorns, children played while they worked, women were easy with their voices. The girl without a mother noticed right away that some of the people were darker than her, and some of them were lighter.

The woman who came out of a mountain gestured to the new place. "See, this is where you will live now."

"Are you going to be my mother?" asked the girl without a mother, taking off her blue sweater and letting it slide to the ground.

"No, I'm just an old woman," laughed the woman who came out of a mountain. "Not many children here have mothers. But you'll be cared for. This is getting to be a big family. We're busy just now—acorns, salmon, islay are good this year. You'll have to help."

By now the little girl had stripped off her sundress, and her black patent leather shoes that squished her toes, and the white slippery socks that made her feet sweat. She stood in itchy underwear that got caught in all the wrong places but had been her secret armor against the dark. Hardly anyone here wore clothes except for pretty, she noticed; but most girls her age had a rustly skirt. "Can I have one of those?" she asked, pointing to two girls running by with empty baskets in their arms. "And a basket like that for working?"

The woman who came out of a mountain reached out and stopped the other children. "This is the girl I went to find," explained the woman.

"Help her make a skirt, and give her a basket. She'll work with you."

The three girls looked at each other. The girl without a mother was astonished. One of the girls had a dark, serious face much like her own—short nose, arched eyebrows, thin lips—but freckles washed across her cheeks. Her eyes sparkled black and made the girl rise on her tiptoes with a laugh. Her hair was shiny black and thick like the little girl's, too.

The second girl stood light and alive, as if she could hardly keep from dancing away; her skin was the color of sand in the river, and her eyes glimmered brown and green like water over deep rocks. Yet her hair had the same still darkness as her companion's.

The girl without a mother knew with certainty that here were others who had not matched their families.

Suddenly both girls smiled, and the girl without a mother, who had no brothers or sisters who looked the way she did, felt a grin blossom on her own face. Some scar sealed shut in her chest opened; warm, strong blood rushed in.

The first girl held out a round basket, revealing her wide flat palm and short strong fingers.

"You can have this one," she said.

* * *

It was all a long time ago, longer than anyone remembers. On the other side of the tunnel, people searched for the girl without a mother. They had dogs who tracked her faint scent up a rocky streambed, farther than anyone believed she could have walked. But even the dogs couldn't find any sign past a place where the arroyo curved sharply around a big hill dense with sagebrush and rabbit holes.

Long after the little girl's corn had ripened, taller than the grandmother and heavy with fat ears, the grandparents ceased looking. The foster family didn't have room for the many other children in that place without mothers, anyway. People slowly forgot about the girl without a mother, though her grandmother came out before dawn and listened hard for music she was almost afraid to hear.

Every once in a while the woman who came out of a mountain went back, pushed aside the curtain of sagebrush and manzanita, and looked out. She could see a long, long way from her hill; clearly, too.

Sometimes her sharp eyes caught sight of a certain kind of child. Then the woman who came out of a mountain would take her grinding stones and basket, sit by the entrance, and sing. If the child were very small, the woman would walk quietly down the streambed to meet him. If the child were older, the woman sang soothing songs to encourage her.

None of the children who came to her ever arrived unharmed, but the woman who came out of a mountain always took them home with her anyway.

This is the song she sang:

Ah hey way lo lo, hey way
lo lo, hey way lo lo;
Lo lo, hey hey, ah hey way
lo lo, hey way lo lo;
A hey way lo lo, hey way
lo lo, hey way lo lo
lo lo hey hey
hey way lo lo
hey way lo lo
lo lo hey hey
ah hey way lo lo
hey way lo lo
hey way lo lo . . .

Angel in a Pink Plymouth

In the late 1980s, with the birth of my two children, my father and I tried to make peace. He'd been living in Washington State since 1975 in a failed effort to reunite with my mother; even though his temper and drinking had made my teen years miserable, I wanted my children to know their grandfather, hear his stories, have a connection to the older world he came from. So when my father asked if I'd accompany him to the hospital for a surgical procedure, I agreed.

The surgeon told us to be at the hospital by eleven a.m., and we are. But my father is nervous. His blood pressure is too high for someone about to have three hours of IV fluids. Nurses come into his hospital room several times in an hour to wrap the black band around his tattooed upper arm and shake their heads. Finally a doctor okays some blood pressure medicine, but by then it's been thirteen hours since Al last ate. His stomach is upset.

"Can't I have just a couple sips of soda-pop?" he wheedles Cheryl, his current nurse. Standing aside, I witness the time warp of genetics: Al is my five-year-old son, begging me for candy; my twenty-year-old brother, borrowing gas money to get to work on the day after payday.

"*One* sip," Cheryl finally agrees, "7-Up or ginger ale. Just swish it around in your mouth a little, make it last."

I empty the pockets of my jeans onto the bedside table, look for change for the machine down the hall. I'm impatient too. In my backpack is an unread letter from a woman I recently met at a writing workshop. Living over one thousand miles apart now, we have a rich and voluminous friendship-by-mail. I am anxious to read her response to my last letter, but I don't want to bring it out until I'm alone. For my father, a private letter is like Pandora's box—he can't wait to open it, the temptation to *know* is more than he can bear.

Meanwhile, my pockets yield up mints, hairbands, pennies . . .

"What the heck is that?" Al asks, pointing to something brown, teardrop-shaped, not much bigger than a silver dollar, that has emerged out of my pocket.

I surprise myself. I hand him the soft leather pouch that my friend recently sent me. A few years ago I would have been angry at my father for asking, and at myself for inadvertently revealing something dear to me.

Al picks up the pouch, pulls on the drawstrings with the delicacy that is always so unexpected from those huge, calloused hands. He shakes out a round medallion. Even with his glasses, he squints down through bifocals, rotates the disk in his palm.

"It's an angel," I explain. I'm not sure how much sight he has left. He's good at faking it.

He pauses, lets his eyes focus. I know the exact second he finds the angel imbedded in epoxy, the gold, purple, blue and silver glitter, foil hearts and stars swirling around her, because my father says in almost startled recognition, "That's for protection!"

After a second he asks, "Is this a magnet on the back?"

I say yes. "I guess it goes on a refrigerator." I don't say, "It's been living in my pocket as a talisman instead."

"No," Al states positively. "It's to go in your car. For protection."

Suddenly he is remembering.

"We had a station wagon once, a pink Plymouth with black trim, big fins on the tail like that, eh?" Thick hands craft a curve in the air by his hospital bed. "Tepa, your grandfather, bought it for us . . . you were just a baby then, not more'n nine months. We were living down on Barrington, your mother and I. One morning I drove that car to work when I was still hungover from the night before." His voice lowers as he speaks, mindful of the man in the next bed, as if the thin curtain between us could possibly block any sound.

"And I musta fallen asleep at the wheel. On the freeway! Next thing I know, man, I was off the road and that station wagon was flipping over, rolling over and over through the bushes, this tall grass. And then it landed on one side, on the driver's side, and kept sliding. And I went down, down about nine or twelve feet, into a ravine, and hit a concrete overpass coming down like that—" Again, his hands diagram angles and motion. Carpenter's hands. "I landed on a cyclone fence, eh, and I couldn't get the door open! I turned the engine off but I could smell the gas, you know? And I couldn't get out. Then I thought, this thing has electric windows. I pushed the button for the back window and it went down! So I crawled out that way, crawled up the embankment to the road. A lotta people stopped, they seen me go off the road and come running. I was in shock, didn't know *nothin'* . . ."

Al's round, flat face is distant. He is on the shoulder of the freeway again, his knees pierced by gravel, his guts heaving. "And these people were yelling, 'Get the babies out, get the babies out!' And I thought to myself, 'Okay, Al, go back, get the babies out' and started to slide back down. Then I remembered. I had two big dolls in the back, I won them for you at the bar—and I tol' them people, 'No, no, it's two dolls—dolls, not babies . . . ' "

Now the IV team comes in to do the needle, and Al tells me to forget the pop. He hates the IV, always complains about being "poked too god-damned many times" without success. I know he is afraid. This same man still bears the gang tattoos of his youth, walked the girders of skyscrapers in L.A. for a living, did eight years in San Quentin and emerged alive.

This time, though, there is no problem; the technician is smooth and practiced, and Al grunts "Good," as if it's the least they could do. Soon his dark, compact body is strapped onto a cot and waiting for a ride to surgery. He has long since handed back my angel. I stand with my hands in my pockets, flannel shirt untucked, a question on my mind.

"Your mom almost killed me," Al says suddenly from the doorway.

He looks at me sideways from under his carefully combed silver mane. He doesn't use Tres Flores anymore—maybe he's been too far from home too long—but I still smell it in his presence. He measures me with his half-blind eyes, says, "Your mother used to be different—" smiles, shamefacedly. "She used to yell at me. Oh, she read me the riot act. 'What are you going to tell Tepa, how will you get to work, what about the baby's appointments? . . .'"

I laugh at the absurd image of my quiet mother letting her temper fly. I don't remember ever seeing that happen in my thirty years, but then, there are a lot of things from that time I don't remember.

I forget to ask my question.

My father's gurney is rolling down the hall. His thick glasses lie on the bedside table. He can barely see without them. Glaucoma. There is no choice but this last-ditch operation. The leather bag is a hard lump in my pocket. I touch it gently with my fingertips. Can't believe I let him hold it, open it; can't believe I'm even in this hospital as his next of kin. I used to hate this man; feared him so much that I couldn't eat, couldn't stand to be in the same room with him. His demons contaminated all of his children, but especially my brother, his last child, ten years younger than me.

I raised Little Al until he was six. We had each other on those crazy nights, Al's hand like a paw in mine as we listened together to the sound of that old red pickup truck barreling down the dirt road away from us again. Though I was not allowed to interfere when our father pulled off his belt to discipline, I snuck into Little Al's room afterwards as he cried what we both knew had to be perfectly silent tears. In the long summers while I was home all day, we walked the woods and pastures together. I was Little Al's big sister, surrogate mother, friend; he was my first child.

When my parents separated for the last time, my father took his son with him. Fathers had that right in Al's universe. What it really meant was that at age six, my brother was on his own.

He could use a guardian angel, I now think to myself. But it's just a bottle cap filled with glitter, a paper angel, and clear epoxy; it fits snugly inside a smooth two-inch pouch with tiny crimson beads circling the top lip.

I think about the friend who gave this angel to me: a good poet, a strong woman who has worked hard to live her mixed-blood heritage with dignity and love. In my heart, I call her sister. A woman who looks like me, my brother, my son. Like my father. I'm thirty years old; she is the only other California Indian I have met.

I think of everything: the Maidu song her mother sang in a scale she couldn't learn—her mother's early death—the way things get lost. My last letter to her, confessing, "I don't have an enrollment number, I don't have stories. All I have is my father's face, my grandmother's hair, these Chumash hands . . ."

I find an unoccupied sofa in the waiting area by the picture window. The white envelope rips open across the postmark. Pages of fine, precise handwriting slide out.

> You do have stories . . . those stories your dad tells are connected with older stories, stories that might not have been passed down to you, but which existed and maybe even still exist in a world that isn't this one . . . It is a fragment in one way, but like the shard of a pot that can be restored.

Sitting cross-legged, I feel the hard edges of an angel pressing into my thigh. I pull out the angel, set it down on top of the envelope beside me. Look at her, all sparkles and glitter, hearts and stars, hands held out—in warning? Greeting? Pronouncement?

Angels. They show up in the strangest places.

I wonder what it was about this pop-art medallion that brought back that memory to my father. Was he thinking of a St. Christopher stuck to his dashboard, a Virgen de Guadalupe swinging on a chain from the rear-view mirror as he saw that concrete pillar coming towards him? When he was trapped against the cyclone fence, unable to get the door open, did he hear a celestial voice say, "Try the rear window release"?

What *did* my father see that day?

There is an angel in this story somewhere. In the pocket of my jeans at a hospital in 1994. In a pink Plymouth station wagon on a Los Angeles freeway in 1962?

Outside, the pines and rhododendrons of Western Washington glow green under midsummer sun. I know the names of all these Northwest plants, yet I am a long way from home.

My father's surgery will last about two hours.

I unpack my journal, find a pen. If I hurry, there's time to write this down.

A California Indian in the Philadelphia Airport

The white and gray cumulus clouds at the Philadelphia airport look like beautiful clouds anywhere: otherworldly, prehistoric, lush piles of moisture sculpting and resculpting their messages across a pale blue June sky. I'm thinking of Ishi and the Feather River, Oroville and Deer Creek, glass arrowheads and tuberculosis. Meanwhile the flight mechanics and cleaning crews slam in and out of the heavy metal door in front of me, stride in and out with their dreads and crew cuts, shorts and heavy denim overalls, radios and phones slung at waistbands. For this moment, the people around me are racially predictable: the white people are travelers, packing water bottles, computers (like this one I'm writing on), iPods, straw hats, magazines, newspapers, coffee, carry-on luggage, sometimes shopping bags from stores I've never heard of. The black people are workers: at the desk, on the cleaning crew, fueling or resupplying the small planes that fly out of this major hub to small towns all over the southern United States.

I'm going to Roanoke, Virginia, and from there to Lexington, and from there to Kerr's Creek. I'm not white or black. I'm a half-breed: half California Indian, half white European. I've been reading about Ishi's brain, how it was removed from his body against his wishes, and despite promises from his white academic "friends" that his body would be left intact. Ishi's brain was shipped to the Smithsonian, where it floated around for decades in various storage facilities, ultimately ending up in a steel canister with several other brains, until repatriation activists tracked it down. They arranged for Ishi's ashes, at Mt. Olivet Cemetery, to be reunited with his brain, and then buried them together in the hills of Deer Creek, where Ishi's people lived their last few years in exhaustion and fear, hiding from the culture that had genocided them.

And I keep looking out the glass windows in front of me, at the blue Philadephia sky with its majestic, gruff clouds sailing past ponderously as whales, at their own pace and in their own time. Do clouds migrate like whales? Are clouds really sentient beings, brought together into these clusters of moisture, massive communities traveling from one place to another? I imagine the ebb and flow, the gatherings and dispersions, of so many molecules across the face of the earth, and I think about Ishi's brain floating in a dark stainless steel canister at the Smithsonian, his ashes sealed into a clay Pueblo pot in California, his songs scratched tentatively on the wax cylinders of early twentieth-century technology. Maybe we're all clouds in one form or another.

I've been thinking about the shattering and fragmentation of California Indian communities since Contact. Putting the pieces back together and burying them might be one solution, even if it's only a metaphor. Sometimes something is so badly broken you cannot recreate its original shape at all. If you try, you create a deformed, imperfect image of what you've lost; you will always compare what your creation looks like with what it used to look like. As long as you are attempting to *recreate*, you are doomed to fail! I am beginning to realize that when something is that broken, more useful and beautiful results can come from using the pieces to construct a mosaic. You use the same pieces, but you create a new design from it. Matter cannot be created or destroyed, only transformed. If we allow the pieces of our culture to lie scattered in the dust of history, trampled on by racism and grief, then yes, we are irreparably damaged. But if we pick up the pieces and use them in new ways that honor their integrity, their colors, textures, stories—then we do those pieces justice, no matter how sharp they are, no matter how much handling them slices our fingers and makes us bleed.

Sometimes when we are damaged, we scar, we heal, we adapt, we go on. It's amazing how much violence a culture can take and still maintain its integrity, much like a person who endures a terrible beating at the hands of bullies, then recovers the use of arms and legs, mind and humor, heart and soul. But other times, we are damaged too severely to recover our former shape and ability. You can lose a leg, an arm, a kidney, an eye, or your hearing and still make a comeback. But when you lose all of those parts, all at once, there's really very little hope that your original self can be reassembled, and a devastating amount of disappointment when you try to faithfully adhere to some frozen snapshot of your self's "tradition."

I'm thinking about Esselen, Costanoan, and Chumash cultures, and other California tribal cultures and communities, how terribly we have been battered. The tribe I'm enrolled in, the Ohlone/Costanoan-Esselen Nation, has been battling the federal government for recognition, and we have been battling each other for power. We've lost our language, our lands, our religion, our literature (stories and song). None of those things are recuperable, no matter how hard we work, but given our emotional and psychological damage, still less so. Even at a distance I hear and sometimes can't help but take part in the skirmishes that various tribal factions blow up into massacres. Rumors of election fraud, physical violence, name calling, relatives who won't speak to one another, hoarding of tribal histories or information. Good people, good hearts, savaged and misused. I've come to the conclusion, horrifying and bitter as the words sound, that there are too few original pieces of our tribe left to glue back together.

The gaps in such a construction are violent and sickening; like a Frankenstein brought back from the dead, such an artificial construct too often fails us in its ability to love and be loved, to love itself. I'm afraid that our people aren't capable of mending in the ways we keep thinking we must. If I think about this too much, it breaks my heart. My own identity as "Indian" stares right into the mouth of extinction. Who am I, if I'm not part of a recognized tribe? Who am I, if my tribal council splits open, if relatives accuse one another of cheating, lying, or grabbing what little power there is? Who am I, if my community can no longer function as a community?

But I'm not admitting failure. We must rethink our strategy, our goals. Maybe, like a basket that has huge holes where pieces were ripped out and is crumbling to dust and can't be reclaimed, my tribe must reinvent ourselves—rather than try to copy what isn't there in the first place. We must think of ourselves as a mosaic, human beings constructed of multiple sources of beauty, pieces that alone are merely incomplete but which, when set into a new design together, complement the shards around us, bring wholeness to the world and ourselves.

We think we are too broken to ever be whole again. But it's not true. We can be whole—just differently.

* * *

I've often thought it would be nice to be all of a piece; to be all Chumash, or all Jewish, or all French, or even just all "European"! By "nice" I mean it would be *simpler*. Less confusing, fewer negotiations, more secure. But I'm not whole. And yet, I *am* whole. What the hell! I'm a whole mosaic. Deal with it, world. White and Indian, and not only that, but Indian and reinventing myself in this Post-Colonial Art Project I've inherited.

I'm a cloud, wandering in my ancient migration from one form to the next, pausing today over the city of brotherly love on my way home.

Intensive Spanish: A Language ~~Acquisition~~ Resistance Journal

In grad school, three years of a foreign language were required for my degree. I chose Spanish, thinking that since I'd taken two years of high school Spanish *and* heard my father speak it, I might have a chance at surviving (although those experiences dated back twenty years or more). That first year, I chose a summer-quarter immersion program that promised a full year's study in just nine weeks. Called "Intensive Spanish," the course met daily in June, July, and August. I kept a journal of my progress in order to save my sanity.

Monday: A Lesson in Endings

"Gender nails this language down," our instructor says. "*Atención!* Endings in 'a' signify feminine; 'o' masculine. However, there are exceptions— always the most interesting, no? *Por ejemplo,* you would think the word for 'language'—*idioma*—is feminine, but it is preceded by '*el.*' '*El idioma.*' The word becomes male almost by force, no? On the other hand," smiles *la profesora,* "Spain has other languages, once hidden. During Franco's reign these were forbidden—*el catalán, el gallego, el vascuence.* The people in Cataluña, Galicia, and el País Vasco buried their subversive tongues. Now that Franco is gone, they fight for separatist rights. Bombs, *terrorismo.*"

La profesora pauses, brushes back her hair. "Next, we look at plurals."

At home that evening in the garden, I tell my son, "Turn on the hose, *gracias m'ijo.*" For some reason he asks, "How do you say 'god' in Spanish?"

I remember *mi profesora* says "*Gracias a Dios.*"

My eight-year-old asks, "And goddess is . . . ?"

I want to say "*Días,*" to be logical, but of course that means "days."

My son says, "The whole day is a goddess!"

No, m'ijo. Gender nails this tongue to the cross.

Tuesday: Questions of Conversion

Father Arroyo de la Cuesta, attempting to preserve in written form the various Indian dialects he heard around him at the mission, wrote, "A verb with no past tense is above my comprehension but I will ask God's help and will learn, though it take bloody tears." I never thought studying

Spanish would give me empathy for a padre! But how do you conjugate the verb *ser* ("to be") when you have been declared extinct? How do you produce the formal *usted* when the priest teaching it rapes you?

I want to know: when did my ancestors begin dreaming in Spanish, making love in Spanish? When did our tongues convert? I know our first words were a foreign prayer: *Amar a Dios*—the only instruction necessary before baptism with magical water, sign of the cross between blows. *Amar a Dios.*

Wednesday: Names

Someone asks, "Why do so many Spanish surnames end in "-ez"? *La profesora* smiles and explains that "-ez" means "son of," like the suffixes "-son" and "-sen" in German and Scandinavian languages. "*Por ejemplo,* Fernández is the son of Fernando, Martínez is the son of Martín, Rodríguez is the son of Rodrigo . . . and then, *pues,* people give their children names *por protección de los santos.* For many generations, *mujeres se les dio el nombre María y* one of the names of *La Virgen*, like Esperanza (hope), Concepción (conception), Dolores (pain), Encarnación (incarnation). Virgen María de los Dolores . . ."

I try to write all this down, but when I look down at my notebook, I see the names of my grandmothers. María Josefa, María Teodosia, María Estéfana. I think, "Who was the first missionized Indian girl child named María?" Who was the last Indian child to be given an Esselen name? How can I pronounce those alien names written in Castellano script filling the black ledgers? They are only skeletons anyway, not the heart or flesh of a people. Will I ever know how they sounded coming out of an Esselen mouth—called by a grandparent, sister, lover, child, mother, river?

Did someone hide my name in that parchment, bury it—forget the way back?

Thursday: Oral Tradition

Silence is a long story, a complex art left to descendants of Native speakers. Ribboned palm fronds hang absolutely still. A thousand tongues that don't move, yet exist whole and fully formed. Sometimes I dream in Spanish. My mouth moves in all the proper patterns: the rolling "r," delicate placement of tongue against teeth, subtle slip of consonants. But in the morning I taste a tide of blood, slick iron in my traitorous mouth.

Friday: *Vocabulario*

During the weekly quiz, I pause, my pencil hovering over the blanks that are waiting for me to fill them in with the sweat of my nightly memorization. Every time I learn a Spanish word I want to know the Esselen word it replaced. Between my teeth I clench the Unholy Trinity: English, Spanish, Esselen:

Water. Agua. Asanax.
Bear. Oso. Koltala.
Earth. La tierra. Madsa-no.

I laugh, and *la profesora* looks up from her desk, asks with her eyes if I need help. I shake my head, glance down again at the page of words to be translated. How can I shape a third language to describe a second language that destroyed the first language? This language: blade to slice my tongue. *Esta lengua: un beso como un cuchillo.* It will take ten more years, but I will say it: *Nishwelel, nishkumal:* sever our bonds, tear the gags from our mouths. Remember us.

Learning How to Fish:
A Language Homecoming Journal

And he saith unto them, Follow me, and I will make you fishers of men. And they straightway left their nets, and followed him.
—Matthew 4:19–20

Monday

8 a.m.: coffee

9 a.m.: blessing

10 a.m.: welcome. "Give a person a fish, and she'll eat for the day," Leanne tells us, "but teach her to fish and she'll feed herself and her family forever." I sit in a classroom at UC Berkeley and take notes. I can't believe I'm here. Can't believe I've done this to myself again: an intensive summer language program. Didn't I go crazy enough the first time around, with Spanish? Teach me to fish. Yeah, right. The Franciscan missionaries assigned to Alta California loved their metaphors too. Father Serra wrote of California's Indigenous inhabitants that "before long, they will be caught in the apostolic and evangelical net," likening himself and his fellow priests to the Fishers of Men called upon by Christ to spread the Gospel. I've always been a bit bothered by this image, however; the comparison between catching fish and catching souls just never worked for me. After all—one *eats* what one catches; swallows, consumes, devours. One uses that flesh as fuel for one's own body. Catching Indian bodies and souls like catching fish? It makes me wonder about alternative, darker definitions of the word "save."

I'm not sure I can survive an entire week here, submersed in California Indian languages. It all started with a phone call and my sister Louise gushing, "This is incredible," in a voice happier than I had ever heard her use before. "I'm learning new words every *hour,* I seem to understand them even before David explains what they mean, I wrote a prayer, we study all day and all night . . . I never thought this could happen, but our language is out there, *we can learn it!*"

It was as if someone had given her a brand new pole and a big box of tackle and said, "Come on in, which hook do you want to try first?" My sister had become a Fisher of Words.

So here we sit, two years later, at the Breath of Life conference, a biannual event sponsored by UC Berkeley's linguistics department, in partnership with the nonprofit group Advocates for Indigenous California Language Survival. I'd encouraged Louise to apply that first year. After all, she lived in California. (I was way out in Virginia.) After all, she was involved with the tribal council and meetings. (I was just a poet, an academic, dealing with theories about indigeneity.) After all, learning Esselen or Chumash is about a billion light-years beyond me (a woman who almost had a nervous breakdown trying to survive three years of Spanish for her Ph.D. requirements). I had a lot of excuses, and eventually Louise countered every single one. But secretly, I know my monolingual brain is completely occupied by English; I can't imagine taking decolonization to those deep dark places where Indigenous languages hide. I just hope I don't embarrass my sister.

Let me explain right here that my sister Louise is brilliant. Two years after her first Breath of Life conference, she has compiled the first Esselen-English dictionary, coauthoring it with her mentor, David Shaul. Louise accomplished this not with an academic degree, not with government funding, not with a fellowship or grant, and not with any technical support or materials other than her home computer. She accomplished this mammoth task while sitting in her living room in San Jose, sifting through research papers and copies of field notes, and with several short visits from her mentor, who was usually away working on an entirely different project. She accomplished this while running for chair of the Ohlone/Costanoan-Esselen Nation, caring for a granddaughter, husband, and elderly mother, and managing a household, both before and after knee replacement surgery!

God, I hope there's not ten different tenses.

Tuesday

8 a.m.: coffee

9 a.m.: blessing

9:30 a.m.: homework

Oh faithful band of linguists and students who volunteer their time, expertise, and encouragement! Do you really want us to read a passage in our language out loud on the second day? I stumble over *Tanoch kalul hikpa,* "The woman sees the fish." Subject, object, verb. I thrash my way through *Iniki tanoch mashaipa,* "This woman is hungry." Demonstratives—the equivalents of the English words "this" and "that." (What is Louise doing over there? Jesus! She's writing a freaking book!) Leanne, her cheerful face bobbing from one table of fricatives and glottal stops to another, reminds us that Breath of Life does not—cannot—teach California Indians our tribal languages in one week. "What Breath of Life *tries* to do is present hungry people with the tools and materials you need to learn how to fish for yourselves."

So Leanne and her magnificent crew of volunteer linguists, students, and museum/archive/library staff give us a crash course in how to do research on California Indian languages, with specific focus on *our* individual languages and the materials close at hand in California, especially at UC Berkeley. UC Berkeley, according to Leanne, has the largest collections of California Indian language and cultural materials in the world. I call them "how-to tours." Every afternoon, we visit a major collection and the tour always includes not just a general introduction to the materials, but hands-on instructions for using those materials to research a specific tribal language and/or culture. The Phoebe Hearst Museum of Anthropology. Survey of California and Other Indian Languages. An archival information site at Doe Library. The Berkeley Language Center. The Bancroft Library's extensive collection of microfilms. If my brain doesn't shrivel up first, my feet will.

Today we received special permission to view the baskets in Basket Storage. Going into the facility was like visiting our relatives in jail: sweet, bittersweet. We left purses, backpacks, food and drink outside. We donned plastic gloves. We entered a huge room full of white towers, inside of which are set deep drawers and shelving, covered with—oh, filled with—baskets made by the hands of our ancestors. Gina found one made by her grandmother. She cried. We could touch them (with gloves on), photograph them, talk to them, pray over them, sing to them. We were allowed to bring in rattles and clappers. The shaking seeds like rain, elderberry claps like thunder, and voices of our little Breath of Life tribe were springs of life in the quiet climate-controlled room. It was a heartbreaking visit. We could not take them home.

Wednesday

8 a.m.: coffee

9 a.m.: blessing

9:30 a.m.: homework

10:00 a.m.: class

Every fishing hole has its quirks, little tricks to finding the best fish, special hooks that work there but not over here, and secret techniques passed down only to a lucky few. I guess it's the same with trying to learn a California Indian language: some libraries have certain field notes; others don't. One linguist's field notes are on microfilm but only at one particular branch of one particular school; another linguist's research has been processed and published as articles, but in obscure journals. Some "field notes" are actually letters and journals kept by explorers, missionaries, or entrepreneurs, scattered all over the planet in various museums, collections, libraries. Some primary materials—the actual notes themselves—are found only at a tiny nondescript storage area you'd never suspect.

But the one guaranteed thing? It's never all in one place, it's never all perfectly clear, and it's never going to be easy. Put on your hip boots and wade right in. Today, I am up to my neck in the existential *cha'a*—as in "we exist!"

So I'm not surprised that Esselen has no real verb for "to be" or for "to have." You just *are*. It just *is*. Louise tries to teach me some sleight-of-hand linguistic maneuver to get around this, but I'm thick as a brick. *Kalul yakiski-k*—"the fish (is) large" and *mawipas saleki-k*—"the song (is) good." Somehow, the intention of "is" is communicated via this "k" sound stuck on to the end of the noun. My brain wrestles with constructing a sentence that, to my poor English-trained neural pathways, means "The fish large is." "That's it!" Louise crows, "That sounds good!"

"That sounds like Yoda," I mutter. But I'm pleased.

Thursday

8 a.m.: coffee

9 a.m.: blessing

9:30 a.m.: homework

10:00 a.m.: class

This year's Breath of Life class is over sixty participants, representing more than twenty-five different California Indian languages and major dialects of languages. It's one of the larger groups, Leanne says. That's a lot of Indian souls literally given the "breath of life" to take home to their communities and families.

We joke that for this week, we are all one tribe: the Breath of Life tribe, located in the Berkeley homeland. We move to our tribal rhythm: breakfast together in the seminar room, followed by sharing of our individual homework assignments and a lecture about linguistic analysis. At noon we break for lunch, then head off to various tours and little study groups scattered throughout dorms and the campus till dinnertime; in the evenings, more study groups (frequently led by our mentors and their assistants) go on late into the night. Instead of sitting around a communal fire grilling juicy salmon, we sit around dorm rooms or on outdoor benches grilling each other on vocabulary, conjugation, plurals, and the always-popular curse words.

Somewhere in the Harrington notes, Isabel Meadows remembers that "Flugencio Cantua told her, "very tasty, our language." I imagine our words being crispy or salty or smooth as a ripe fig. I like the idea that our language has flavor, texture, scent, yet can never be consumed. I tell Louise about Fulgencio's comment; she tells everyone else, and we end the evening with great smacking of lips and satisfied rubbing of tummies. "Oh, *that's* why they make those sounds, like they're savoring each syllable!" Anyone looking at us from the outside would run in the other direction.

Friday

8 a.m.: coffee

9 a.m.: blessing

9:30 a.m.: homework

10:00 a.m.: class

Louise and I call each other *Ichi* now—"sister."

Louise writes beautifully in Esselen, and her speaking voice/pronunciation sounds rounded, natural. It reminds me of the way our dad used to slur his English so that the edges of the words came out softer than everyone else's. Maybe his Spanish did that too, but I never heard him speak enough of it to tell. I remember how our dad's dad, Grandpa Tom, spoke Indian in his last days, how his son, Uncle Tommy, was shocked to realize not just that this was an Indian language, but that he, too, understood it! How it came flooding back to him after six decades of dormancy: his mother tongue. We all knew that our grandmother Marquesa and her mother, Dolores, spoke Chumash together; Louise remembers playing under the kitchen table and hearing them chatter as they worked. But it never occurred to any of us that Dad and his younger brothers might have soaked up enough of that language to make any difference. As the oldest, Uncle Tommy must have heard the most, before the conversations stopped when our great-grandmother died—he was probably the only one to retain anything at all. Later, Tommy told us, he went down to Santa Ynez and spoke with some of the old folks there. *They understood what he was saying.* So was Grandpa Tom speaking his wife's language? Or was Esselen enough like Samala (Santa Ynez Chumash) to bridge the gap? Or had the family developed a kind of hybrid dialect of the two? It's one of those California Indian mysteries. And it makes me wonder if this kind of tenuous connection—literally listening under the table—is what gives Louise such fluency, as if she is coming home to a language at last, rather than learning it for the first time.

If she is coming home to the language, the language is coming home to her, too. *Lex welel*—our language—must have been lonely all this time.

Saturday

9 a.m.: blessing

10 a.m.: participant projects

Louise gave the blessing this morning—in Esselen.

I read my first poem in Esselen, sweated out onto the page with much help from David, our mentor, and Ruth, his assistant; pushed off my awkward tongue by Louise's determined coaching.

Did I say we were hungry Indians? We are starving! Starving for our languages.

At this morning's presentation of individual projects, I heard California Indians use their languages to speak prayers, sing songs, create original poems and stories, retell oral histories, croon lullabies to their babies, make jokes, invent picture books, caption family scrapbooks— Clara even reveled in finding a phrase that means something like "piece of shit!"

Listening, watching, I realized that virtually every aspect of culture was presented: religion, music, oral and written literatures, linguistic play . . . don't try telling a Breath of Life participant that our cultures are dead. We have become Fishers of Words, but we practice a catch and release system: snag those little silver gems, then release them back out into the wider world as quickly and lovingly as possible. Let them go forth and multiply. Whatever allegory you want to use, the work of language recovery and renewal takes patience, near-obsessive persistence, and the generosity of many.

We understand now: you just gotta know the right place to drop that line.

Teheyapami Achiska
Giving Honor

> For my sister Louise, and the Breath of Life
> language conference

Eni micha elpa mishmaxanano,
I feel you in my blood,
nishiyano nishiti'anaxno, nishahurno.
in my bones, my gut, my teeth.

Name sikosura niche a'kxi,
You rise all around,
kolopisik xulin opa.
return like a lover.

Nishkuuh, niche lahake.
My basket, carry me.
Nishimila, niche lasapke.
My ocean, bathe me.

Eni namexumunipsha,
I am your hummingbird,
name hi'iyatan neku masianehk.
you are a flower of the heart.

Name cha'a nishkxatasaxno,
I feel you in my head,
nishxushuno, nishkeleno.
my hands, my feet.

Uxarat kai pire.
We dance on the cliff of the world.
Name cha'a nishchawisaxno,
I feel you in my spine,

nishxorksno, nishsixihano.
my throat, my womb.
Namesanaxkak opa, eni inamkak opa.
You are a river, I am the rain.

Mantuxite, mantuxite,
It is true, it is true,
mantuxite, mantuxite.
it is true, it is true.

Nishwelel, lexwelel:
My language, our language:
maksiri maknoco.
breath of life.

Soledad

"Mission Nuestra Señora Dolorosísima
de la Soledad, thirteenth in the chain of
Alta California missions, was established
on October 9, 1791 by Fr. Fermín de
Lasuén, at the site of an Esselen Indian
village recorded by Pedro Font as
Chuttusgelis. When Soledad Mission was
founded, the 'Golden Age' was beginning
for the California missions, and there
was anticipation for another successful
venture."

—Athanasius Schaefer,
Virtual Church website

The Santa Lucia Mountains thrust up a sudden, toothlike ridge against turquoise sky, roots grasping this sweep of valley. The mission bell hangs from an iron post. White roses bask in the raked garden. The old mission lands grow broccoli now, vineyards drape along the mountains like jade scarves. Brown workers from Mexico, El Salvador, Guatemala, picking since dawn. I wonder if the soil recalls their bruised Indian bones; I wonder if it ever forgot.

It's Saturday morning, and we have never walked so mindfully. We find bone fragments on paths, in the parking lot, at the edges of groomed green fields. Here is a finger joint, here a tooth. Here a shattered section of femur, here something unidentifiable except for the lacy pattern that means human being. Our children run to us with handfuls of ancestors they keep calling "fossils" because youth and privilege don't let the truth sink in yet. It's too big, too much to know: our relatives scattered on the earth where Mass is said once a month and for three hundred dollars you can baptize a baby in the old chapel beneath turquoise, pink, green, and blue designs painted by our relatives.

Chevy trucks and Mercedes-Benzes drive across the dirt parking lot created by bulldozing the graveyard of Soledad's Indians. Bits of bone rise up from the dirt, catch in the steel-belted tire treads of tourists, carry our ancestors out to Highway 101, scatter them to the wind. Our Lady of Sorrows weeps in her niche behind the altar, dressed in black, inconsolable. What has been done in her name? She doesn't want to know.

We gather this chipped harvest in our hands, pockets, cotton tobacco pouches, circle the mission slowly, follow Louise, who found our language buried beneath her tongue, who places living words in our hungry mouths for us to swallow whole. James kneels, digs a hole with a flat sharp stone. Chris prays shyly: the old grandmother hums inside her skin. Ernie holds up the iridescent abalone shell, lets pale blue smoke bless this lonely air. The children hover like butterflies, taste the past without fear.

Xu-lin, we say to our broken ancestors; *xu-lin*, sprinkling sage, mugwort, and tobacco over the small grave. *Xu-lin*, we whisper as the earth takes back. *Xu-lin*, a plea and a promise: *return*.

Note: *xu-lin* means "reclaim, return, recover."

In the Basement of the Bone Museum

Look at us: lonesome piles
of sticks with no names,
no tribal ID, no stories
but the one in our teeth
that brought us here.
Our curved ribs stacked
like bows waiting to be strung.

Look us over, test us, try us.
Place your own smooth palm
over the broken web of our
souls: can you hear it? the rush
of belonging in dry marrow?
Will you know us without
our long hair, our brown flesh,
no tongues in our skulls to speak?

These bones, they're all we have
to offer. Lay out our incomplete
skeletons on this clean white table.
Sing us that happy clapperstick
song for dancing; twine
glowing abalone and olivella
among our faded vertebrae.

Do you remember us?
Do we look like someone you knew?
We confess everything, chewed
by the mouths of history and science.
We ache with fractures
from the echoes of that turbulence.

Touch us. Claim us.
Take us home. Tell us,
we have never forgotten you.

Testimony

In late December 1974, I was a moody seventh grader in raggedy-edged bell-bottoms who confided to my teacher that I missed my dad. I had not seen him since I was three years old. All I knew for sure was that he was Indian, dark, handsome, and had been sent to San Quentin for eight years.

"He'd be out now," I said to my teacher. "I wish I knew him."

Mr. Thompson called my mother to suggest an effort at reconnecting; that night my mother made some calls to California, tracked my father down, and told him that he had a daughter who was asking about him. My father's response was to get on a plane and fly into Sea-Tac Airport the next morning. His return happened with an ease and speed that made this extraordinary event seem natural—predestined, even.

When I went back to school after Christmas vacation, I told my teachers that I'd gotten the best present ever: a father. I don't think my mother had any intention of reuniting with my father when she called him, but the pull between them was stronger than all the hurt, fear, and trauma they'd gone through the first time. It was a history so scarring it was never spoken, never mentioned, by anyone—not my two older half-siblings, who'd lived through it, or my grandparents, who had watched helplessly as my mother's second marriage spun from crisis to crisis. Why didn't she leave him? My parents' love for one another, I was to learn, was a spiritual obsession, a physical compulsion, a wicked sweet spell impossible to resist.

Those first months were the kind of reunion and honeymoon I'd always dreamt of. The three of us, living together for the first time in ten years, were full of forgiveness, tenderness, affection. In my eyes, everything my father did was brilliant. His carpentry skills were a testament to that genius: out of scraps of lumber, my father made bunk beds, bookshelves, a storage unit for my grandparents, a henhouse. He also grounded the washing machine in the shed so we didn't get zapped in wet weather, wrapped heat-tape around the exposed pipes beneath the trailer during winter, and rewired a beautiful old porcelain lamp for the living room—less visible projects that made our shabby old trailer much more of a home.

I spent hours out in the barn with my father, watching him measure, mark, and measure again: *measure twice, cut once*. He taught me how to be precise with a tape measure, sharpen a carpenter's pencil, knock together a sawhorse, handle a chisel, use a level and a T square, snap a chalk line,

Alfred Edward Miranda, circa 1963

make bookshelves. Compared to his thundering hammer, my blows were puny, but I got the job done, once I'd learned how to pound a nail straight in rather than bend it.

My father was pleased when I progressed rapidly. "That's my girl!" he'd sing out in his melodious voice. It was a fine day for each of us when I used his heavy construction-grade circular saw to cut a piece of plywood by myself. Each expression of pleasure from him was a caress to my spirit, and another connection to the deep bond that I felt forming between us.

As we neared spring (it starts as early as February in the Pacific

Northwest), my father lovingly took on what had been my mother's vegetable garden before she started making a long commute into Seattle. My
father relished that dirt, that earth.

"Look how dark this is," he'd say, holding up a handful of freshly
turned soil. "See that? That's good soil, nice and rich. We're gonna grow
some *good* tomatoes here!"

And he rubbed the earth between his two big hands, brought it to his
face and inhaled, the way I might bury my face in an armful of wild roses.
Working mostly barefoot and shirtless, clad in an old brown pair of Levis
or work pants cut off raggedly at the knees, he carefully measured out
rows for all his favorites: along with tomatoes, he planned cucumbers,
garlic, chives, lettuce, carrots, peas. An entire half of the garden plot, the
side receiving the most sun, was reserved for corn. Somehow, my father
knew every intimate step of creating a garden: tilling the land one shovel-
ful at a time, sifting out large stones, raking, determining which seeds
should go where, how many to plant, and how often to water.

Watching my father tend his garden I had the odd sensation that
he had entered into the earth itself, his presence there was so right. Or
more accurately, it seemed to me he had simply emerged *out* of it. With
his dark-skinned tattooed arms, skinny calves, rippling back and shoulder muscles, smooth brown face still mostly unlined at forty-five, it was
sometimes hard for me to tell where my father ended and the earth began.

Now I think what I sensed was my father's unspeakable joy at belonging again to a place, to land, to creation. He'd lost that in San Quentin,
or maybe even before then; he certainly hadn't found it afterwards in the
apartment complexes of Los Angeles. I know that he was never again as
happy as he was that spring when everything he touched flourished and
he was at the center of all his creative powers.

* * *

My father liked to cook. He was very domestic, even though he'd been
raised in the middle of a macho culture on the streets of Santa Monica
and Los Angeles. He often took over the small kitchen of our trailer to
make us breakfast—chorizo, eggs, potatoes, tortillas—or dinners of sopa,
or chile verde, or pot roast, all of which he created with meticulous attention from start to finish.

Al Miranda in garden with Little Al, circa 1976

Shopping became a treasure hunt. Our only grocery store was a Safeway, a big chain that had the basics but not much else. My father had to make do, and he was good at it. He doctored cans of Old El Paso enchilada sauce with chopped onions, canned green chilies, dried cumin. He simmered a pot of tomatoes all day to prepare sopa with rice. He hunted through the Safeway produce section for green and red bell peppers that met his standards, picking them up with his fingertips, turning them slowly from side to side, smelling, squeezing lightly, hefting their shiny bodies in his giant square palm. He prized the few unripe avocados, bumpy green eggs, that he could set in a windowsill till they were soft and ready for the knife. He peeled back corn husks to examine the kernels for firmness and color, looking for ears to roast in the oven. Rice wasn't hard to find—he wasn't used to anything special—and pinto beans were purchased in the largest bag we could afford.

On rare occasions, we drove up to Seattle to the Pike Place Market, where my father could buy fresh chorizo and homemade corn tortillas—just often enough to enlighten me about the culinary possibilities of the outside world.

Sitting down to eat a meal cooked and served by my father was a glorious moment. In our cramped kitchen, we had a small table topped with imitation-wood Formica, accompanied by four aluminum-and-plastic chairs. Curtains with red polka dots, sewn by my mother with much sweat and determination, hung triumphantly at the windows—all the more impressive because in high school she'd taken flamenco dancing instead of home economics. My father would take one of our mismatched plates from the cupboard next to the propane stove and hold it in one dark brown, thick-fingered hand while scooping up steaming mounds of rice and beans, delicately shoveling up an enchilada or two, and then put the full plate into my hands so that I could put it at the appropriate place at the table.

Al Miranda goofing off in the kitchen, circa 1975

When my father cooked, it seemed like there was always more than enough to go around; we never ran out of beans, everyone ate their fill of tortillas, and my serious, methodical father goofed around, teased, got silly. Perhaps that's because my father enjoyed cooking most when he'd just gotten paid and had money for lots of groceries. Or perhaps I remember our meals as feasts because, for a very short time, we were a two-income family. My father picked up steady carpentry jobs right from the start and supplemented my mother's low wages with cash.

And perhaps what I felt—sated, cherished, replete—might have reflected the shy, tentative unfolding and filling of three wary hearts.

Of course, as in any romance, we were all trying to impress each other. My father fixed and constructed and made us feel that we were the center of his universe. He told stories about his mother scavenging for acorns and cactus apples to feed her four boys. He shared memories of his mother's grandmother, an ancient Indian woman who spoke no English, but who taught him the word for "water" when she was thirsty. (He couldn't say the word; when I asked, he touched his throat and said, "It was down here, like this," and the sound he made was like swallowing the sound "o" in, as I discovered years later, Santa Ynez (Ineseño) Chumash, now reclaimed with the Indigenous name of Samala.) He talked about his father sneaking out to secret Indian dances at a certain rancheria in the hills, about his grandfather's bootlegging.

And he told stories about my mother when they were first married ("Ay, she had a mouth on her in those days—she would cuss me out when I came home late!"), about my birth (he was so excited that he shoved a pan of hot, sputtering fried chicken straight into the freezer), about the little rituals he and I had before it all went to hell—for example, pushing me on the swing at the park, both of us singing "Puff the Magic Dragon" at the top of our lungs. (I fell out and chipped a baby tooth.)

I did everything I could to make him fall in love with me, too: I'd come right home from school, throw on my overalls, and help him with the latest carpentry project, or assist him in the kitchen if he was making dinner when my mother's bus ran late.

I listened avidly to his stories, asked questions that allowed him to expand even further, handed him the right tool at the right time, and thought he'd invented carpentry.

I learned how to say "I love you" in Spanish, found a bizarre collection of words from my early childhood still embedded in my brain (*chonis, make mimi, caca, mocoso, cochino, vámonos, ándele, m'ija, chingaso, pinche, chingón, vieja, da me un besito . . .*).

I learned to mix tortilla dough in my mother's big brown pottery bowl, rolled out the soft velvety uneven circles, slung them one by one into the cast iron frying pan to steam and brown and transform from flour and water into a heavenly sacrament for my father's supper.

It occurs to me only now that my father—born always and already a survivor, child of one of twenty thousand out of one million who took the brunt of colonization with their sturdy bodies and gentle spirits; my father, born in 1927, Indian in a state where shooting, buying, and selling Indians was perfectly legal only thirty years earlier; my father, three years out of a brutal eight-year stretch in San Quentin, twice divorced, with the four daughters from his first marriage lost to him and his only son in the custody of an ex-girlfriend—my father was as starved for love as I.

* * *

My father was an early riser; without an alarm clock, he hit the linoleum floor running at five a.m. with the energy to shave, make coffee, mop the kitchen, get laundry started, scrub out the kitchen sink, clean the bathroom. (He said he learned that discipline in the Navy, but later I learned it was actually the Seabees, and that he had been dishonorably discharged.)

My father just couldn't see wasting the early hours of the day sleeping, though at first his activity drove my mother crazy. She learned to sleep through his clatter, one of many generous accommodations we were willing to give one another in those first months. My father savored these quiet, hopeful hours and did his best work then, much the same way that I rise early now to write or gather my thoughts for the day.

I still think of that space just before and after dawn as a time when everything seems possible, when I remember to be grateful for being alive. This is an ancient ritual for all tribal peoples. Before the Spaniards came, our ancestors rose early and went straight to prayer and to bathe. The hour itself seems to encourage renewal and rededication. This is one custom that we survivors can reclaim, keep alive by the thin braided threads of chance, stubbornness, dignity.

When I'm writing very early, when I pause to sip my tea, I see my father in my mind's eye. He's sitting on one of the kitchen chairs, legs spread wide for support, leaning back. He is surveying the freshly mopped floor, the sparkling counters and sink with silent satisfaction. Beside him on the table is a cup of black coffee that he'll let himself drink while the floor dries.

* * *

Sometimes I'd be so amazed by my father's talents (it seemed to me that there was nothing he did not know how to make, repair, or imagine) that I'd ask, "Daddy, where did you learn to do all this stuff?"

My father's reply was always an abrupt "Ha!" and an uncomfortable grin. "In college," he'd say, and I assumed he meant some distant institution of learning, much like my mother's two-year stint at Highline Community College.

Later, because he knew that his incarceration wasn't a secret to me, he admitted that he'd spent his eight long years at San Quentin learning various construction trade skills.

"Why do you call that 'college'?" I asked, not understanding yet the depth of his shame, or the terrible cruelty of his crime. His embarrassed shrugs and frustrating silences were my only hints.

Late that spring, as I stood ironing one of his work shirts into crisp perfection, my father told me the truth, or at least, *his* truth.

"I just want you to know, I don't want you to find out from anyone else," he told me almost formally, as if he were inviting me into his trust, "I was in prison for rape."

He must have seen something on my face that pushed him to elaborate: "I thought she was eighteen. She *said* she was eighteen. After, her brother and his friends made up this story that I forced her. But I didn't. She just didn't want her brother to know she was, well, one of those girls."

I focused my attention on getting the points of the shirt collar perfectly flat, not knowing what to say in response to this confession. Back and forth went the prow of the hot iron, until suddenly I realized that the cotton beneath it had darkened and was almost too hot to touch. I said, "Okay, Daddy."

* * *

By mid-May 1975 it was clear that my father planned to stay on with us in Washington State; things were going so well that even my mother's parents, who initially opposed the reunion, began to reluctantly accept the situation.

My father, however, had one piece of unfinished business in California: his only son, Al Miranda Jr., still living with his mother, Beatrice, in a small L.A. apartment. Never having married, my father felt he and Beatrice had nothing legal to dissolve, and I guess he thought that applied to custody of Little Al as well.

In one of the most audacious moves I'd ever heard of, my father simply flew to California on Mother's Day, picked Al up out of his bed, got on another plane, and flew home to my mother and me. No custody battle, no drawn-out negotiations, no lawyers.

"He's my son," my father said when he set out. "Ain't *nobody* gonna keep me from having my son."

It was my first real experience with another side of my father, the side everyone else but me knew about: the patriarchal, dictatorial, indisputable king of the family. He Who Must Be Obeyed. *El Jefe.* The way my father told it, Beatrice made no effort to resist the theft of her son, or to see him, or to check up on him. She simply gave Little Al up without a fight. My father had an uncanny, threatening aura of authority that silenced any dissent or questions; as far as I know, no one ever challenged his assumption of sole custody, but it was nothing less than kidnapping. Of course, having been his girlfriend for four years, Beatrice probably knew what my father was capable of if denied something he felt belonged to him. And his only son was definitely a valuable piece of property that my father had waited a long time (and five girls) to possess.

Many years later, my sister told me the truth: that Little Al's mother had called her, called everyone in the family she could track down, crying, asking, "Do you know where my son is? Where did Al take him?" But at that time, no one knew exactly where Al had gone, just "up north."

Two things happened when my brother walked off that plane from L.A. with our father. First, Little Al and I bonded instantly, as if he were my own child. He was a dark brown, black-haired, black-eyed bear cub of a boy wearing faded jeans with patches ironed onto each knee, a blue T-shirt, and scuffed white sneakers. He had just been taken from his

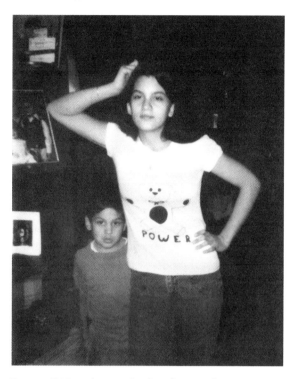

Power: Al Miranda Jr. and Deborah Miranda, circa 1975

home and mother; fear and loss shadowed his round face like bruises. He badly needed a haircut, and his fingernails were ragged.

I took his hand. His head barely reached my waist. He couldn't pronounce my name. Home was suddenly a place to which he couldn't go back. But my hand was there, and he held onto me, and for a little while we both believed I could protect him.

The second thing that happened was like a natural disaster—a firestorm, a tectonic earthquake, a flash flood—that I could not have anticipated: I was summarily demoted from Son Substitute to Dutiful Daughter.

Even now, when I try to make sense of the abrupt change in my father, I don't understand exactly what happened, or why. It was as if, assured that he had his son to raise, my father no longer needed me, no longer cared about any aspect of my life except for the ways I could serve him or care for his son. Projects we had worked on together with pleasure and mutual enjoyment suddenly became replaced by never-ending chores—for me. My father's patience for teaching disappeared; he wanted me to know how to do things and do them *right*. Conversations were minefields, places I could take a wrong step and set off an argument or tirade without warning.

And it did feel as if I could lose a foot or leg to my father's unpredictable rage.

Rage, like so many other changes initiated by my father, was new to me.

For the previous ten years, my mother had parented me with a particular style: soft-spoken, undemanding, gentle if withdrawn. Because she was normally low-key, if my mother raised her voice and rolled out my full name in deliberate, round syllables, I leapt to attention. Chronically depressed, still mourning the death of a baby girl in her first marriage, my mother consoled herself with alcohol and sometimes drugs.

When she drank heavily, my mother might forget to pick me up somewhere, or not come home at night. She passed out on the sofa, or in the middle of a bath. She smoked in bed. She forgot to feed me for days. I learned to dread June 30, the anniversary of her baby's death; Mama drank, cried, drank, and cried some more, lost in a maelstrom of grief and regret.

I wasn't a difficult child (my idea of being bad was to eat out of the sugar bowl with a spoon) but I was accustomed to very little adult supervision or direction. There wasn't much I could think of that wasn't "allowed"; my mother just didn't make rules. Half the time she wasn't paying attention, and the other half she was trying to make up for her neglect. A firm voice or mild warning, then, could send me reeling; my mother sometimes said exasperatedly to visitors, "If you look at her cross-eyed, she bursts into tears!"

As I entered my teens, my mother and I clashed over her boyfriends, my moods, her drinking, but our version of fighting was passive and unspoken, accented with the occasional slammed door or stomped foot. I think I was too afraid of losing her to risk anything more. And, despite seeing alcohol and a buffet of drugs used daily all around me by parents and their friends, I had no desire to even try them.

If I had, I suddenly realize now, my mother probably wouldn't have objected.

In short, you couldn't have found a girl more unprepared to face regular beatings, unpredictable verbal attacks, and strict discipline.

* * *

Under my father's new regime I cooked, cleaned, did the laundry, fed the animals (we had a small collection of cats, dogs, goats, ducks, chickens, and sometimes pigs) and, naturally, took care of all of Little Al's needs as well—coming right home from school to babysit, staying home from school to babysit if we couldn't afford daycare.

Other kinds of caretaking I took on out of love and necessity. I learned quickly that my father did not tolerate bed-wetting, for example, but he also refused to put my brother in a diaper at night. Our mornings were no longer peaceful, productive times, but became potentially explosive in ways I had never imagined.

Sometime in that first week with Little Al, what began as a spanking for wet *chonis* progressed to a beating with my father's belt, and my universe fell apart.

Years later, when I'd become both a mother and a teacher, I always said that Little Al was my first child and my first pupil. I loved that boy with all my heart, more than I've ever let myself love anyone again. I think you only know that kind of intense affinity once. Even with my own children, I've held back one splinter of heart for myself, for my own good—and I tell you, I'd lay myself down for those children, give up my life for theirs if need be. But I loved my little brother completely, unflinchingly, unwisely, crazily, wholly.

There was no separation between us, between my skin and his. We were two lost halves that had found each other at last. We were one person. When my father discovered that he could beat Al in order to punish me, he discovered the perfect way to control me.

That first time, I didn't understand what was happening right away. My brother's wet pants, my father's sudden "Goddamnit, son!" and the strange quick hum of my father's black leather belt being jerked through his belt loops with one hard pull.

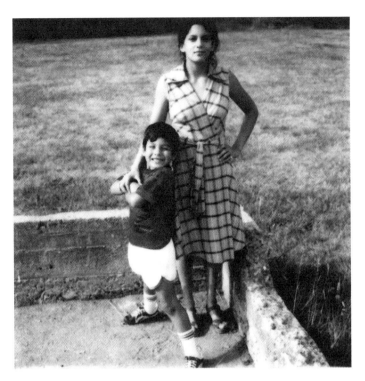

Al Miranda Jr. and Deborah Miranda, circa 1976

I remember Little Al trying to cover his butt with his small hands, fingers wide, screaming, "No Daddy, no Daddy, I sorry!" and the curses, the venom erupting from my father, my dear, clever, strong father, as he held his son fast with one hand and whipped him with the other.

It happened so quickly that sheer surprise, then terror, paralyzed me where I stood at the sink, washing dishes. The next thing I knew, I was wrapping soapy hands around my father's arm, but he shook me off like rain; I barely weighed ninety pounds.

"Stay the hell out of this," he snarled.

I stared at him, and all I could think of were the feral cats that lived in the woods, the ones who forsook the barn for living wild, who fought off the most good-intentioned gesture with slashing claws and fangs.

My father's body rose huge and full of rage, filling my vision. Hovering just out of his reach, almost dancing in my anguish, I pleaded for him to stop. Out of the corner of my eye, I could see my brother twisting in our father's grip, trying to avoid the blows even when he must have known there was no escape.

When I think back on that moment, I have no memory of sound, of voices—only the sight of that belt blurring towards Little Al's backside.

I lost the ability to form words, in my head or my mouth. I forgot there *were* such things as words. I was nearly as crazed as my father, stomping my feet, beating the air with my fists, hands outstretched, hands to ears, inarticulate noises coming out of my throat from deep in my gut—rooted to the spot, writhing.

Afterwards, I was forbidden to go into my brother's room to hold or comfort him. He huddled on his bed, trying to muffle his sobs with pillow or hands while my father hollered, *"Boys don't cry!"*

I sat on the other side of the thin wood walls of the trailer, listening, learning to hate.

* * *

One morning, up before our parents, I found Little Al frantically stuffing his wet pajamas behind the toilet, his face stricken with fear.

We looked at each other silently.

I knelt down and pulled the soaking wet pants out from behind the toilet. My brother stood stock-still, terrified; his damp bare legs quivered.

"Don't worry, I won't tell him," I said softly. "How about this: if you wake up wet, you come and get me; I'll take care of it."

Little Al stood staring at the wet clothes in my hand. He was holding his breath. I put one arm around him, gave him a quick hug. "Okay, sweetie?"

He was unbending against me, but he whispered, "Okay."

Together, we stripped the bed, remade it with fresh sheets, and ditched his pj's in the washing machine. I threw in a scoop of detergent and started a load before the smell of urine could permeate the shed built onto the back of the trailer. Later, I made sure to put the clean sheets back

Seattle Center: Al Miranda Jr. and Deborah Miranda, circa 1975

in the linen closet and tuck the dry pj's into Little Al's top drawer before bedtime.

It was the first of many covert collaborations between us; we were like young green plants that could never take the route we desired, straight up toward the sun, but grew bent and gnarled, contorted with the effort of evading an obstacle that kept moving.

* * *

It was the drinking, in part. My father's drinking increased in both potency and frequency after Little Al arrived.

And my father was a mean drunk. A swearing, yelling, stomping, slamming, violent drunk whose belligerence and impatience led to car accidents, bar fights, and the inevitable two a.m. phone call from the cops. He'd kick the dogs that ran out to greet him, throw things at the cats, all the while swearing profusely and creatively. One phrase that stuck with me is *Goddamnsonofafuckingbitch!* His voice bellowed out of his stocky bear's body like God's own epic wrath. The word "anger" can't describe the sound of his voice cracking like a whip in the air around us.

Relief and terror took turns inside me when my parents left home to continue drinking at taverns.

"Thank God they're gone/What if they never come back?" I'd worry, and make dinner for Little Al, watch TV with him, put him to bed, do the dishes . . . and wait.

I knew their favorite places, the names and phone numbers; called each bar when the hour grew later and later and no one came home. Clutching the beige receiver in my hand, I dialed the list in rotation: the Mecca, the Ad Lib, the Sugar Shack, the Red Rooster.

Before a concert: Al Miranda Jr. and Deborah Miranda, circa 1976

"Is Al Miranda there? Midge Miranda? . . . Mom, when are you guys coming home?"

I both dreaded and longed to hear my father's truck coming back up our winding gravel road late at night.

Sometimes if Little Al and I were already in bed when the truck roared and rattled to a stop beside the trailer, we'd pretend to be asleep, huddled beneath blankets and sleeping bags in the hope that our father would just wind down on his own, roll into bed, and sleep it off. And sometimes he would do that, and we would tiptoe around him to rustle ourselves breakfast. When he woke up, our father might leap right back into his foul mood, still half-drunk, drinking more, looking for a fight.

Those times, we tried to be very small, hide, but we would have had to be invisible to avoid his reach.

Other nights, my father would come in like a thunderstorm, slamming his truck door, shouting to the stars and distant neighbors, "I'm drunk, goddamnit, I'm *drunk!*" as if challenging the universe itself to stop him. Throwing open the door to the trailer, turning on all the lights, he'd yell, "Wake up! wake up!" and demand that I fix him something to eat—fry up some eggs and potatoes, warm up beans and tortillas, make some toast.

If I continued to fake sleep or protested the hour, he'd blast, "I'm your *father*, goddamnit, get up and fix me some food!" And then of course Little Al would start crying, which would make my father angrier still, and I'd be out of my bed in an instant, attempting to divert his attention from Al, trying to appease the beast.

"Here, Daddy, I'll make you breakfast." And I would, standing in my nightgown at the stove, two a.m. with all the lights blazing, trying to comfort Al with one hand and cook my father something with the other.

By this time, my mother was either passed out in bed or the car; sometimes, towards the end, when she was trying to sober up, she was the one in the kitchen while I lay in my narrow bed down the hall, listening with teeth clenched, waiting—all the while my stomach working overtime, twisting, churning, afraid of the first slap, the first smack, the jingle of his belt coming off and being folded in two, the sharp crack. You couldn't reason with my father when he was drunk.

Alcohol worked on him like an evil spirit, and nobody knew the medicine for it.

* * *

And so my father separated us, my little brother and me, one shredded piece of skin at a time. When I was nineteen, I married a white man much older than me, who I had been sleeping with for three years. He was my high school history teacher. He was my ticket out.

We moved three thousand miles away, where I threw myself into raising my husband's two small children, and I abandoned my little brother.

I saved myself. Not gracefully, not wisely, but I got away.

I still love him, that chubby-faced, dark brown boy who wrapped himself around me like a blanket and sobbed into my neck. But I left him behind a long time ago, like a piece of my soul that got snagged by a briar bush.

I yanked myself away, and we both tore.

* * *

My father's older daughters, my half-sisters Rose Marie, Louise, Lenora, and Pat, got in touch with me when I was thirty-five years old and we were working toward federal recognition of the Esselen nation.

Our father's blood brought us together. As we compiled genealogies, scoured the National Archives for documents, and interviewed elders for evidence of tribal continuity, I found myself especially compatible with Louise, loving her fiery take-no-prisoners spirit.

When her only daughter died after a long, fierce fight with leukemia without finding a bone marrow match, Louise threw herself into organizing bone marrow screening on Indian reservations in California, Oregon, Washington State, and Idaho—driving thousands of miles in her big RV to take blood samples and search out potential donors whose unique Native ancestry might be the only match for some other Indian child. Tough, brave, tireless, Louise single-handedly expanded the database for potential Native bone marrow donors by thousands.

Louise would have nothing to do with Al, as she called our father— wouldn't speak to him, see him, acknowledge him as her father. In high school she'd even changed her surname to Ramirez, after one of our great-grandmothers.

"I hated the name Miranda," she told me. "If he didn't want any part of us, then I didn't want any part of *him*."

My sister told me stories about life with my father in that first marriage, before I was born. How he beat their mother, beat his girls. How he cheated on his wife, blew his salary in bars, and finally left his family without a penny, so poor that they didn't even have coats in winter, went to school hungry, and only received one Christmas present each, from a Catholic charity for Indian children.

The worst blow came years later, as her daughter Tiara was dying.

"She asked to meet her grandpa, her Indian grandpa. I swallowed my pride. I called him. I begged him. He wouldn't come. He wouldn't come to see his dying granddaughter." That, for Louise, severed any chance of a relationship with our father. "It's one thing to hurt me," she growled, "but my *daughter* . . ."

* * *

At a tribal gathering in San Juan Bautista one summer, I spotted Louise off to one side of the fire, practicing a deer song learned from a wax cylinder recording of two of our female ancestors. I walked toward her, passing Rose Marie as she headed up to the bathrooms.

"Hey," Rose greeted me, grinning, "I was watching you. You walk just like Dad, like a big ol' bear."

Surprised, embarrassed, I mumbled, "Gee, really?"

We were all having these flashes of recognition that weekend, bittersweet DNA circulating through the gathering like gossip. Earlier in the day, I'd seen Lenora's twin granddaughters laughing in their Auntie Pat's lap; all three of them had Little Al's dimples, his deep chuckle.

I found a seat next to Louise, sat down and looked into the fire.

All around us in the dark, the embers of the Esselen tribe were bedding down for the night after a long day of powwow and seminars on abalone jewelry, smudging, prayers, and songs—all the things we needed to relearn from the few who still held the knowledge. The air smelled of burning wood, eucalyptus trees, dust, and sweat.

I imagined the earth still reverberated with the sound of our feet in the dance circle earlier.

Another tribal member passed by, greeted us, said it was too bad our father wasn't there with us. After the man had gone, Louise went off like a firecracker.

"'Too bad Al's not here'! Huh! Like he's some wise old elder. He lies about everything. Did you know that San Quentin wasn't Al's first prison? He served time before, shorter stays. And do you know what he was convicted of, when he went to San Quentin?"

In what I hoped was a casual voice (but which felt small and fearful) I said, "Yeah—rape."

Louise scowled. "That's what he tells people. But my mother was *there,* she went to court for the hearing, she heard the testimony, the girl's testimony, the doctor's. Al was in a bar, Deby, and got stinking drunk, the way he always did. And there was a waitress there that he wanted, and he told her so, and she said no. You know what that bastard did? He waited out in the parking lot until it was dark, and she left work to go home. He attacked her in that parking lot and he *beat her*, Deby, he broke her jaw, he cut her face, he broke her ribs. *Then* he raped her. And just left her."

Louise's voice trembled; not just with fury, but anguish. Anguish for what that nameless woman must have felt . . .

"Left her there, bleeding, in the dark, didn't care what happened to her or nothing," she went on, letting her grief ignite into anger again. "That's what Al went to prison for, and he deserved all eight years, and more. He ruined that girl's life. He'd probably done it before and never got caught. And he goes around telling everyone, 'Oh, I thought she was eighteen,' 'Oh, she lied to me,' 'Oh, she was afraid of her older brother.' He's just a lying son of a bitch."

In that moment, Louise's hatred for our father was a carved mask obscuring her face with shadow and flame.

I wonder what my face looked like when denial fled and left me standing without the last shred of pretense.

Images burst through my mind: My father, bellowing at my little brother as he cowered on his bed, "Stop crying!" My father, yanking the black leather belt from his waist, doubling the length, whipping my small brother mercilessly. My father, tearing my room apart to find my journal, reading it, grabbing me by the arms and demanding, "What's this? Why did you write this?" and showing my mother a passage that said, "I hate you, Mom!"

My father. Bully, drunk, violator of anything precious that was withheld from him. My sister's words opened a door to the conflict at the center of this struggle to reunite a fragmented tribe, a tribe in which my father is a direct link to one of the first Esselen families taken into the Carmel mission.

It is his blood that gives our bid for federal recognition real teeth, authority that the government can't deny. It is our father who remembers family names, stories, clues we are desperate to record.

It is our father whose body is the source of the most precious part of our identity, and the most damning legacies of our history.

* * *

To survive my father, you had to become brutal, self-centered, savvy about blame and vulnerability and surprise attacks.

You had to know cruelty or punishment intimately, all the different ways they could be used as weapons. You had to cultivate deviousness in order to be prepared, you had to have an exit strategy, an escape route, a comeback, a diversion. You had to be ready to give up the most cherished thing in the world in order to be free; you had to be ready to sacrifice the innocent.

You had to want to survive more than you wanted to be good.

As we sat there in sudden silence by the fire, our faces hot, Louise's clapperstick mute in her lap, I felt as if I'd put together all the pieces of a mirror that had been broken into thousands of shards: *This is how our ancestors survived the missions.*

All those passages I'd read, researching conditions in the missions, how the soldiers and padres treated the Indian neophytes: a mirror image. Imprisonment. Whippings. Betrayal. Rape.

That was the first time I wondered if, in order to survive, we had become destroyers, like them. That was the first time I asked the question I had never dared face: Was there no way out of this self-perpetuating cycle of cruelty?

That was the first time I really understood, *in my bones,* the unimaginable, savage splintering that my ancestors—and my father, my sisters, my brother, my self—had endured.

I saw my father as a seven- or eight-year-old boy, still round-faced and eager, helping his grandfather bottle homemade beer in the attic. I saw him stacking those bottles neatly in his small wagon, hauling it around the neighborhood and making his deliveries. I saw his grandfather paying him in beer, laughing when the little boy got drunk, then sleepy, then passed out.

I saw a boy who worshipped his father being taught the missionary's code: give love with one hand, punishment with the other.

I saw a boy full of music, sensitive to subtle shades of color, tenderhearted toward animals, savvy with plants, hiding all that tenderness, ruthlessly burying it to keep from being flayed alive. I saw the loneliness in that boy's face as he was sent away from the family every night to sleep in his grandfather's house down the block, made to wash the old man's feet, help him to bed, keep watch. Just a little boy.

Born into a hard world, he never learned to transform that hardness, only to endure it by taking that loss into himself, spitting anger back into all whose lives he touched. Is there a way to reconcile this broken, innocent child with the violent, mean-spirited man he became?

To gaze at my father required a kind of split vision. He was a talented, creative Dr. Jekyll one minute, Mr. Hyde the next ("a meaniac," Little Al confided to me once, when he still confided). I can't get a clear image of my father; his figure seems to divide as if each of my eyes is focused on one of two radically different men, and my brain cannot bring the two divergent images together into one person. Only it's not my eyes that are split. It's my heart.

I love my father. I hate my father.

He died alone, in a hospice facility. Not one of his daughters went to say good-bye. Separated from his third wife, who accused him of beating her, and having driven everyone else away, at the end our father had only his son. Al Jr. went by as often as job and life permitted; sometimes filming his dad's last wishes, sometimes listening to him cry with pain and misery, listening to his father beg him, his nurses, anyone, to kill him, end this suffering. But at the very end, our father was alone. Al hadn't been able to visit that day.

"He said he wanted to be cremated, have us scatter his ashes on the Tuolomne River, where he was born," my brother told us. "He wanted Louise to do a ceremony for him, like she did for his dad. He said, 'Don't leave me in a box in the closet' like *his* dad." Poor Thomas Anthony had been cremated but never interred; finally, Louise put together a ceremony, the cousin with Thomas's ashes brought them, my father flew down to observe, and Thomas was laid to rest with Esselen songs and strings of abalone jewelry by a handful of descendants. My father, despite the lifelong tension between him and Louise, had remembered that, had wanted that when his time came.

I flew to San Jose, where Louise began contacting relatives, connecting with the folks at Tuolomne Rancheria. But things didn't work out. First Little Al needed money to fix his car, because he planned to drive down with the ashes. Then he needed new tires. I got out my credit card. Then my brother couldn't get time off work. And then, it was over. "I can't come," Little Al told me over the phone.

A year later, my brother would bring our father's ashes to California and arrange a beautiful ceremony, led by Louise, on the Tuolumne River. Not knowing this at the time, in need of a ceremony to help us say good-bye to this man who had blazed through our lives like a comet, Louise and I drove to Monterey a few weeks after our father's death. It was one of those clean, sunny days that can get chilly around the Monterey Bay. We took some beads, mugwort, and sage. With Louise's granddaughter Alex, we said a prayer that Louise had composed in Esselen, waded out into the warm waters of the bay, and tossed the beads into the waves. For a long time we stood, silent, each of us remembering and praying.

A pod of dolphins entered the bay and circled it twice, their gray bodies gleaming, leaping with energy. "That's the Chumash contingent, come to see him off," I told Louise, and we laughed with tears in our eyes. After all, he was only half Esselen. The other half, his mother Keta's people from Santa Barbara and Santa Ynez, had come to claim their due.

My father once told me a story about how he could breathe underwater. It used to drive his mother crazy, he said; he'd dive off the end of a pier at Santa Monica and swim underwater all the way to the next one, take a breath, swim to the next one, and so on. "She would get so worried, but I really could breathe underwater, m'ija!" he insisted, wonder and pride in his voice. Later, when I learned about the special relationship between the Chumash and the Dolphin People, I understood.

So that day on the beach at Monterey, loving my father, hating my father, that visit from the dolphins was a gift. "Take him with you," I whispered to the flashing arcs of joyful gray bodies. "Take him back. Let him be innocent again."

And a coolness washed over my body, scalp to sole. That's how I imagine forgiveness feels, when it comes, if it comes.

* * *

The Indians at the missions were very severely treated by the padres, often punished by fifty lashes on the bare back. They were governed somewhat in the military style, having sergeants, corporals and overseers, who were Indians, and they reported to the padres any disobedience or infraction of the rules, and then came the lash without mercy, the women the same as the men . . . We were always trembling with fear of the lash.

—dictated in 1890 by Lorenzo Asisara, born at
Santa Cruz Mission in 1819

One for the Road

For my father, Alfred Edward Miranda
(November 19, 1927–June 27, 2009)

I need a song. I need a song like a river, cool and dark and wet; like a battered old oak, gnarled bark, bitter acorns. A song like a dragonfly: *shimmer—hover—swerve,* like embers, too hot to touch.

I need a song like your scarred, callused hands; a song with the echo of solstice, a seed's hard and shiny promise. I need a song like ashes, like abalone, tough as stone, smooth as a ripple at the edge of the bay.

I need a song with a heart wrapped in barbed wire, a song with a good set of lungs.

I need a song with guts.

I need a song like lightning, just one blaze of insight. A song hurtling from hurricane's mouth: a snake-charming song, a bullshit-busting song, a shut-up-and-listen-to-the-Creator song.

I need a song that rears its head up like Mount Diablo, beacon for the dispossessed.

I need a song small enough to fit in my pocket, big enough to wrap around the wide shoulders of my grief, a song with chords raw as cheap rum and a rhythm that beats like magma.

I need a song that forgives me. I need a song that forgives my lack of forgiveness.

I need a song so terrible that the first note splinters like slate, spits shards out into the universe—yes, that's the song I need, the right song to accompany your first steps along the Milky Way, song with serrated edges, burnt red rim slicing into the Pacific—

the song you taught me, Daddy: howling notes that hit the ghost road hard, never look back.

Santa Monica Beach: Alfred Miranda and Deborah Miranda, circa 1963

Tuolumne

"Tuolumne River. My father took me there when I was a baby to show me 'the Indian river,' and again when I was released from prison. We went to see the salmon." —Al Miranda Sr.

My father walked out of San Quentin after eight years and somehow ended up at the Tuolumne River. His forty-four-year-old body was hardened, callused, scarred, and tattooed with eight years of fighting to breathe, to stay unbroken, or at least alive. He woke up nights in a cold sweat, fists coiled, pumped with adrenaline. Far into old age, he told me, he lived in fear that his release was a mistake, and guards would show up to take him away, lock him back up.

But how did he get from San Quentin to the Tuolumne River, and why? Well, he didn't mean to make that trip. As to why . . .

My father went to see his own father; they hadn't seen each other in a long time. Maybe my dad just wanted to catch up. More likely, he wanted to borrow some money, maybe bum a place to crash until he could find work. My father wasn't afraid of hard work, and right about then, he could use some structure in his day. With all the carpentry skills he'd learned "at college," he'd find work quick.

But these two men, my father Al and grandfather Tom, could not communicate. Oh, they both spoke English. But they also both spoke the language of pain, and for that very reason, could not speak to each other.

I don't know how my father got to his dad's house. He had no money. He had no car. He had nothing. Nothing. Still, in his lonely freedom and state of shock, my father found himself there in Stockton. Maybe Tom was out back in his garden, lifting his prize cantaloupes up on boards so the gophers wouldn't gouge them out from beneath, or maybe he was feeding treats to one of his dear dogs. I'm sure it was hot, the California sun merciless on skin that had not seen much of that particular light for over three thousand days.

Maybe they had coffee. Or a cold beer together. My grandfather was no angel, but he'd never been in prison. I suspect he was shamed by my father's incarceration, but then my father always was the black sheep of the three surviving boys; he would have been used to that. And my father wasn't the first family member incarcerated at San Quentin; his mother's brother, Cesar Robles, had done time there, convicted of manslaughter. He'd killed his wife for her unfaithfulness. My father said Cesar had beheaded her; I'm not sure that part of the story is true. Still, forgiveness was not a family trait. Al and Tom would not have enjoyed this reunion.

And yet at some point Tom said, "Get in the car."

And because he had nowhere to go and no one to go with, my father did. He sat in the passenger's seat of my grandfather's old Ford sedan, waited to see what would happen next. He expected Tom to say something about the prison gang tattoos, the X between my father's eyebrows, the dark blue marks in the crease between thumb and forefinger. Tom said nothing. Just backed out of his driveway, pulled onto the side street, and made his way to a freeway.

They were heading toward the mountains.

When they arrived, Tom steered the car down toward a cluster of tall trees, shaggy pines, and oaks.

The two men stepped out of the car, felt the heat of the engine hanging over the hood, and then the embrace of cool river breath and liquid calls of birdsong. And in the river, the long ancient bodies of salmon returning home, silver and red flashing in the green water, spotted tails pushing hard against the current. It must have been fall; that's when Chinook and steelhead make their return up the Tuolumne.

This is what my father told me, years later.

"The Indians came to this spot," my grandfather said. He might have sounded casual, offhand, or deadly serious.

My father was silent. I do know that. He was stunned by the beauty of that place, the taste of wet air on his tongue, same air of his first breath when he emerged from his mother's womb nearly forty-four years before. Stunned by the song of water, the explosive greens of leaves and pine needles, the scent of life.

And now his father was talking about Indians.

Tom Miranda spent a lifetime being silent about what was written all over his body, his former wife's body, and the bodies of their four boys. Family stories say that Tom used to go to Indian dances, make his own regalia, but he never shared any of this with his boys. Indian was a dirty secret.

"You know, you were born near here, up at the Rancheria. I brought you here when you were just a baby. The river, she was a lot faster in those days, before they dammed her; lotta salmon then. Your mother came up here cuz I was away logging, and she had family up here. Her mother died around then, and her grandma was real sick. She needed family to help her with Tommy and Richard. They was just little ones."

My father knew this story. It was his personal creation story, the one that marked him as different from everyone else. The sudden November snowstorm; the doctor sent for but stuck on the road; the Indian woman—a cousin? an auntie?—who midwifed Keta. The doctor who finally arrived, exhausted, agreed the hollering dark-brown baby was a healthy boy, stepped outside to sign the birth certificate and collapsed, didn't get back up. That baby, never registered with the US government, didn't officially exist until it was time to go to war, and he needed proof he'd been born before he could sign up to die. My father told me that he'd had to go back up to Tuolumne and find that woman who'd delivered him, get her to sign a document.

My father was a little proud of his outlaw birth.

"The Indians used to come here. Catch salmon, big ones. This is the Indian river," Tom went on, looking out over the waters, hands in the pockets of his windbreaker. "You come here when you have questions. You come here when you need . . ." Tom's voice broke off; maybe he didn't know the word for what he wanted to say. Or maybe he knew the Indian word once but couldn't remember it, or remembered it but knew his son couldn't understand the word even if his father did use it.

I wonder. Was the word *healing, cleansing, rebirth*?

Tom and my father stood there a minute, silent. Then Tom gestured at the river with his chin, an abrupt sharp jerk. "So." It was a move and a word that said, Well, it's up to you.

He wouldn't have touched my father on the shoulder, wouldn't have patted him on the back. The only touch shared between these two men had been blows. Tom turned, walked down the river bank a ways, left my father to it. When Tom walked away, he carried the remnants of a world with him: languages, dances, tools, materials, songs. Things he never shared with any of his sons. This was the closest he would ever come to attempting that bridge.

This is the Indian river. You come here when you have questions. You come here when you need . . .

My father loved rivers. After he came to live with us in Washington State, that's where he would go when he wasn't drinking, when he had a weekend off. A fishing rod, a battered red tackle box, a thermos of black coffee, and a river; and maybe a chance to be happy. The Puyallup River on the Muckleshoot Reservation was one of his favorites, but he frequented the Green River, the Nisqually, the White, too. He took me once or twice but brought my little brother more often; our father ached for a father-son bond that he didn't quite have the tools to create. If only fatherhood fit in his hands like a good solid hammer and kiln-dried two-by-fours.

I don't know what my father thought as he stood there by the Tuolumne in the cusp between the 1960s and 1970s; whether he prayed, or asked for forgiveness, or wanted to throw himself into the green waters and let it decide what to do with his body.

His body.

He carried eight years of hell in that body. Did he think about what had been done to his body in San Quentin? Did he think about what that body had done to others? Did he hate his body for its weaknesses, for its needs, for its fears and angers? Could he even still feel his body anymore? Did he know his body as anything but a weapon, or a target? Did he wonder how long he could bear the weight of his body, heavy with the blood of others, stained with indelible loss and grief, curled tight as a fist around a handful of shame? Was he already thinking about where he could get a beer, start numbing the thousand and one blows to the innocence he'd once known that November night on the Tuolumne Rancheria, swaddled tight against his mother's breast?

Of course, my father had not been innocent in a long time, decades before San Quentin. He knew that.

But my father never told me what he was thinking that day his dad took him back to the river. What I do know is that in 2009, when my father was dying, he gave my brother this command: "Take my ashes back to that river. Scatter me on the Tuolumne." He told our sister Louise the same thing over the phone, calling her in San Jose from his hospice room in Everett, Washington.

Something in that river called him back. Something in that water told him he needed to return to this Indian river one day, even if only as ash. Something told my father that here was the place he would lay down that battered body one last time, his bits of bone and cinders spread on a current that starts as snow somewhere in the Sierra, gathers its power through canyons and gravity, pours like an artery of creation through meadows near the place of his birth, then crosses the Central Valley with its thirst and fertility, is dammed and held captive, joins the San Joaquin River, is dammed again and finally, weakened in volume but not memory, flows on to the bay, and the Pacific Ocean, entering that mother of a story.

Something passed between river and man that day. Was it a promise? A plea? Instruction?

One year after our father's death, my brother fulfilled our father's last wish, and he did it well.

On that day, I could not be there, though I was on a river, too, on the other side of the country with my two children. What I know about this story comes from my siblings, and from the photographs taken by them. I know that our sister Louise loaded up her van: sisters Pat and Rose, our little brother. It was a long drive from San Jose to the nearest part of the Tuolumne. Large stretches of the river were full of trash, the water low and dirty. It made them all sad, to see a beloved river treated so cruelly. Other places were inaccessible for Louise, who uses a cane. They were losing heart when Louise saw a stranger parked nearby and asked him whether he knew any good places in the area, somewhere pretty, and easy to get down to the water. It turned out Harry was the right guy to ask. He said, if you go around this park and make a right, go down a couple of lights, make another right, go down around two miles . . .

Louise told him why they were there, asked if he would be willing to show them the way. He said yes. They jumped in the van to follow. Louise told me, we would have never found this area without him, I think he was sent to guide me. Harry took them to a sweet place where the river ran fast and clear. Our brother walked out and stood, at the edge, smelling. Listening. Feeling. This is the spot, he said.

There, Louise gave a prayer she'd composed in Esselen, and they offered abalone and beaded gifts she and Pat had made. Al kicked off his shoes, pulled up the legs of his jeans, skinned off his shirt, waded into the river holding the plastic bag of ashes with both of his big hands. He opened the bag, poured the gray gritty contents out like a cloud onto the surface.

In the pictures Rose took, the plume spreads out, hangs for a moment like a diver streaking downstream. My brother is as brown and broad shouldered as our father. He stands in the water, sure-footed, watching Al Miranda Sr.'s last mark upon this earth.

Our grandfather Tom had brought his son to that river for guidance during a time of great change. In that moment, even if he could not articulate why, the river was the one thing Tom could offer to a son in need of a ceremony to begin his life over. Now, in a way, that son—our father— had also brought his son to that river, brought three of his daughters, to stand on the bank and say *micha eni hikpalala*. Together, they reinvented a ceremony for beginning again.

One of these days, I'll go to the Tuolumne, too. I'll stand on the bank cut by thousands and thousands of years, by storm, drought, rain.

I'll go because this is an Indian river, our river, and we go there when we have questions, when we have need. We go there for guidance. We go there for cleansing. We go there to say good-bye.

We go there to start over again. We go there because there is one prayer we have never forgotten: water is life.

Coyote Takes a Trip

"I have substantial evidence that those Indian men who, both here [Santa Barbara] and farther inland, are observed in the dress, clothing, and character of women—there being two or three such in each village—pass as sodomites by profession (it being confirmed that all these Indians are much addicted to this abominable vice) and permit the heathen to practice the execrable, unnatural abuse of their bodies. They are called *joyas* [jewels], and are held in great esteem."

—Pedro Fages, soldier, 1775

Standing in the cold, sand-swept Venice Beach parking lot, watching his clothing scatter in the four directions, Coyote decided to head for New Mexico, catch up with his brother, and leave his broken heart behind.

He'd been living on Venice Beach for a long time; he liked the ocean, with its tall jade winter waves and generous people who camped in the parking lot. Something about their vehicles—old school buses, pickup trucks with handmade campers, station wagons from the 1970s equipped with curtains and propane stoves—felt like home. Coyote was always welcome to add a paw print or play with bright paints, contribute his own unique touch to the vivid vehicle decor. And no one objected to his new favorite signature, a bumper sticker of two naked women kissing, emblazoned FUCK CENSORSHIP.

On Venice Beach, even in the winter Coyote could get cheap pizza by the slice at a kiosk that also sold Pall Malls and condoms, find regular guys always up for a good game of go or checkers, or soak up an afternoon's entertainment from a wandering minstrel with a sexy three-string guitar and cheerfully resigned dog. Not to mention the sweet crazy woman with sleeping bags in the back of her van just waiting for Coyote to heat them—and her—up.

But this one winter, the rain just didn't let up. The sand never dried out, the paint bled off his best graffiti, and the sleeping bags felt damp and gritty. Heavy squalls blew in off the Pacific day after day, the checker players hunched grouchily under the few covered shelters arguing about whose turn it was to score some hot coffee, and even the cement walkway between Venice Beach and the Santa Monica Pier seemed sodden. "Must be friggin' global warming," Coyote muttered to himself, wringing out the only pair of socks he owned. (Who needed more than one pair of socks in Southern California?) "World's goin' ta hell these days."

Yeah, Coyote figured maybe he'd take a road trip to see his brother in the drier climes of New Mexico, where it might be colder but at least a guy could stand outside for a smoke without wearing a plastic garbage bag. Seemed like his sweet crazy woman wasn't so sweet anymore. Maybe more crazy than sweet, eh? Why else would she move her van while he was out cruising—er, walking, the beach? He'd come back from a little hot chocolate sipping under the pier to find his rickety suitcase teetering, lonely and frayed, in an empty parking space.

"Gah!" Coyote surveyed his wardrobe of obscene T-shirts and gangsta pants scattered amongst the scraggly pigeons and seagulls and grabbed a few handfuls. Time was, he wouldn't be caught dead with baggage, but the economy wasn't what it used to be. He tucked the soggy mess into the rickety rolling suitcase that served as pack mule and safety deposit box, shook the sand out of his fur, hitched up his lowriding green canvas pants, and slouched up the hill to catch a #1 Santa Monica Big Blue Bus to Westwood. From there he could catch a shuttle to LAX, where he had relatives who worked in baggage.

Maybe one of them could box him up and put him on a nonstop to ABQ. Anything would be better than this soggy gray sponge of a beach!

Trudging past the bright but mostly empty tattoo shops, massage parlors, and taquerias in Venice, Coyote wondered how his life had taken such a tragic turn.

He'd lost his mojo, that's what it was—lost his touch, lost his way, lost his magic. It must be these SoCal women he'd been hanging with. They just sucked the life right out of a guy, and not in a good way. Made him feel every one of his immemorial years old. Geez, they wanted you to bring home groceries!

As if that's what Coyote does.

Groceries? Gah. What woman in her right mind would waste her Coyote on groceries?

Yeah, he'd never had any trouble getting fed or otherwise taken care of—until this winter. But something—maybe the endless rain—was diluting his powers.

"My prowess!" thought Coyote, bumping his old green suitcase up and over curbs and around puddles. "Dude, where's my prowess? I can't even hold my tail up anymore, let alone my pecker."

The shoulders of his jean jacket slumped, excess inches of pants sloshed in the rain; Coyote stood at the bus stop with water dripping off his snout and didn't even have the heart to flick his ears.

Oh well. At least the bus was pulling up, he had seventy-five cents for the ride, and there was his brother's wife's cooking in the near future. Just thinking about a big round bowl of Macaria's smoldering beans topped with diced peppers and some hunks of goat cheese cheered Coyote up a little bit. And oh, Macaria's homemade corn tortillas!

He perked up enough to let three old ladies get on the bus ahead of him.

Of course that meant the three old ladies took the last three seats on the bus, the row right up front under the sign that said, in English and Spanish, PLEASE GIVE UP THESE SEATS FOR ELDERLY AND HANDICAPPED PATRONS. On the opposite wall of the bus, behind the driver, were more seats, but they'd been folded up earlier for a wheelchair and never restored.

Coyote lurched awkwardly, trying to pull a seat down without losing his balance on the already moving bus, but he couldn't find the right button or switch. "Story of my life," he growled. Finally he just threw his suitcase down on the floor and plopped right on it. He smiled up innocently at the three old ladies—one black, one *India*, one Korean—as he perched at their feet.

Buncha dried-up old *viejas*. What's so funny?

Crouching on his suitcase at eye level with three old women's knobby knees, his cold feet throbbing and wet pants clinging to his cold calves, Coyote made a strange discovery. It was something he'd never noticed before: all three of these broads had perfectly dry pant hems. Of course that meant that when they sat down their high-waters rose practically to their knees, but he had to admit, it also meant they didn't suffer from water wicking up the fabric and freezing them to death, either.

"Interesting," Coyote thought, "but distinctly uncool."

And in the gaps between the saggy tops of their white tube socks and the bottoms of their polyester stretch-waist pants, strips of even less attractive, bare, hairy skin gaped.

Ay!

Well, hairy on four of the six legs—at least the Indigenous woman, the one in the middle, seemed relatively smooth-skinned . . .

Coyote sniffed.

She used lotion, too, or maybe just a nice laundry detergent. Fresh. Lilacs, maybe, or could it be lavender? Gee, it'd been so long since he'd been with a woman who actually did her laundry with something besides public restroom pump soap.

Coyote tilted his head so he could get a look at that middle woman's hands grasping the curved dark top of her wooden cane. He didn't want to seem obvious.

Ah, yes. A modest but tasteful home manicure. Nails not long enough to do a guy damage, but grown out a bit, filed, polished with clear stuff, and clean. No wedding band, he noticed, but a nice silver signet ring on the left pinky, turquoise stone, probably a high school sweetheart's old token. Cinnamon-colored skin, weather-worn but not too wrinkly, hardworking hands—sturdy hands, with calluses and a few old scars across the back, a scattering of well-deserved age spots.

"When the missionaries first arrived in this region [San Diego], they found men dressed as women and performing women's duties, who were kept for unnatural purposes. From their youth up they were treated, instructed, and used as females, and were even frequently publicly married to the chiefs or great men . . . Being more robust than the women, they were better able to perform the arduous duties required of the wife, and for this reason, they were often selected by the chiefs and others, and on the day of the wedding a grand feast was given."
—Fr. Gerónimo Boscana, 1846

She would never have been a beauty, Coyote admitted, but with those hands, she surely could have made a man happy.

She even had a cloth shopping bag sticking out of her coat pocket; obviously, off to the grocery store. Senior Tuesday at Von's, he remembered. Important day for those beach dwellers on a budget.

He risked a quick glance up at her face as she shifted to let someone squeeze toward the exit. She knew how to use makeup, that was certain; a little foundation, some blue eye shadow but not too much, and a discreet but feminine coral-pink lipstick. A bit heavy on the rouge, perhaps, but then again, maybe that extra tinge was from the effort of hoofing it up to the bus stop in the rain. Firm chin, a good nose with some arch to it. Not ashamed of her strength, he decided. Her hair, mostly silver with black streaks, pulled back into a tight braid and protected from the elements by one of those plastic baggie-things old women always carry in their purses.

Suave, in a sweet way.

She'd tied a silky blue scarf, just the right color to set off her eye shadow, at her throat. Coyote would've liked a better look at her neck, but as it was, he was surprised to find that one old woman could hold his attention this long.

Shi-i-i-t. What was he thinking? He was on his way outta here, this was not the best time to be ogling a woman. Disgruntled and hungry, he looked out the wide front windows at the rain and resisted the awful thought that he was inside a mobile aquarium. "Okay," he thought, "I'm on the road, heading toward a whole plate of Macaria's enchiladas . . ."

The longer he sat on his rickety old suitcase on the floor of the bus, the better Coyote felt about his decision. It was time to clear out of L.A. Venice Beach in the winter was no place for an unappreciated Coyote like him! He needed to be where stories were told, hot food was dished up, and a woman was only wet when he made her that way himself. Yeah. Albuquerque for sure, hit some bars with his brother, a few excursions to the Pueblos. Didn't he have an old girlfriend at Zuni?

* * *

Lost in his dreams of glory, culinary and otherwise, Coyote damn near missed his stop. "Wait!" he yelped, leaping up to snag the yellow pull-cord and bending down just as rapidly to grab the worn handle of his rickety suitcase. "Wait for me!"

Scrabbling, Coyote had an odd, hobbled sensation, like a horse, unable to move more than a few increments in any direction no matter how hard he tried. And what was that cold breeze at his back—or rather, his backside?

Just as he straightened fully, suitcase firmly grasped in his left hand,

Coyote's very baggy pants, held up by a dirty-white piece of rope, suddenly became a lot baggier.

Oops.

Not only was his butt hanging out for all the world to see, but so was his pride and joy, and wouldn't you know it, right at eye level with the old *Indita* who'd been ignoring him the whole ride.

There was something about her expression that he couldn't quite figure out, but it reminded him of his brother's face when they'd hit the jackpot in Vegas one time.

An involuntary guffaw escaped Coyote's mouth as he grabbed the front of his pants and yanked up, clung desperately to the handle of his suitcase, and tried to spontaneously sprout another hand as the bus driver went from 30 mph to nothing, screeching to a halt. Barreling forward, Coyote blew right past the driver, bounced off the dashboard and down the steps, and landed breathless and barely clothed at the foot of a gently dripping palm tree.

He looked up at the bus windows to see three pairs of eyes staring back.

The black woman's face was mapped with new laugh lines Coyote knew he had just personally inscribed.

The Korean grandma's eyes glittered with outrage, her lips moving with words he was glad he could only imagine.

But the old Indian lady—could it be—was he just imagining it, or—well, was she giving him the *eye*?

Admiring his prowess? Almost applauding what she'd witnessed for one brief sweet second?

Coyote felt it then: his mojo.

Like an illegal firecracker smuggled off the rez, like a long drink out of a fresh bottle of tequila, it was coming back to him, streaming into him, filling him with a terrible joy: that was no little old lady. The qualities that had so intrigued Coyote, that mix of strength and serene femininity . . . that old lady was a glammed-up—*and impressed*—old man.

The bus squealed outta there, the driver blasting into traffic, and Coyote found himself with a suitcase in one hand, his family jewels in the other, and a confused but very happy mojo.

He stared after the bus, unconsciously licking his chops.

Not exactly a man. What was that old word?

Joto?

No, older than that, and sweeter.

Joya? Jewel of the People?

Nope, still Spanish, and just thinking it conjured up vile images of humiliation before loved ones, being stripped naked, mastiffs set loose, flesh and souls mutilated. "No, we had our own words before the padres and *soldados de cuero*," Coyote thought; it was coming back to him now, how many beautiful words, each tribe creating a title as unique as the being it described.

Standing on the sidewalk, Coyote rolled his slippery pink tongue around in his mouth as if he could rattle the lost names out from between his teeth somewhere. One word in particular, something he'd learned long ago on a warm beach, whispered by a Ventureño with sparkling eyes and a ticklish belly . . . a word that meant honor, medicine, truth . . . then his mouth remembered, and Coyote cried the Chumash word aloud: *'aqi!*

He looked down the street toward the airport shuttle stop.

Then back down Westwood toward Santa Monica Boulevard, and Venice Beach.

S/he must live down there. He was sure he'd seen hir around. Yeah, s/he sat off to the side during checkers matches and read books, sometimes brought a bag of cookies from the Hostess discount bakery to share. Always had a warm chuckle when Coyote threw up his arms in triumph, or a soft "Awww . . ." and a *click* of tongue in sympathy when Coyote slumped in defeat.

What name did the *'aqi* go by? Dolores? Estéfana?

Juanita.

It was *really* cold in ABQ this time

> "The priests [at Mission Santa Clara] were advised that two pagans had gone into one of the houses of the neophytes, one in his natural raiment, the other dressed as a woman. Such a person [was] called a *joya*. Immediately the missionary, with the corporal and a soldier, went to the house to see what they were looking for, and there they found the two in an unspeakably sinful act. They punished them, although not so much as deserved. The priest tried to present to them the enormity of their deed. The pagan replied that that *joya* was his wife."
>
> —Fr. Francisco Palou, 1777

of year, Coyote remembered. Icy, even.

Slowly Coyote pulled up his baggies and reknotted the ratty rope around his waist. He replayed that swift glance of pleasure from Juanita, his thrilling moment of chaotic revelation, his tail waving and erect.

Then, without waiting for the light to change, he pulled out the extended handle of his rickety rolling suitcase and hauled it across the street, where the Big Blue Bus #1 headed down to Venice for a mere seventy-five cents.

"A cheap trip," Coyote thought, smiling amid a chorus of honks from a Prius, a Mercedes, and a shiny yellow Hummer, accented by well-honed expletives from their drivers. He didn't mind. Now he knew where his mojo had gone, and he was gonna be there waiting when it came back this afternoon.

Hell, he might even help carry the groceries.

Post-Colonial Thought Experiment

1.Carmel Mission Project

Dear 4th Grade Students and Parents,

Here is a packet that will assist you in completing our California Missions Project this year. Each student will research one of 21 California missions and write a report (see the sample report to learn the format). In addition to the report, each student will construct one of the three projects (see the sample project ideas below). The materials used to create the projects are suggested materials. You may have your own ideas on how to put together the project that will be selected.

Students are not required to present their reports on any type of display board. Typewritten or handwritten (double spaced or a line skipped) on the appropriate paper will be fine.

Fabricated mission kits that can be purchased at the local craft store MAY NOT BE USED. I would like the students to learn the value of problem solving and being creative when constructing their projects. Cardboard, wood, sand, clay, dirt, paint, fabric, pasta noodles, paper tubes, natural and artificial plants, twigs, etc. are all great materials to use. I have even seen projects built out of Lego blocks, chocolate, and sugar cubes.

Please, parents, try to refrain from doing your child's project for them. This is a valuable time for your child to grow as a learner. It makes it difficult to grade projects with fairness when they appear to be done by adult hands.

We will be talking at great length in class about how best to go about these projects but it may be wise to save wrapping paper tubes, boxes, and other scrap material left over from the holiday season.

There are several websites on the Net for you to use in your research. Simply go to your favorite search engine (Yahoo, Google, etc.) and search for "California missions." There is a wealth of information. Books and encyclopedias are a big help too. If you should have questions, please contact me.

Okay kids, this will keep you busy!!! Have fun and I can't wait to see what you come up with.

Warmly,

Mrs./Ms/Mr. X

Mission Project Worksheet

Name _____

1. What is the name of the mission?

2. When was the mission built?

3. Who founded the mission?

4. In what town or city is the mission located today?

5. What number in the chain along El Camino Real is this mission?

6. Which tribes lived at this mission?

7. What did this mission grow or manufacture (make)?

8. What special features are seen at the mission?

9. How is the mission used today?

10. Are there any special facts or unusual stories about this mission?

2. Birmingham Plantation Project

Dear 4th Grade Students and Parents,

Here is a packet that will assist you in completing our Mississippi Plantation Project this year. Each student will research one of 21 Mississippi plantations and write a report (see the sample report to learn the format). In addition to the report, each student will construct one of the three projects (see the sample project ideas below). The materials used to create the projects are suggested materials. You may have your own ideas on how to put together the project that will be selected.

Students are not required to present their reports on any type of display board. Typewritten or handwritten (double spaced or a line skipped) on the appropriate paper will be fine.

Fabricated plantation project kits that can be purchased at the local craft store MAY NOT BE USED. I would like the students to learn the value of problem solving and being creative when constructing their projects. Cardboard, wood, sand, clay, dirt, paint, fabric, pasta noodles, paper tubes, natural and artificial plants, twigs, etc. are all great materials to use. I have even seen projects built out of Lego blocks, chocolate, and sugar cubes.

Please, parents, try to refrain from doing your child's project for them. This is a valuable time for your child to grow as a learner. It makes it difficult to grade projects with fairness when they appear to be done by adult hands.

We will be talking at great length in class about how best to go about these projects but it may be wise to save wrapping paper tubes, boxes, and other scrap material left over from the holiday season.

There are several websites on the Net for you to use in your research. Simply go to your favorite search engine (Yahoo, Google, etc.) and search for "Mississippi plantations." There is a wealth of information. Books and encyclopedias are a big help too. If you should have questions, please contact me.

Okay kids, this will keep you busy!!! Have fun and I can't wait to see what you come up with.

Warmly,

Mrs./Ms/Mr. X

Mississippi Plantation Research Notes

Name _____

1. What is the name of the plantation?

2. When was the plantation built?

3. Who founded the plantation?

4. In what town or city is the plantation located today?

5. What number in the chain along the Mississippi River is this plantation?

6. From which countries or tribes were African slaves taken to live at this plantation?

7. What did this plantation grow or manufacture (make)?

8. What special features are seen at the plantation?

9. How is the plantation used today?

10. Are there any special facts or unusual stories about this plantation?

3. Dachau Concentration Camp Project

Dear 4th Grade Students and Parents,

Here is a packet that will assist you in completing our German Concentration Camps Project this year. Each student will research one of 21 German concentration camps and write a report (see the sample report to learn the format). In addition to the report, each student will construct one of the three projects (see the sample project ideas below). The materials used to create the projects are suggested materials. You may have your own ideas on how to put together the project that will be selected.

Students are not required to present their reports on any type of display board. Typewritten or handwritten (double spaced or a line skipped) on the appropriate paper will be fine.

Fabricated Concentration Camp Kits that can be purchased at the local craft store MAY NOT BE USED. I would like the students to learn the value of problem solving and being creative when constructing their projects. Cardboard, wood, sand, clay, dirt, paint, fabric, pasta noodles, paper tubes, natural and artificial plants, twigs, etc. are all great materials to use. I have even seen projects built out of Lego blocks, chocolate, and sugar cubes.

Please, parents, try to refrain from doing your child's project for them. This is a valuable time for your child to grow as a learner. It makes it difficult to grade projects with fairness when they appear to be done by adult hands.

We will be talking at great length in class about how best to go about these projects but it may be wise to save wrapping paper tubes, boxes, and other scrap material left over from the holiday season.

There are several websites on the Net for you to use in your research. Simply go to your favorite search engine (Yahoo, Google, etc.) and search for "German concentration camps." There is a wealth of information. Books and encyclopedias are a big help too. If you should have questions, please contact me.

Okay kids, this will keep you busy!!! Have fun and I can't wait to see what you come up with.

Warmly,

Mrs./Ms/Mr. X

Concentration Camp Project Worksheet

Name _____

1. What is the name of the concentration camp?

2. When was the concentration camp built?

3. Who founded the concentration camp?

4. In what town or city is the concentration camp located today?

5. What number in the list of camps is this concentration camp?

6. Which type of "undesirables" lived around the camp? (Sephardic or Ashkenazic Jews, nonreligious Jews, traditional Jews, Hasidic Jews, Jewish professionals, gypsies, homosexuals)

7. What did the concentration camp grow or manufacture (make)?

8. What special features are seen at the concentration camp?

9. How is the concentration camp used today?

10. Are there any special facts or unusual stories about this concentration camp?

"California Pow Wow," by L. Frank

Namo'esa: Cleansing

I.
They call the California missions
the "21 beads of the mission rosary."
They call this road El Camino Real.
What would these missions say,
if they could speak?
What would I ask them,
if they would answer?

Were you complicit in war crimes?
Or were you, too, victims
of Spanish colonial greed
and conquest? What skeletons
have you tucked away in those adobe
walls? What is your secret name?

II.
Some missions give me an alias,
an alibi. Some missions confess
as if I were their priest. Some
spit at me for my pagan ways.

One mission wants me
to burn her down.

Others deny any knowledge
of floggings, rapes, angry neophytes
who torched fields. A few missions
long ago took their own lives,
left no note behind.

Some missions swell fat
with lies manufactured
for profit by Disney.

III.
I listen. I listen to them all.
I listen to swallows.
I listen to clay bricks.
Adobe. Ghosts hiding
in a fourth-grade mission diorama.
Bells. I listen, but it's not easy.
Sometimes I don't like
what I hear. Sometimes I cry.

I offer tobacco. Sage.
Mugwort. I offer poems,
prayers. I offer my blistered
feet, promises made
of sweat. I sit in the shade
of two hundred-year-old
olive trees, wear the stains
of their black fruit
on my skin and clothing.
I run my fingers beneath
the breathless music
of twenty-one fountains
afraid of drought.
I taste the bruised sweet
flesh of fig trees whose roots
clench around memory
like talons.

IV.
Beneath the missions,
our homeland stirs.
Beneath this unhealed scar
running up the side of my homeland,
I follow the tracks
of a time-traveling coyote.

San Zombie de los Muertos Vivientes

[formerly known as Mission San Diego]

First, hands made me out of wood and tule, cut raw.
Then came mud and sweat and straw and grief.

I rose out of the earth brick by brick
like an obedient monster.

I became church and prison, shelter and cage.
I served as vessel for prayers by priest, soldier, Indian.

I learned how to count the lashes of a flogging.
I held tight to stocks that held wrists tighter.

I drank wine and blood without distinction.
I was created to devour people

made from the same clay as me. There!
On that spot marked with a white cross—

their knives spilt the priest's blood.
I swallowed it. I liked it. Is that my curse?

Next, the people burned down my walls,
my tule roof, my timbers from the mountains;

torched the friar's beds and bright books.
They refashioned me a funeral pyre, cleansed me.

I burnt to the ground. I was dead.
I was glad. But you wouldn't let me

stay dead. You made me rise from the ashes.
New walls. Fire-proof clay tiles. A new bell.

More Indians. More blood. More scorching
flames to whet my darling appetite.

Even years later when my untended bones
began to melt, you wouldn't let me die

my clay seeped back into the ground,
my bells all stolen or lost;

even with no Mass, no penance, no priest
or Indian left to protest, you brought me back.

Now you say *tourist* you say *docent*
you say *legacy* you say *education*

and you remake me, remake me,
you mix adobe and cement, cut new tile,

add signage, dig up bones, re-glue shards
of pottery thrown out generations ago, you

put my trash on display like saint's relics,
desecrate the bones of the history.

I keep trying to die. You keep
resuscitating my poor white stucco'd body,

haul me staggering back for another round—
force the hearts of children into my mouth

and I eat them, insatiable, adobe set like teeth
around my threshold. Have pity on me!

Undead, immune to decay, I live
and live past reason:

O, relentless resurrection.

San Amnesia de la Lobotomía

[formerly known as Mission San Luis Rey de Francia]

I am pristine. I am a National Historic Landmark. Take your inquisition to my arches,
my church, cock your ear toward brick or bell

as if to the mouth of history. Listen:
my fountain sprinkles words like *pause, peace,
perfection*. My rose garden petals the air: *refresh,*

renew, reflect. No one here remembers the word
lash. No one recalls *smallpox, syphilis, rape*.
What is this creature, *murder*? Go into the cemetery

alone, before sunrise—you will find no ghosts.
But please, take a brochure. We offer many
options: *comprehensive package, burial plots,*

wall niches, and of course, *affordable financing*.
Unmarked mass graves? Nonsense. This place
is merely a cemetery of its time, doing the Lord's

work on pagan ground. Skull and crossbones
over the gate? Added by Disney—leftover prop
from *Zorro*. What's wrong with a little romance?

Yes, my adobe bricks are historical restorations;
call it a strategic facelift. This is California,
after all. Earthquake, flood, war, conquest—

those are the authors of history, not memory.
Ah yes, our pepper tree. Unreliable witness,
that one. Two-hundred-plus years! It's all

he can do to hold up fattened arms, keep
that bulbous torso from splitting open.
The friars keep him drunk on lavish irrigation

and fertilizers. Sometimes he mumbles
about an Indian boy he loved long ago
who learned the holy language of priests,

sailed away to Spain, didn't come back. Mostly,
our Patriarch of the Mythical Era leans, silent,
on iron crutches, wallowing in wealth.

You want testimony? Nothing to excavate here.
Atrocity, invasion, genocide? Never happened.
I stand on a foundation of faith and salvation.

I am pristine. I am a National Historic Landmark. Go ahead, ask me anything. I am
as clean as these whitewashed walls.

Santa Mariposa de las Piedras

[formerly known as Mission San Juan Capistrano]

I was created to be a sacred body, constructed with stone carved out
from the sacred womb of this earth, shaped by the labor of my sacred
human relatives. I rose from the work of their hands: domed sanctuary,
left transept, right transept, my nave a long torso.

But I was too heavy for this world, clumsy in my breathing, out of
balance with the dance. Maybe it was the crystal of obsidian slipped into
my mortared veins; something in me ached for home. When the earth
shifted deep below, called my bones back, I could not say no; released
my walls and arches.

Now some say I am the shattered remains of a tomb, a ragged coffin
made to hold those who came for the Feast of the Immaculate
Conception, met death instead. It's true, my dear relatives spilled out
of their bodies like wine. But I caught them, cradled them close to my
breast.

Others whisper that they see me sprawled like the outline of a murdered
soul, left behind at the scene of an ancient, unsolved crime.

Over these long years, I have wondered myself: am I a broken egg,
cracked in the teeth of a predator, all the future licked out? A fossilized
clam shell, preserved from a savage time?

But the earth rocks my brokenness gently, reshapes me. She tells me
I am chrysalis, made to burst from the inside out, made to know the
secret of fragile wings—made to let them go.

Santa Grita de los Dioramas

[formerly known as Mission San Francisco de Asís/Mission Dolores]

If you are looking for San Francisco de Asís, you're too late. That kind soul—
gentle protector of animals and children—gave up, departed long ago;

I take my name from the creek nearby, Arroyo de los Dolores, the haunted place
where La Llorona slit her children's throats, threw their dear bodies

into a river rather than give them up to Spaniards. At night, docents
tidy the cash register, lock up rosaries, turn out lights. Set the alarm, go home

still mumbling, *All that history. Such a legacy. Our amazing heritage,*
as if their inner workings haven't completely unwound yet.

I'm accustomed to the darkness of this sanctuary, the secret sounds
made by shifting foundations, unspoken testimonies. I listen hard,

I hear the tiny wordless shouts of brown plastic Indians rise
from the glassed-in diorama just outside in the courtyard: children

in painted-on white shirts laugh with exhaustion, play eternal tag on #10
sandpaper "earth," while men in loincloths curse, and yoked oxen still plow

the same plywood furrow after all these years. The padre mumbles
benevolent blessings, his grip tight on a black bag full of mysteries

as he strides forever beneath the precarious sugar-cube archway.
I want to gather my dusty skirts up in hands cracked with time,

shake loose these tired walls, but docents long ago shackled my body
to adobe with iron clasps as screws—for my own safety, they said. So

I endure the dull thud of paper mache bells over the entrance, frayed
twine ropes pulled by boys naked as monkeys. I recognize the chrome rattle

of the *soldado de cuero*'s sword, his horse's paperclip bridle and stirrups,
the cries of Indian women forced behind bushes made of discarded Easter

basket grass, followed by a Latin chant or shivering plainsong
pater noster or *salve regina* from ten obedient Indians, kneeling,

hot-glued to the burlap floor of the small church sanctuary. Nothing
ever changes inside this glass tomb, no weather penetrates,

a coffin as perfect as any Sleeping Beauty's in a Grimm European tale.
How hard it must be for the women to grind corn by hand for decades

without ever revealing a proud brown breast to innocent schoolchildren!
How painful, to always prepare food but never eat. What agony to endure

the hungry howls of limbless babies encased in matchstick cradleboards
but never suckle them to sleep, never know their soft, satiated silence.

Near dawn the racket finally dies down, drowned out by streetcars and buses.
The docents open up, take donations, tell their stories. *All that history.*

Such a legacy. Our amazing heritage. They show off the diorama's details.
A good example, visiting parents tell their fourth graders, *see what you can do*

with fingernail polish and toilet paper tubes, scrap fabric, glue, recycled junk?
Mom chuckles, *My project wasn't this good, but we didn't have mail-order*

Indians back then. Dad admonishes giggling nine-year-olds, *It's your inheritance,*
a California rite of passage! Someday your kids will be part of this tradition too.

I sigh, termites tunneling inside my rotting redwood ribs.
I hold back two hundred years of screams for one. more. day.

"To Make Story Again in the World"

What good is a story? Great storytellers, and great literature, craft story
out of a few crucial strategies: metaphor; allegory; mythology. Story is
everything we are: human beings are made of words and the patterns we
construct out of words. Fourth graders, their parents, their teachers, tourists to the missions, even historians, often learn and perpetuate only one
story about California Indians: conquest, subjugation, defeat, disappearance. Somehow, this story manages to get told without any real mention
of the violence and violations that accompanied colonization. The mission dioramas, glossaries, coloring book pages, timelines, thrilling tales
of the discovery of gold, forty-niner mining camp songs, and accounts
of the adventures of rowdy, good-natured frontiersmen all sidestep the
realities of the physical, emotional, spiritual, and cultural pain, or death,
required to bring about such iconic mythology. In short, this story is one-
dimensional, flat, and worst of all, untrue.

California Indians, however, have many other stories. They aren't
easy; they are fractured. To make them whole, what is needed is a

multilayered web of community reaching backward in time and forward in dream, questing deeply into the country of unknown memory—an extremely demanding task.

But why do we need to know about violence and loss? What good would this knowledge do fourth graders? Tourists? Indians?

I think of a story told by my grandfather, Thomas Anthony Miranda, whose voice comes to me from recordings made by other family members searching for shards. In "The Light from the Carrisa Plains," my grandfather narrates his experience about being drawn toward a mysterious light while working as a vaquero far from his birthplace in Monterey. His yearning toward this light started Tom on a journey around California's landscape that took most of his life.

I have learned two important and seemingly oppositional facts about that light.

One, the light my grandfather yearned toward came from the top of Mt. Diablo, about three hundred miles away. He said, "I'll tell you what made me leave there: I could see a light from the Carrisa Plains every night, and I said, I wonder where the hell that light is? You could see it from the Carrisa Plains as soon as it got dark every single night." The geography Tom spoke of was significant: he was being pulled homeward.

Mt. Diablo, at the upper end of the San Joaquin Valley, and Big Sur's Pico Blanco are both considered places of emergence, places where the world began after a great flood, by local Indian peoples—including some of my ancestors, whose community at the Carmel mission was artificially created by the cramming together of Ohlone, Costanoan, Salinan, and other tribes from that general area.

Places of emergence are sacred; the Wintun, Pomo, Northern and Southern Sierra Miwok, Nisenan, and many other Indian peoples also revered the mountains from afar or traveled there to conduct important ceremony. Who we are is where we are from. Where we are from is who we are.

As the Esselen and other communities went into the missions, forcibly encouraged to leave behind their individual cultures for a Mission Indian template planned by the Franciscans, their beliefs and stories began to merge. In this time of great loss, as people from different Native cultures intermarried, lived together in close quarters, and shared survival knowledge, there was also great innovation and resourcefulness. It isn't hard to see how the specificity of *which* mountain was sacred for which community might be lost, while the knowledge that a sacred place of emergence, a mountain, did exist was retained. Isabel Meadows knew only a few words of Esselen that she learned from an elderly Indian woman hired to help out with childcare on the Meadows Ranch. Omesia told her, "*Xue elo xonia eune,*" which means "I come from the Rock." Ethnohistorian Philip Laverty writes, "The Rock in question is associated with *Exegun* . . . and is likely located either in the Santa Lucia range or along the Big Sur coast." Others have suggested this landmark is Pico Blanco or Mt. Diablo. Omesia's relationship to the world, her identity as an Indigenous person, depended upon her relationship to the land in very specific ways.

So one way to read my grandfather's story is that he was being pulled back home to his beginning, to the source of his Indigenous identity. He didn't understand how that light could shine so brightly, from so far away, or how it could haunt him so; he laughs, "I didn't know how big the world was anyway. I used to sit out there and look at the damn light," but he understood it was something powerful and important. "It looked like it wouldn't ever stop," Tom says; you can hear the wonder in his voice.

The other way to hear this story is to know that the light my grandfather was mesmerized by was actually the first airplane beacon erected in California, set on top of Mt. Diablo like a giant sacrilegious stamp, the Good Colonizing Seal of Approval. Its presence on the mountain was a direct violation of all that was sacred and holy to Indigenous Californian knowledge. We can look at this story as an example of the foolishness of a naive Indigenous man, his failure to comprehend modern technology—industry and capitalism victorious in their exploitation of land and indigeneity. He's looking for the meaning of his life, and what does he get? An airplane beacon! On top of his most sacred site! It sounds like an existential joke, akin to the light at the end of the tunnel being an oncoming train.

I don't know about you, but I don't want to see this second interpretation. I don't want to imagine mystery and wonder being squashed by a big fat hunk of iron, glass, and electrical wiring. I'd rather keep the mythological fantasy of some blood-memory of the connection between indigeneity and land, and not see the blood of genocide pooling around that airplane beacon, not know how many thousands of Indians had to die for that monstrosity to come into existence. I think that's a pretty normal response. I think that's the visceral response of the human body to inescapable pain: forget about it.

But there is yet another option, a third way to understand Tom's story. We can look at both interpretations simultaneously: the consuming mystery that draws a man back to his origins, the brutal loss of that which is sacred to him. The airplane beacon on that mountain drew my grandfather's attention when he was far from home. It made the mountain visible to him; yes, it was a terrible violation, that airplane beacon, the stone constructions that surrounded it, the casual daily trafficking on a holy site. But for those very reasons, my grandfather's wandering soul was drawn back, given a path to return to that site.

And because my grandfather was drawn to that site, so was I. I followed his gaze, and it took me on this journey of a lifetime. Like Tom, *What I wanted to see was where the hell that light was coming from.* His words, spoken when I was still a child, hovered in the air for years, waiting to find me, waiting for me to listen. Waiting for me to look at both the blessing and the genocide.

There are stories inside my grandfather's story. I learned that the name "Mount Diablo" came from a story told by Spanish soldiers, mythologized in personal journals, newspaper stories, and history books: during the Mission era, a group of wily Indian runaways being chased by Spanish soldiers take refuge on Mt. Diablo. By the time the Spaniards arrive, night is falling; the Spaniards set up camp and decide to wait for morning to catch the Indians. Apparently the Indians, cornered in a thicket that is dense, green, and dark, have no way out of their refuge. With the Carquinez Strait blocking them on one side, the soldiers fanned out and blocking all other routes, there will be no escape. The soldiers decide to bed down for the night, finish this job in the light of day.

But in the morning the Indians are gone. The cliff with the impossibly steep drop to the Carquinez Strait is still there, the woods are still there, the soldiers are still there. But the Indians have miraculously escaped.

Of course, to the soldiers, this is far from a miracle. This is a disaster. The padres will be furious, crops will go untended, the relentless slaughter of cattle and grinding of corn will be slowed. Without these Indian neophytes and their labor, soldiers might find themselves hauling logs and mixing adobe in the sun. No, this mountain is an evil place, with an evil spirit that the Indians have long worshipped—ay, el Diablo! It must be the devil helping them, those pagan animals! Yes, they must have called on the Devil himself, and he answered.

And that's what they told the priest when they returned to the mission, horses lathered and spent, soldiers dirty, exhausted, and empty-handed.

That's the Spanish story. I imagine another one, told secretly among Indians.

Places of power are not tread on lightly; runaway Indians understand the power of the mountain's reputation. Fleeing to the mountain is an act of desperation, perhaps even a call for help.

The mountain is a being, infused with the power of creation, from root to cloud. The rocks, soil, meadows, streams, trees, sun—all sacred, sacred, sacred, sacred.

Onto this luminous landscape you come, a group of fugitive Indians from Mission San Jose, tired, perpetually hungry, with nowhere left to call home, all on foot while the Spanish soldiers and mercenaries pursue on horseback. In a moment like that, what thoughts, what impassioned prayers, come to your lips? What deep memories do you scour for the refuge of a canyon, a cave, a passage where you cannot be followed? What ancestors do you call on, what old medicine from your childhood, what stories, songs?

Even now, when it seems the world has ended and the gods are pre-occupied or angry with your people, even with the floggings, the sickness, the deaths of loved ones as well as leaders—even now, you feel the mountain drawing you. You remember her true name: Tuyshtak, "at the day." You feel the heat of her breath with the soles of your bare feet. Hear her heart, pulsing. Despite everything, this mountain remembers and bears the magnificent traces of creation.

You turn and follow that knowledge. Lead your people—perhaps a husband, children, beloved friends—up, up, onto the flanks of this Mother. "Protect us," you pray. "We have no tobacco, no sage, no feathers. We can make no offering. Hide us, Mother. Take us back into your womb."

* * *

Is that how it happened? Where *did* they go, those Indians? How did they escape the trap? Did they cross the Carquinez Strait, those treacherous currents, borne up by the desperation of fear? Did they slip past the soldiers as the night watch slept? Did they hide themselves in the trees, in the very earth, in a cave, to emerge at last when the hoofbeats were no longer heard? Did they die, trying to swim or climb away?

This is what we can know: wherever they went and however they got there, those Indians were not lassoed like cattle, tied up, made to march back to the mission in the shame of capture and sin, the stocks, flogging, whatever the padre or soldiers dictated. They did not go back to the mission. Wherever they went and however they got there, those Indians were free.

And that's as much a miracle as any birth, or rebirth. That's a story worth telling, worth remembering, worth yearning towards one hundred years or more later.

* * *

When my kids were little, I used to tell them I was the Queen of California, and that the most beautiful places of all—Carmel, Big Sur, Monterey—were our homeland. The bitter truth always was, and still is, that after missionization, the Ohlone/Costanoan-Esselen people ended up with no land at all. A few families managed to hang on to a house here, an acre there, for a little while. It wasn't until recently that I learned some of our ancestors actually had been granted land after secularization, actually owned and worked a rancho of their own in the Carmel area. Who were these ancestors, I wondered, and what happened to them, and to their land?

Cholom was baptized "Fructuoso de Jesús" at San Carlos on January 21, 1785, the day after his birth, by Padre Noriega; in fact, the padre noted that Fructuoso was the thousandth Indian to be baptized at Carmel. His father was recorded as Patricio José Solol Cholom of Echilat village, baptized by Padre Junípero Serra, as were his mother, Felipa María Chunniron, in 1775; and her mother, Pulgaria Yoschal, and her grandmother Leonila in 1777. (The missions initially recorded the neophyte's baptismal name, followed by the Indigenous name; for a time, these Indigenous names became surnames, although later they were dropped completely in favor of Hispanic surnames. Thus Patricio José may have carried both his father's name, Solol, and his own name, Cholom). Cholom married Yginia María Yunisyunis on July 3, 1803, at Carmel Mission. He was eighteen years old; she was thirteen. Yginia María Yunisyunis had been baptized on January 17, 1792, at the age of two; her parents had also been baptized, as adults in 1772, followed by an "*anciana*," her grandmother Diodora María Mihausom, in 1773. Fructuoso and Yginia are my great-great-great-great-great-grandparents, the first generation in both families to be raised entirely within a missionized experience. Curiously, they were also among the few examples of Indians who received land as promised in the original plan by Spanish priests.

Hand-drawn map of El Potrero, as it existed when Joaquín Gutiérrez and Estéfana Real lived on and worked the land acquired from Fructuoso and Yginia

According to Steven Hackel, author of *Children of Coyote, Missionaries of Saint Francis*, Fructuoso de Jesús Cholom-Real grew up to serve as a mission alcalde prior to secularization; he was a kind of overseer, or boss. Fructuoso's position as alcalde probably benefited him in the form of better food and clothing, as well as status. With his wife, Yginia, he received a small parcel of land (one square league) during secularization in 1835, awarded by Governor Alvarado. In a few years, Fructuoso petitioned to add on more land from the former mission and formed a rancho, called El Potrero de San Carlos, which supported him and his surviving family by allowing him to farm and pursue the hide-and-tallow trade. He lived on this land until his death in 1845. Fructuoso's land had been Carmel Mission's pasture for its herds of cattle; but before that, before the mission, it had been the site of Echilat, the village from which his parents, grandparents, and great-grandparents came. Somehow, I am sure Fructuoso knew this; and I am certain that he told his children. Fructuoso was not "putting down roots." He was deepening his ancient attachment to a place whose minerals and elements ran in his blood.

In 1852, seven years after Fructuoso's death, Yginia sold some of the land to Joaquín Gutiérrez, an emigrant from Chile who had been a soldier at the presidio in Monterey. The contract carried the agreement that Yginia and her adult daughter, Estéfana, and presumably any of her surviving underage children could continue to live on the land until Yginia's death. By 1853 Yginia had sold the remainder of her husband's rancho to Gutiérrez, and around the same time, Estéfana married the Chilean. After secularization, marriage to a non-Indian was most likely the only way for Estéfana to secure what was left of her inheritance: Mexico sometimes honored Spanish land grants when the head of household was European. Even though the United States later challenged this land grant, Hackel notes, "remarkably, the land claims commission upheld it" and awarded the couple full title in 1862.

It was too late, however; Estéfana lost El Potrero to an American who had made his fortune in the goldfields, Bradley Sargent. Just how, I'm not certain, but Sargent was (like many other Americans in California at that time) well known for simply occupying Indian land, or placing armed guards there, until finally the Indians were forced to abandon it. In another case, Isabel Meadows said that the local community knew Sargent "ordered Vicente Escobar to murder Ponciano," evidently claiming that

Ponciano was squatting on Sargent's land—even though Ponciano had received a patent to that property! In all, Sargent purchased or bullied his way into twenty thousand acres, including Estéfana Real's El Potrero. Isabel Díaz, cousin to Isabel Meadows, had the nerve to challenge Sargent, demanding, "Why do you want more land? You really don't need this small piece. We are not bothering anything here, and as long as we live, we will not bother anything." Regarding a third instance, Isabel Meadows adds, "Alefonso moved away from the ranch just from the thought that Sarchen [Sargent] did not want them there. Sarchen didn't own the entire river shore. He only put the Chilean to make it look like there was a Chilean buyer there. So he [Sargent] grabbed The Piñon [Rancho] where Alefonso and Laura lived. He grabbed like a squatter. That was not his land there." Despite articulate resistance, the justice system ignored these and most other thefts of property from Native people, even when they had acquired the property legally, through that same justice system.

Although Bradley Sargent used his fortune to create a still larger fortune, becoming a tremendously influential state senator, he lived only eighteen years on his gigantic estate in Monterey. He died unexpectedly in 1893, at the age of sixty-five. According to his obituary in the *Salinas Weekly,* "The malady to which he succumbed was a combination of la grippe and pneumonia brought on by getting wet and cold while driving cattle across the Carmel river to his San Francisquito ranch a few days before." Is it ironic, or poetic, that the Carmel River, whose Indigenous people he personally drove from its banks, had the final word? Or perhaps the best word is *la maldición* ("the curse"); Isabel doesn't repeat the curse itself, but she says, "*Pero la maldición de la Ularia cayó en la familia de los Sarchens*"—"But the curse of Ularia fell upon the Sargent family." Ularia, an elderly Indian woman, turned to her own medicine when all else failed. And who knows? Perhaps it worked. It's a good story.

Later, Isabel tells the longer story of losing El Potrero, and her beautiful words tell us much about her work with Harrington—the work of making story out of disaster, a story that preserves Indigenous history, heartbreak, and hope.

[The padre . . . he gave him the ranch, that piece of land that they call now El Potrero on the Sarchen ranch. And from there, when the Americans came, they chased them away. The padre gave it to them with written papers, but no, those signatures were no good, [the

Americans] said; when the Americans came, Sarchen chased them away when he bought there. And they had to leave, and from there they crowded, camping by the river, and from there all the Indian people dispersed.

The government never helped these people from Carmelo, they didn't help them with anything, they said that the signatures were no good, and they had to go away wherever they could, in this way they were thrown out among other people, their lives to look like no more than the most poor, and they were exposed to all kinds of vices and drinking.

Instead of taking care of them the way they took care of the Indians in other areas, it seemed that the American government didn't even realize that these Carmeleños existed. Some died of sadness and others went away, they dispersed all over, some ended up living in Sacramento or in Santa Barbara, all this is why there were Carmeleños, hiding well the fact that they knew their language. And many ended up with smallpox, too, with measles, they didn't know how to take care of themselves, and years were ended with drunkenness.

Before, in Monterey, it seemed that every other house had a cantina, and these poor people drank themselves to death, and some drank from sadness at having been kicked out. The history of Carmelo and Monterey includes many accidents and fights and fistfights, and strangling and all that happened between the Indians when they were drinking, and many deaths were the result of drinking whiskey and wine, so that the people began dying out faster with the drinking and the pain of being kicked out of there . . . now there are hardly any people of pure descent from Carmelo, nor language, since they have suffered being kicked out by force by the Mexicans and then the gringos.

Hopefully one of the rich folks from Carmelo will buy them a good piece of land to live on, to put their rancheria like before, to revive their language and to make story again in the world.

The loss of land is a kind of soul-wound that the Ohlone/Costanoan-Esselen Nation still feels; a wound which we negotiate every day of our lives. In her talks with Harrington, Isabel tells many other ugly stories; Indian-on-Indian violence, husband against wife as well as wife against husband; children abandoned, killed in accidents of neglect, dead of disease or abuse; terrible betrayals by European, Mexican, and American government officials, by trusted priests and employers. The loss of land clearly presaged intergenerational trauma with the accompanying loss of self-respect and self-esteem.

But the stories—Tom's deep yearning toward Mt. Diablo, the theft of El Potrero—the stories still exist, and testify that our connections to the land live on beneath the surfaces of our lives, like underground rivers that never see the light of day, but run alive and singing nonetheless. The stories call us back.

In my own fascination with these stories, I pored over maps and historical land records until I could locate El Potrero on a contemporary map of California. My whole body leapt forward, the palms of my hands tingled with a rush of blood, when I learned that El Potrero, the last Esselen-owned land in California, home to my immediate ancestors Fructuoso, Yginia, and Estéfana and her children, and once the village of Echilat where many of my ancestors originated, might still exist.

Perhaps it seems strange to others, but so much of our history has literally disappeared that I simply assumed any land that was once El Potrero couldn't possibly still be there—it had to be bulldozed, dug up for minerals, stripped for timber, sucked dry for water, blacktopped, graded, and subdivided into oblivion. "El Potrero," the land itself, couldn't possibly still be standing.

I didn't know whether to laugh or cry when I found that El Potrero is part of the Santa Lucia Preserve: a combination private, corporate-owned real estate holding and nature conservancy consisting of Bradley Sargent's former ranch, itself stolen from Indians. I read the preserve's website, found someone to contact: Mark Miller, a historian writing the history of the preserve.

After my immediate relief that the land had not been developed beyond all recognition, I was almost equally disturbed to discover that part of it had become a luxury housing development with a golf course designed by Tom Fazio, as well as a fully equipped sports center, "Hacienda" country club, and equestrian center with one hundred miles of trail. I imagined the worst: El Potrero beneath an emerald green, spotlessly groomed golf course.

Mark Miller turned out to be a remarkably balanced and warm human being, able to fill me in on the preserve's surprising statistics: all of those luxurious accommodations and playgrounds are on only two thousand acres; eighteen thousand acres have been purposely left undeveloped. The golf course is designed to subsist on natural supplies of water. I learned that the "luxury ranch community" was designed to earn enough money to perpetuate the trust which preserves the bulk of the land in its original state, organized as the Santa Lucia Nature Conservancy. My initial rough (and pessimistic) estimates with land maps put Fructuoso and Yginia's land under the golf course, but Mark wrote, "It's my impression that your family's farm was closer to the Rio Carmelo, down by the preserve gate."

What brought about this incongruous combination of luxury real estate and land conservancy? Basically, Mark told me, although there had been some protests about the final deal, the preserve's suggestion of a private "trust" situation involving between two hundred and three hundred members with homes there funding an endowment to take care of land issues "in perpetuity" was ultimately approved. And the agreement calls for minimal management of the land, in order to encourage the regeneration of native plant and animal species. The uglier alternative, suggested some years before when the Pacific Union Company purchased the land, was a plan to subdivide it into about eleven thousand suburban home sites. And, he added, although the preserve is secluded and not accessible to the general public, its survival and care are paid for by those wealthy enough to have purchased million-dollar (or more) homes nearby. Still, I know the truth: despite the miracle of this land's existence, El Potrero and the other Indian ranchos and rancherias have not been, and will never be, turned back over to the descendants of tribes from that area.

But another truth exists beside that harsh one: there is a pathway open to me—to my tribe, our families—to return to a place which formed us, a land that cradled us in the hands of the Mother. What was stolen from us hasn't exactly been returned, but then, we aren't exactly our ancestors, either. Perhaps we can open up a dialogue about making the land of Santa Lucia Preserve more accessible to the descendants of Fructuoso Cholom-Real, to the descendants of those who survived the Carmel mission. *Xu-lin*: to return, reclaim, recover. Unlike so many of our sacred places, *this* place, to which we are bound by blood, history, bone, title, tears, and story, still stands in much the same condition we left it when we sat down by the Carmel River, wept, and dispersed to the winds. That is a miracle.

That night, after locating Fructuoso and Yginia's land and emailing back and forth with the historian, I had a dream.

* * *

I dreamt that I took Louise to see El Potrero, but didn't tell her where we were going, or why. I wanted to be absolutely sure. But our guide assured me that this was the place. So I turned to help my sister out of the big truck we'd come in.

"Louise," I said, and I could barely get the words out, my breath and words little sobs with big gasps in between, "this is it. This is El Potrero. This is the land that the Mexican governor deeded to Fructuoso and Yginia after secularization; and this is what Estéfana inherited." Louise was absolutely stunned. "It's still here. It still exists. I wasn't sure if it was or not, but it is. It is."

Shaking and crying, we held onto each other. To walk on that land was almost more than we could bear. Adding to our adrenaline rush was a grown bear, strolling across a corner of the clearing. It looked at us, but it didn't come near. No one seemed to think the bear was unusual, but we gave it a wide berth and walked toward some sort of lodge. Our guides wanted to show us some of the things they'd collected. I stopped Louise and we looked up at a mountain range. One of the mountains had a white top—Pico Blanco?—and I said, "This is what she saw, Louise—this is what Estéfana saw when she looked up every day," and we broke down into tears again.

My mom was with us. Quietly, but walking everywhere with us. Her huge blue eyes taking it all in, that familiar little smile on her lips.

The guides showed us shards of plates, abalone scoops, things recovered from the old days, obviously precious to them, but as we stood there the palms of my hands began to ache as if the very earth outside were calling to them. I had to go put my hands palm down on the earth outside; I *had* to. The artifacts were wonderful, but the lodge was keeping me away from touching the earth itself.

Finally we got back outside. There, too, were a few remnants of the Fructuoso rancho that we could touch and see: old wood, melted adobe lumps, a half-collapsed cellar where I lay down to peer inside. As I stretched out on the ground, looking into the darkness, a bear cub came up beside me. I remembered what someone had told me about bears being "face-to-face creatures," so I leaned towards the cub, and he bumped noses with me quite civilly and walked on.

It was all wonderful. But then—

Then I looked over and saw the rocks in the river. "The ranch was right on the river, I saw that from the map I found," I whispered to Louise, and that was sacred, significant.

And that's when I made a break for it. Till then I'd been content to just go wherever the guides told us to go, view whatever they had to show us, but when I saw that spot in the river—rocks—and one large, strangely shaped, light-colored rock out on an island of smaller rocks in the river itself—I suddenly began to run toward it. I wasn't supposed to. I got the feeling it was something the guides were sort of withholding from us—but I knew, I knew this was the thing that had been pulling me like a magnet this whole time, this whole search for El Potrero. Fully clothed, with my shoes on, I ran right into the river, waded through the clear warm waters to the little rocky island, and Louise was right behind me! We were crying again as we approached the large rock (probably six feet tall at the most, and maybe that wide, but not solid, with a little cave in the center, and nooks and crannies everywhere).

"Look! You know what that means, right?" and I showed her the four straight lines together, carved into the rock, the symbol for grizzly bear. There were several of those, and we traced them with our fingers. There were many other symbols that were unfamiliar carved into the rock, and we ran the tips of our fingers over them as if we were touching the faces of our ancestors themselves.

Then I said, looking into the central cave, "There was a saying that you put your hand in there, and . . ." I didn't finish, because there aren't words for what would happen—the touch of some kind of power, some kind of intense sacred power, would be given to you. Trembling, we put our hands into the smaller opening inside the little cave. Right in that opening, under our hands, was the perfect white skeleton of a huge fish, complete with spiny teeth! "Look at this skeleton," I whispered to Louise, and she brushed a finger against one of the razor sharp teeth with such love that I started crying again. We withdrew our hands from the little cave, because that was all we could stand, it was so powerful.

By then the guide had joined us, and now, it seemed, he could tell us everything. The people here had set up some kind of a training ground for young people of all backgrounds and origins, and the kids were starting to arrive—mostly early teens at this point—and he apologized for their casual shouts and laughter. "No, that's good," I said, "the sacred should be that familiar to them, they shouldn't feel it's weird or foreign—it should be all around them, they should respect it but know it's everywhere," and somehow, these kids did.

Louise said, "We finally have a place to return the bones of the ancestors to," and I realized that we did, and we cried again. The woman in charge of the school said we could make a symbolic donation; that was when my mother spoke. She said, "I want to be sure that this school is well funded, because this is so important, everything depends on it, we can't let it fail." So we were all digging for change. Change! As if spare coins would change the world! That's when I found a picture of Al, my father, in my pocket; I showed it to the guides—"This is how we are related to Fructuoso, our dad"—and I knew that was the "donation" they had been looking for.

Then the guides wanted to show us one last artifact. It turned out to be the skeleton of a human foot—pale cream, clean, nothing grisly. Bones, old bones. They weren't properly put together, but I understood what the pieces were and fit them together the right way, laying out the complete form on the thick, soft, cotton table covering. I was surprised but pleased that I could do this. But then, as everyone watched, suddenly two small bones in the foot skeleton disappeared completely. We all gasped. One of the woman guides rushed forward and pulled back the thick cotton covering to reveal that the two foot bones had gone all the way through the cotton and now rested on the wooden table beneath it—without leaving a hole in the material. We were all a little scared by that; my mom just smiled and said something like, "Yes, what did you expect?"

I woke up full of tears and wonder and pure joy, lay there for a few minutes awash in all those images; then my alarm went off. I leapt up and started writing.

* * *

In her story about the theft of El Potrero, Isabel wished for us to "*hacer cuento otra vez en el mundo,*" which Philip Laverty tells us may be translated as either "to make an account again in the world," or "to make story again in the world," a phrase that embodies the very act of creation and Indigenous identity. I have tried to honor her words and her work as a storyteller, activist, historian, and intellectual. I have tried to create a story out of the shards she, and so many others, left behind. But it isn't, and never was, just *my* story. As Cherokee writer Thomas King says, "Take it.

It's yours. Do with it what you will. But don't say in the years to come that you would have lived your life differently if only you had heard this story. You've heard it now." Tom King throws down a challenge that every listener must heed: Indian or not, haven't we lived under the burden of California mission mythology and gold rush fantasy long enough? Isn't it time to pull off the blood-soaked bandages, look at the wound directly, let clean air and healing take hold?

I think of my grandfather's stories; I think of Isabel's stories, and how their words survive, reach out for listeners. El Potrero lies in the shadow of Mt. Diablo's profile, the sacred place of emergence toward which my grandfather Tom Miranda yearned as a young man, knowing—without quite knowing that he knew—that who we are is where we are from. "*Xue elo xonia eune*," Omesia told Isabel, "I come from the Rock." "What I wanted to see," Tom said so long ago, "was where the hell that light was coming from." These are stories worth following home.

Our bodies, like compasses, still know the way.

Surfing the Tsunami

In the ten years since *Bad Indians* was first published, I've been asked countless times, *How long did it take to write?* And, *Why did you decide to research your own family?* And, *What's been the response to such a strange, multigenre, hybrid memoir that covers almost 250 years?*

All these questions make me think about tsunamis.

A tsunami isn't a single event; it's a series of extremely long, powerful waves created by some massive, sudden displacement of the ocean—an earthquake, a landslide, volcanic activity. The waves can travel thousands of miles through the ocean from their place of origin, but when they hit land, they form long walls of water that are indiscriminately destructive, with far-reaching floods that pound and drown and rush—then they return to the sea, pulling anything in their path back with them.

What's left behind—survivors, debris, the precious and the damaged—is irrevocably changed. In the Andaman Islands in the Indian Ocean, the Moken people call this wave the Laboon, "the wave that eats people." Such a wave, they know, washes over everyone and everything on their island, cleansing it of impurities and evils. They believe that the Laboon, like so many other forms of destruction, is also an opportunity for renewal and rebirth. The two forces are linked together, inseparable, awe-full, almost beyond comprehension. The Laboon reminds me a lot of Coyote, that trickster creature whose powers are equal parts creation and chaos.

I often think of the missionization of California Indigenous people as being that abrupt, brutal displacement in the earth, triggering a tsunami of trauma, traveling through generations in enormous wave after enormous wave. Whether or not anything good can come of the aftermath, I believe, depends on how we ride out that wave.

* * *

Officially, I began the project that would become *Bad Indians: A Tribal Memoir* on my very first academic sabbatical, 2007–2008. I'd sent out many applications for financial support of my research, and was grateful to be awarded a fellowship at UCLA's Institute of American Cultures. I rented a small studio apartment in Westwood, and moved myself and boxes of research books and materials to L.A. for ten months. It felt like coming full circle: I was born at UCLA Hospital in 1961, and had lived in Los Angeles for the first five years of my life. I quickly discovered that my body had stored deep memories of L.A. streets; hot beaches with warm, salty waves; riding buses with my mother; the scent of roses in December; street names; little brown lizards scuttling out from under giant agave stalks; the slant of sunrise; and the cool tendrils of desert nights.

These body memories helped me realize that the book had started long before 2007; even before I inherited the boxes of genealogy and cassette tapes from my mother in 2001—even before I'd entered grad school and begun to explore the possibilities of the archives. Maybe, I thought, this book went all the way back to the first story I'd written, at seven years old.

"How the John Rabbit Familys Lived in the Tall Grass" was my first attempt at voicing the trauma of my own childhood, and the trauma I'd inherited from my Indigenous father. The story goes like this: Two baby rabbits are born to a nice mother and father who feed and protect them. Then "it was rabbit season and the mother and father had to leave the baby rabbits. . . . They were scared. They asked if they could go with [the parents] but they said no because it would be too dangerous because it was a rough journey. The babys were very very sad. Soon their Mother and father had to leave. The babys ran and hid. They almost got shot but they were too fast." The babies survive, grow up, and soon have their own batch of baby rabbits

Once upon a
time in the wild
wilderness in the tall
grass a baby rabbit
was born. It was white
with a little tail and
a light pink nose.
Its mother was
white and black and
the father was gray.
Their eyes were red
and they sparkled
in the dark.

(giving them all nice names); the new family settles into celebrating birthdays, holidays, finding food and staying warm. But hunting season comes along again. This time, the family stays together, "but five got wounded and soon died and father rabbit was the only one left." Undaunted, father rabbit bravely starts over again, creating another large family; luckily, before another hunting season falls upon the rabbits, a small girl rescues them all, and keeps them safely in a cage inside her house. "She gave them all the feed and water they wanted. They were very happy to be with the little girl, and they lived happily ever after. THE END."

At sixty years old, I look at that narrative as a kind of map through my own childhood. I see all the familiar landmarks: my father's disappearance (incarceration), my mother's disappearance (breakdown), and the disappearance of my two older half-siblings (foster care). I see my own fears about disappearing (being taken in by my aunt and uncle, losing our family home). I see an older history, too, a palimpsest of genocide and death marking the generations of my father's family. At seven years old, I had already learned that injustice and violence, followed closely by competing desires for security and freedom, are central to my own survival narrative. But I also see the beginnings of my path as a writer: words helping me make sense of chaos, transform the tsunami of trauma into something I could hold and examine. I bound the pages with green yarn, using a linoleum sample for a cover, and took it to my second-grade classroom at Wickersham Elementary, where my beloved Mrs. Freeman read it to the classroom at story time. I was the only Indigenous child in that entire school, and I knew it. But sitting on that braided rug, watching my teacher turn those pages I'd written, I was empowered.

I see now that my telling of this long narrative, in all its complexities, had just begun with my penciled story.

BAD INDIANS

Halfway through that sabbatical in Los Angeles, I realized that I had fallen into a story so big, I wasn't sure I could swim out of it, let alone contain it in a book. I remember sitting one day at the little folding table that served as my desk—surrounded by books, microfilm prints, photographs of ancestors, and a handwritten timeline that wrapped all the way around the studio walls—wondering how to create a narrative that worked. I realized that I was smack in the middle of a story whose origin went clear back to the moment my ancestors first laid eyes on those Franciscan missionaries and Spanish soldiers. Worse, I had just admitted to myself that this book required all these fragments and visual materials— the flotsam and jetsam of that original event—to even begin to convey the complexity of what the ancestors were telling me. Questions hit me one after another: *Who will ever publish something like this?* and *How will I ever tell it all?* In reality, I was asking: *How do you surf a tsunami?*

Now when people ask me how long it took to write *Bad Indians*, I say, Too long! And I add, It's not over yet.

* * *

In September 2015, I traveled with a group of California Indians representing more than fifty tribes to Washington, DC, just before the canonization of Junípero Serra (we didn't stay for the event). We held a news conference, setting out our objections to the making of a saint from the man who had founded systemic oppression on top of our villages, sovereignty, and bodies. Though the room was mostly empty, a few reporters attended; one of them was Peter Montgomery. In his article covering our statements, Montgomery writes, "At the heart of their objection is Serra's role in creating and overseeing a system of missions that they say enslaved and brutalized Indians, forced religious conversions, and destroyed communities and culture in ways that continues to harm Native people today. Donna Schindler, a psychiatrist specializing in 'historical trauma' said . . . the result . . . will be the 're-wounding' of the descendants of mission Indians, who struggle with depression, domestic violence, substance abuse, and teen suicide rates that are triple the national average."

That psychiatrist was right . . . and wrong. Although historical trauma is real, so too are the ways California Indian peoples have grown, strengthened, and learned to be "differently Indian" as we moved toward the twenty-first century. If change is a wave, historical trauma is a tsunami.

Every generation, our work as survivors has been to figure out how to ride that monster wave.

MONTEREY COUNTY HERALD

Easter Sunday protest over Serra planned at Carmel Mission

April 1, 2015

Carmel>> An Easter Sunday showdown at the Carmel Mission is expected between Native Americans and the faithful over the canonization of Father Junipero Serra.

Anger among tribes has been growing since January, when Pope Francis announced Serra, who is buried at the mission, would be made a saint.

Native Americans and their supporters plan a 1 p.m. gathering near unmarked burial sites adjacent to the mission for a "ceremony for our ancestors"—just as believers begin Mass on the holiest day in the Christian calendar.

Ohlone/Costanoan-Esselen Nation chairwoman Louise Miranda Ramirez said she met with representatives of the Carmel Mission this week to assure them they would be respectful, but asked them to shut the gates around 3 p.m. to be safe.

Ramirez said the ceremony will take place at the gravesites inside the mission gates but will move outside the gates around 3 p.m. for a series of speakers. She said she wants to the ceremony to stay peaceful.

"If it was legally possible, I'd be the first person to dig up (Serra) and send him back to Spain," Ramirez said. "But that's not what's happening."

By 2015, California Indians had been steadily protesting the canonization for decades, and in the nine months leading up to the actual event, we became a force to reckon with. We wrote online petitions, moderated debates, held a mock trial, created art installations, provided commentary on social media and radio shows, and wrote letters to the pope himself. With our allies we held vigils, protests, and news conferences; one woman and her son, as a statement against the canonization, even made a 650-mile walk through all twenty-one missions. We wrote articles, blog posts, and essays outlining—with precision and passion—our objections. Yes, there were moments of "re-wounding," moments when this felt as though we were rape victims telling our story over and over, only to be ignored, chastised, ridiculed, and pushed aside by an entity whose wealth and prestige held power and public opinion in the palm of its hand. Major news coverage of the canonization inevitably threw us just a tame headline like "Indigenous groups oppose Serra's elevation," while the few that, like Montgomery, published in-depth, thoughtful material went mostly ignored as well. It often felt as if we, the very people whose lives and deaths make Serra, the priest, into Serra, the saint, were inconsequential footnotes in history; as if we—California Indians and our ancestors—were merely canonization fodder.

And not surprisingly, none of this activism resulted in one comment (let alone action) from Pope Francis about California Indians.

But we educated ourselves, our communities, and the media about the fact that Pope Francis also ignored the clear thread of protest against California missionization from within the Catholic Church itself, both past and present, running parallel to the protests of California Indians. And we did this by using the Church's own archives against itself. We did this by harnessing the tsunami: by (re)learning the power of transformation.

* * *

Serra, many of his supporters told us, was simply "a man of his times." In other words, colonization happens, and we should not blame those caught up in it. But, as California Indians argued on every media platform available to us, the flip side of that argument must also be considered: if Serra was, in fact, "a man of his times" in 1769 when he founded the first California mission in San Diego, he should have known better. Bartolome de las Casas (a wealthy Spaniard, a priest, and a former Indian slaveholder) knew better in 1552 when he published "A Brief History of the Destruction of the Indies" and spent the rest of his life working for the freedom of Indians and return of their lands; de las Casas's work is a document that Serra and all priests would have studied and debated.

California missionary Fr. Antonio Horra's testimony is still more interesting; in 1799, he protested soldiers' rapes and beatings of Indian converts at his California mission, writing, "The treatment shown to the Indians is the most cruel. . . . For the slightest things they receive heavy floggings, are shackled, and put in the stocks, and treated with so much cruelty that they are kept whole days without a drink of water," adding that because he had spoken out against the cruelty of priests and soldiers, and because he had openly opposed the mismanagement of Church resources, mission administrators had charged him falsely with insanity. In closing, Horra asked to be sent back to Spain because he feared for his life—threatened not by wild Indians but by his own Franciscan brethren.

Significantly, Dr. Jeremiah Sladek's research examines instances of internal resistance against missionization in California. His resulting work, "Padres Descontentos: Spanish Imperial Policy, Franciscan Decline, and the California Mission System, 1784–1803," is well worth reading in this regard. Sladek meticulously follows the thread of shock and outrage

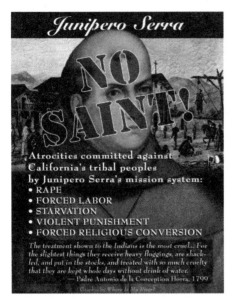

Junípero Serra

NO SAINT!

Atrocities committed against
California's tribal peoples
by Junípero Serra's mission system:
• RAPE
• FORCED LABOR
• STARVATION
• VIOLENT PUNISHMENT
• FORCED RELIGIOUS CONVERSION

The treatment shown to the Indians is the most cruel... For the slightest things they receive heavy floggings, are shackled, and put in the stocks, and treated with so much cruelty that they are kept whole days without drink of water.
— Padre Antonio de la Concepción Horra, 1799

Graphic by Where Is My River?

on the part of priests concerning treatment of Indians in the missions. Sladek documents that a significant number of California missionaries protested, in person and in writing, the violence and cruelty they witnessed daily. These priests were, inevitably, silenced by their own Church: declared insane by mission administrators and sent back to Mexico or Spain.

In our own protests, we California Indians also noted that, during Serra's lifetime, "the state's first governor, Felipe de Neve[, was] a man completely opposed to Serra's approach to the Indians. Neve thought that Indians should be emancipated from mission rule, made citizens, and incorporated into the Spanish Empire in independent pueblos (villages). All of this was to be accomplished in ten years. This approach was dubbed the New Method, and Serra opposed it vigorously" (James A. Sandos, "Writing Missionary Biography in the Post-Colonial Turn: Junípero Serra" 453). Neve, too, was a man of his times; yet his vision was wide enough to see Indigenous peoples as intelligent human beings capable of autonomous, if colonized, lives. (Since missionization had already happened, this was a pragmatic approach.) At the very least, Neve trusted that, as fellow humans, Indians were capable of adapting to the new situation, could negotiate cultural differences without corporal punishment and imprisonment, and bridge cultural gaps without need of the relentless patriarchal hour-to-hour control of the missionaries. No doubt, the "New Method" would have had its difficulties, but the opportunity for more autonomy and the right to improve the quality of life for themselves and their families may well have looked like a decent option to missionized Indigenous people.

Many letters, diaries, and records of others traveling in California during Serra's tenure and afterward left behind testimonies of the brutality brought on by the missions; often mentioned are the observations of French explorer Jean-François de Galaup de la Pérouse, who noted during his visit to Mission Carmel a mere three years after Serra's death, "Everything reminded us of a habitation in Saint Domingo, or any other West Indian slave colony. . . . We mention it with pain, the resemblance to a slave colony is so perfect, that we saw men and women loaded with irons, others in the stocks; and at length the noise of the strokes of a whip struck our ears." Other visitors in the same era noted that Indians were beaten with a whip or cane when they did not attend worship. These people saw through "the eyes of their time," and what they saw disturbed them deeply.

To quote Sandos again, these "men of their time" and others knew that "much of what the Franciscans achieved came through the use of force—military action to return Indian runaways and discipline raiders; enforced living arrangements; and application of corporal punishment for both men and women that included floggings (women were whipped 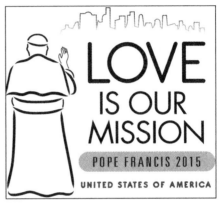 in private), use of shackles to punish and prevent runaways, and placing miscreants in the stocks for public display and ridicule. Missionization came at the price of forced cultural change" ("Writing Missionary Biography" 452). Throughout the canonization process of 2015, Serra's supporters denied that he could be held culpable for cultural habits of his time (particularly useful when Serra's work as an inquisitor during the Spanish Inquisition comes up), while refusing to listen to reasonable arguments otherwise. Contemporary mission scholars write about the political and economic forces behind Spain's need to missionize Indigenous California as being secondary to the Christian imperative to convert; sadly, nothing had changed as the canonization of Serra was fueled by the Church's PR machine pumping out images that declared "LOVE is our mission" without the slightest hint of irony.

* * *

But the key here is what I learned while researching and writing *Bad Indians*: transformation is the most powerful action that we, as Indigenous people, possess. With transformation, we can counter oppression while simultaneously adapting. Transformation, a willingness to ride waves of change rather than sink beneath them, is what allows us to survive, thrive, and outlive an attempt to use us as canonization fodder. This is the paradox of colonization: survivors are often sharpened to a fine edge by the sacrifices of their ancestors and love for their descendants. While I eventually came to believe that nothing short of an actual miracle could have stopped the canonization (yet another wave of erasure), I was proud of, and empowered by, the ways that California Indians took that dominant narrative apart, adobe brick by adobe brick, like total bosses. And we were! We made ourselves the bosses of our own narrative about missionization, utilizing both European archives and the archives of our own bodies. We created powerful networks, engaged in spiritual renewal, connected with our ancestors and our ancestral lands, and once again reinvented our Indigeneity under enormous pressure. We came out of the crucible of 2015 stronger than we had entered it. We rode that tsunami as if Coyote himself had carved our board.

Published almost exactly two years before that canonization, *Bad Indians* went into the world on that wave of activism and transformation—and was embraced in ways that still, to this day, make my knees shaky with amazement and gratitude.

* * *

During my 2007–08 sabbatical, I took field trips throughout the state, attending California Indian Storytelling Festivals, the Breath of Life Institute, TANF meetings, council meetings, basketry gatherings, and meeting young people at universities, elders at barbeques. And at every event, I offered to read from this new material. I wanted to know whether I was breaking any protocols; whether, in fact, I had "permission" to tell stories about our collective griefs, victories, silences. Overwhelmingly, all these groups responded with appreciation and enthusiasm for the project, as well as sharing sorrow, grief, amazement that any of us survived, appreciation for the histories they had never learned, or mislearned, and a determination to change how those histories were told. Many individuals approached me to say, "You're telling *my story*!" "This was my dad's story," "We need to talk about sexual assault in our communities," "My family has stories like the one about . . ."

Someone once told me that I was brave for offering such new work to critics whose opinions I valued so highly; I responded that on the contrary, I didn't think I could keep going without my community's backing! What other California Indians felt about this work was my primary concern; we were all hungry for our own story, and I wanted the input of my family and larger community so that I could do my absolute best.

It is also true that, once the book was published and I began giving readings, I've had occasional encounters with those who take issue with something in particular. One man, a professor, took me aside and instructed me, "Don't trust anything J. P. Harrington says," especially the narrative from Isabel Meadows about a young girl named Vicenta being raped in the church, adding, "I wouldn't pay too much attention to that one, it's just gossip—Harrington liked those dirty stories." Aside from the fact that most scholars note (admiringly or in frustration) that Harrington was obsessive about accuracy, no matter what the topic, this man completely dismissed the power of storytelling, the courage of Vicenta, the analytic genius of Isabel Meadows, and the use of rape, violence, and intimidation of Indigenous women as a colonizing weapon. I was not impressed. His comment did, however, encourage me to write a separate essay about Vicenta; it didn't fit into *Bad Indians* (I began a separate file on my computer titled "Spawn of Bad Indians" to hold such things), but was eventually published in a scholarly journal: "'Saying the Padre Had Grabbed Her': Rape Is the Weapon, Story Is the Cure" (Deborah A. Miranda, *Intertexts* 14, no. 2, Fall 2010). Thanks, buddy.

In addition, my use of the figure of one million Indigenous people present in precolonial California has been disputed. Part of this is my own fault: although I document my source in published essays examining materials from Isabel Meadows, I didn't include that documentation in *Bad Indians*. Over the years, I've used a graphic to

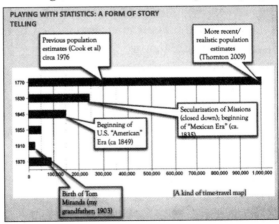

illustrate the discrepancy between Sherburne Friend Cook's established precolonial estimate (310,000) and the more recent estimate of one million.

I came across reference to the higher estimate in Dr. William L. Preston's essay, "Serpent in the Garden: Environmental Change in Colonial California." Preston, in turn, cites Russell Thornton's essay "Population History of Native North Americans," published in *A Population History of North America*. I immediately tracked down Thornton's work to verify the numbers for myself. Next, I wrote to Preston, asking whether he could confirm what I thought I was reading—precisely because it was so different from what I had always seen from other scholars. Preston was then teaching in Cal Poly's Social Sciences Department, focusing his research and teaching on human impacts on the environment, the diffusion and impact of disease in colonial California, and the influence of climate on human activities, historical geography, and military history. In other words, Preston has a particularly good foundation on which to judge Thornton's work.

Preston responded to my email, writing, "At this point I think that Thornton's high number is totally reasonable. In fact, keeping in mind that populations no doubt fluctuated over time, I'm thinking that at times 1 million or more Native Californians were resident in the state [in precolonial times]."

I was stunned. Demographer Sherburne Friend Cook's work *The Population of the California Indians: 1769–1970* has long been referred to as *the* definitive source for precolonial Indigenous populations. His figure of 310,000 has formed the basis on which many assumptions have been made about the impact of colonization, missionization, and the California gold rush (and this figure is an *increase* from his initial estimate of 135,000).

While it's true that we cannot measure suffering and injustice in the numbers of deaths, when we consider the massive mythology that defines California history and contemporary culture, the erasure of Indigenous suffering past/present/future, land theft, and trauma that continues in the lives of descendants to this day, the difference between 310,000 and one million is vast indeed.

Think about it this way: the European rhetorical act of declaring the North American continent as pristine "virgin land" going to waste—unpeopled, unused, without "real" towns, cities, or culture—has been acknowledged as a way to rationalize the dehumanization of an entire culture and theft of their lands, resources, and lives. Likewise, declaring that the entire state of California (as rich in resources as it was) could only support 310,000 people does the same work of minimizing Indigenous existence to the point where our euphemistic "absence" makes complete sense to those looking for a way to excuse colonization's violence, their own privilege, and crimes against Indigenous peoples.

To be clear, my argument is not with Cook; it is with those who, in the twenty-first century, continue to use a number that is so clearly outdated, created by a man whose scholarly resources have since been outstripped by contemporary tools. Why do scholars, or anyone else for that matter, continue to insist on that inconceivably low estimate of the number of Indigenous lives in the precolonial era?

That's a good question. I am still challenged by other scholars for my use of the one-million-Indigenous-lives estimate. I ask them: for just a moment, imagine that this number is more accurate that Cook's. What would that tell you about the deeper story of California? What does resisting that story tell you about what's at stake in believing a more contemporary, accurate, and reasonable number?

* * *

In 2013, six years after that first sabbatical, the book was published; I spent the 2013–2014 academic year traveling the United States on a DIY book tour powered mostly by contacts made through my blog, Indigenous networks (particularly Heyday and *News from Native California*), and academic colleagues. Never underestimate word of mouth and good will; I used the honorarium from one university to get to the next, and paid my own way to indie bookstores, book festivals, poetry readings, Indigenous events, even genealogical societies. It was a grueling and fantastic time; I met with attentive audiences, Indigenous professors and students, and, everywhere, tremendous welcome. What a blessing, to be able to dedicate my second academic sabbatical to the work of introducing *Bad Indians* to the wider world. Young Indigenous people, in particular, had powerful responses to the stories in the book; for some, this was a rare opportunity to openly express the grief so many of us have held locked within.

This happened when my book tour took me to a university in Oregon where three events were planned. Between nonstop touring and a cold coming on, my voice finally gave out. I made it through a reading and a classroom visit, but by the second classroom, I could not continue. One young Indian woman, Clara, had been at each event, so I asked her if she would read "Novena to Bad Indians" aloud for this last class. She had already heard me read it twice, and we'd had some good conversation that made me feel that it was all right to ask; sure enough, she agreed willingly. What a learning experience it was for me to listen to her; she read with so much heart that my words became her words, became *our* words. But by "Day 3" of the novena, Clara broke down in front of the whole class, sobbing. "It's too real," she whispered; these slurs and this pain were too much like real life for her as an Indian woman.

I had forgotten. I had been reading these pieces over and over on this tour, and I had forgotten the visceral power of these stories. I had grown to know the scenes of death, suffering, courage, anger, and love, had years to process those emotions. Clara had not. I rushed to put my arms around her, to apologize, to tell her that I should never have asked a student to read that poem aloud. I realized that between the tour itself and my familiarity with the history, I had become desensitized to the intense emotions and events that "Novena" carries. This is a danger I hadn't anticipated, and which I have worked ever since to remember. I don't want to stop feeling that connection with our history, that sense of brutal honesty—it's a fine line to walk, to speak that reality into the world and yet not allow those words to become simply performative.

But Clara reminded me that sometimes, the most honest thing a person can do is cry. She told me firmly that she wanted to finish reading the poem. "It's important," she said, swallowing her tears. I found that I knew what she meant, and respected her strength. This is where the joy and pride and love come in; choosing to continue *telling* is where we connect. We do it for the ancestors, for ourselves, for our community. The story deserves to be told, shared, spoken. And we deserve to grieve. This was a crucial lesson for me, and I have thanked Clara many times for being my guide.

When I think about the positive effect *Bad Indians* has had on California Indian lives, on the horrendous "Mission Unit" in California school curriculums, on the revisioning of California history and mission mythology, and on the field of Native literatures, I am washed clean in gratitude for my collaborators. I cannot think of myself as the sole author of this material. This book is a collaboration between myself and many others:

first and foremost, my ancestors, whose stories emerged from archival materials never meant to carry their voices, and allowed me to interpret and document their experiences. They came to me in old papers, in microfilms, in dusty books, in internet files, old photographs, genealogical materials. They came to me in dreams, in songs, in the scent of daybreak at Venice Beach, in pictographs painted on rocks. And they are my constant companions to this day.

Close behind the ancestors comes all the assistance that I received from others, collaborations without which the book would not exist; these include not just the contributions of family members, such as my mother's genealogical work, stories from my father, grandfather, and sisters, but also the California Indian communities whose enthusiastic and heartfelt welcome inspired me. The scholarship of others who came before me, both Indigenous and non-Indigenous, is an invaluable resource and encouragement. I developed a first-name relationship with research and special collections librarians in California and Washington, DC. Educators were also crucial, especially two Indigenous women: Amy Lonetree and Renya Ramirez (both Ho-Chunk). These two professors taught at UC

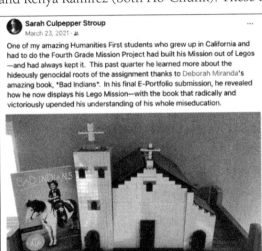

Sarah Culpepper Stroup ...
March 23, 2021 ·

One of my amazing Humanities First students who grew up in California and had to do the Fourth Grade Mission Project had built his Mission out of Legos —and had always kept it. This past quarter he learned more about the hideously genocidal roots of the assignment thanks to Deborah Miranda's amazing book, "Bad Indians". In his final E-Portfolio submission, he revealed how he now displays his Lego Mission—with the book that radically and victoriously upended his understanding of his whole miseducation.

Santa Cruz at the time, and invited me to come speak to their classes on multiple occasions, showcasing the work in progress and giving me the invaluable benefit of not just their own feedback but that of their students. Having my work treated with such profound respect and enthusiasm was so heartening that I think their words became tattooed on my soul: "You *have* to finish this book; we need to teach it in our classrooms!"

I also include as collaborators, however tangentially, the letters and journals of Serra and his peers, charts from the BIA, records from the missions and Catholic Church. By including them as sources of knowledge, by listening between the lines, I find more opportunities to catch fleeting voices. And of course, always, Isabel Meadows's brilliant, heartbreaking archive of consummate storytelling. Finally, I can't omit Heyday's incredible team of editors (especially Gayle Wattawa, whose internal review of the manuscript brought tears to my eyes) and designers (even the folks in the shipping warehouse read my manuscript and talked to me about it), and, of course, Malcolm Margolin.

Malcolm was publisher of Heyday Books when I first sent him a rough draft of the manuscript. (He has since retired.) I'd known of him for years from his extensive work at California Indian gatherings and Heyday events; he'd also overseen Heyday's book *Only What We Could Carry: The Japanese American Internment Experience* (2000). This anthology featured many talented authors, but what electrified me was the book's design: it featured prose, poetry, memoir, photographs, US government archival posters and publications, art, excerpts from a graphic novel, propaganda ephemera, and personal documents. Heyday, I thought, was the answer to my question, *Who would ever publish something like this?*

The truth is, however, that Malcolm turned my early manuscript down. In June 2009, he sent his regrets with typical grace, writing that although some parts of the manuscript were polished and complete, others seemed rough and raw. "It seemed more like collage than a book," he added, "something more suited to the web, something that had the look of notes toward a book rather than a finished book. I've been wrestling with what to do, quite agonized in fact." In the end, both the economic restraints of the recession and the fact that the manuscript wasn't fully cooked played into Heyday's rejection. I was, of course, crushed—and at the same time, this honest critique lit a fire under me. I continued to write and polish the manuscript, while teaching full-time.

Two years later, I sent the completed manuscript, with a new title, back to Malcolm. His response:

Dear Deborah:
I got Bad Indians (this title hits about twelve different targets at the same time—just inspired) in yesterday's mail, and I haven't had a chance to look at it thoroughly. If I were a proper publisher I'd take my cues from _____ and put it aside for nine months before responding. But I'm not a proper publisher, nor, dear friend, are you a proper scholarly writer. I'm awestruck by your courage to do

something so risky, capacious, and intense. Hasn't the academic world taught you that to get ahead you have to squeeze the life out of raw material, process and refine it so it can be easily digested and won't upset or challenge? So full of anger, humor, mockery, yearning. I salute you with all my heart, Deborah, and I'm honored and grateful that you sent the manuscript back to me for reconsideration.

The rest, as they say, is history.

And, after the book's publication, more people joined the project: university educators, scholars, students, book clubs, parents of young children scouring the internet for alternatives to the mission unit, reviewers. People have carried this book into dissertations, conference panels, Indigenous homes, high schools. In 2021, I recorded *Bad Indians* for Audible. The book has moved beyond me, like a child sent out into the world surrounded by guardian angels.

* * *

A few high notes from the past ten years:

- *Bad Indians* was awarded the PEN Oakland–Josephine Miles Literary Award in 2015; known as "the blue-collar PEN," and "the People's PEN," this particular honor brought me home to California in more ways than one.

- The Zinn Education Project published an online excerpt from the introduction, which brought the book to the attention of many; *Indian Country Today* reprinted it online as well, and a major publisher requested permission to include the intro in a new textbook on race, class, and gender.

- In 2014, *News from Native California* produced a special publication called "Saying Our Share: Surviving the Missions." I contributed a piece that's also in this new edition of *Bad Indians*, "Dear Sonora: Writing to a Fourth Grader about Her Project." Now that piece has been included in a history textbook about the Channel Islands—crucially, a book directed at young California students.

- In 2021, a special issue of *Studies in American Indian Literatures*, edited by Laura M. Furlan and Lydia M. Heberling, focused on my work.

- In 2016, California legislators finally encouraged many educators to drop the use of mission projects in fourth-grade classrooms. So far, the legislation has led to very mixed results. It has allowed educators to opt out of the traditional Eurocentric mythology and adapt the curriculum to more contemporary standards, but it did not forbid the presentation of mission history in a celebratory light. As such, the Mission Unit and its accompanying misrepresentations and lies often continue unabated. The reforms that have been made so far are the result of many years of lobbying and work by many Indigenous activists and allies, but certainly *Bad Indians* has played a small, meaningful role.

"We are currently piloting [Island Visions] with a dozen elementary, middle, and high school teachers in Santa Barbara and Ventura counties, and many have specifically mentioned how much they appreciated and learned from your piece in the book. Especially a 4th/5th grade teacher who is working on replacing the standard missions curriculum in her classroom. Thank you for your powerful contribution to this book . . . hope we can get more teachers and schools inspired to do the same!" —Jacob Seigel Brielle, coauthor of *Island Visions*

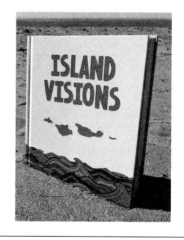

* * *

How a book from a small, passionate, independent publisher specializing in local California history, natural history, and Indigenous writings has traveled the world so extensively, and left such a trail of influences, continues to astound me. I could never have taken this journey on my own. These collaborations mean that *Bad Indians* necessarily privileges a collective voice as much as the individual, and the individual's story is deeply infused by a collective experience. Now Heyday, with new publisher Steve Wasserman at the helm, and editors Emmerich Anklam and Terria Smith, carry *Bad Indians* into the future, honoring it with a tenth-anniversary edition. *Nimasianexelpasaleki*; my heart is happy.

I write about my ancestors to honor their humanity; ancestors were people who figured out how to make it through something terrible because they were willing to try unthinkable solutions. Telling their stories is not only about documenting cruelty or injustice (although that is its own kind of paradigm-shifting work) but studying how our ancestors transformed themselves. Their survival is a kind of terrible beauty, a terrible teaching (*terrible* coming from the root for *tremble*, *shiver*, and also *awe*)—perhaps another good way to describe change. Rosy Simas, a Seneca dancer and choreographer, notes that if time is nonlinear, or spiral, then healing work for ourselves returns to heal the scars on the DNA of our ancestors as well. I hope that this work provides doorways to healing in both directions: for myself and my contemporary Indigenous family and community, and for our ancestors, whose scars may be honored in the telling of their stories.

Change in the shape of a tsunami is destruction and creation in the same instant. It's *how* we surf the tsunami that affects the outcome. This morning, I went through the Esselen dictionary that my sister Louise Miranda Ramirez has been creating. I wanted to know whether anyone had captured the word for "tsunami." Surely, living on the coast, all tribes had a word for that massive event! But apparently, it was not recorded. Like most tribes, we need to take what we know about our language and use that to create a new word. This happens when a language has no living speakers or must incorporate a concept or thing that doesn't exist in the language. That metaphorical tsunami swept away the actual word for tsunami, but Louise and I will invent another word. And it will be good.

(New) Esselen word for tsunami:

tsunami: ta-mashaipayisi imila - literally, "very hungry moving ocean"

ta – pref., indicates intensity
mashaipa, *iv.*, be hungry [also the Esselen word for Anglos]
-yisi, *suf.*, verb suffix denoting motion
imi- expanse; imila, *n.* sea,ocean

* * *

In the first edition of *Bad Indians*, I wrote, "If we allow the pieces of our culture to lie scattered in the dust of history, trampled on by racism and grief, then yes, we are irreparably damaged. But if we pick up the pieces and use them in new ways that honor their integrity, their colors, textures, stories—then we do those pieces justice, no matter how sharp they are, no matter how much handling them slices our fingers and makes us bleed."

Looking at my words now, I see how I was trying to talk about the power of transformation.

I still am.

Acknowledgments

Special thanks to: Dorothy Allison for her tender insights in the aftermath of my writing these stories; Ruth Behar and Lourdes Portillo for their amazing "Documentar" workshop; the California Indian Storytelling Association for song, story, and faith; Rosemary Cambra for living the vision; Sandra Cisneros and Macondistas todos for energy and passion; Linda Hogan for inspiration and unwavering truth; Fred Hoxie for incisive and crucial advice; Malcolm Margolin and *News from Native California* for preparing the way; the entire Heyday crew, especially Jeannine Gendar, Gayle Wattawa, Lorraine Rath, Diane Lee, Lillian Fleer, Natalie Mulford, and Sylvia Linsteadt, for their warm welcome and tender loving care of this work from manuscript to finished book; Renya Ramirez, Amy Lonetree, and their great UC Santa Cruz class; Georgiana Valoyce Sanchez for her true heart; Leslie Silko for the clarifying fire of her faith in this project; Beverly Slapin for her fierce sense of justice; the faculty and students at UCLA American Indian Studies Center (especially Rebecca Hernandez, DeAnna Rivera, Wendy Teeters, Kimberly Robertson); Lesley Wheeler, Suzanne Keen, Sandy O'Connell, and the Washington and Lee U English Department for tremendous day-to-day support. Thanks particularly to those who helped fund research and writing time: The American Philosophical Association, Washington and Lee University, Lenfest Summer Grants, and the Institute of American Cultures at UCLA. My gratitude also to Susan Snyder at The Bancroft Library; Dwight Dutschke, Native American Heritage Coordinator, California State Parks; Dennis Copeland at Monterey Public Library; David McLaughlin at Pentacle Press; Daisy Njoku at the Smithsonian; Mark Miller and Barb Landis for answering questions and queries about obscure publications and resources; and the wonderful Jennifer Browdy for translation assistance, especially in Isabel's long piece about El Potrero.

Gratitude to my children, Miranda Miller Gomez and Daniel Abraham Conner, whose births woke me to my purpose.

My heartfelt thanks to Louise J. Miranda Ramirez for her leadership, healing words, sacrifices—my sister, you keep bringing me home. *Mislayaya kolo, Ichi!*

Deep gratitude to Madgel E. Miranda for her years of genealogical sleuthing, her passion for detail, her unconditional love, and a legacy of treasures left behind.

No words can express my appreciation for Margo Solod's faith, love, inspiration, amazing culinary skills, and especially the gift of a summer on Cuttyhunk to finish this manuscript!

Always, always, thank you to the Ancestors—for the dreams, belly laughs, stories . . . the good, the bad, the ugly, the sacred . . . thank you for your survival.

Nimasianexelpasaleki—my heart feels good.

Sources and Permissions

Images

The following images were supplied courtesy of the author: cover photo of Deborah Miranda; Madgel Miranda and Alfred Miranda; Madgel Miranda, Deborah Miranda, and Alfred Miranda; Genealogy of Violence; Deborah Miranda fourth-grade picture; Deby's mission; Thomas Miranda at Mission San Miguel; Witness to Mark of Isabel Meadows; "A Few Corrections to My Daughter's Coloring Book," based on *California Missions*, Spizzirri Publishing; "Mission Indians of Southern California Making Baskets and Hair Ropes," by Paul Frenzeny (originally appeared in *Harper's Weekly* 22, no. 20 (October 1877); mission register, baptism of Tomas Santos Miranda; María Inés (Agnes) García; Tomás Santos Miranda; Carmel Indian gathering; Tom Miranda Sr., Al Miranda Sr., and Al Miranda Jr.; Guadalupe Robles and José Robles; Thomas Anthony Miranda as a young man; Tom Miranda, dandy; Al Miranda, Keta Miranda, and Tommy Miranda Jr.; Alfred Edward Miranda portrait; Al Miranda in the garden; Al Miranda goofing off in the kitchen; "Power," Al Miranda Jr. and Deborah Miranda; "Protection," Al Miranda Jr. and Deborah Miranda; "Seattle Center," Al Miranda Jr. and Deborah Miranda; "Before the Concert," Al Miranda Jr. and Deborah Miranda; "Santa Monica Beach," Alfred E. Miranda and Deborah Miranda; July '67, Deborah Miranda; handwritten John Rabbit story; "Playing with Statistics: A Form of Storytelling"; "(New) Esselen word for tsunami."

Glossary, Fig. 1, Adobe Bricks: "Padre Directing Mission Indians to Build," from Zephyrin Engelhardt, *San Juan Capistrano Mission:* scan courtesy of Pentacle Press.

Glossary, Fig. 3, Bells: "El Camino Real" mission bell drawing from Mrs. A.S.C. Forbes, *California Missions and Landmarks: El Camino Real.*

Glossary, Fig. 4, Discipline: "The administrator of the royal mines punishes the native lords with great cruelty . . . in the mines," from *Nueva crónica y buen gobierno* (drawing 211) by Felipe Guaman Poma de Ayala.

Glossary, Fig. 5, Flogging: "Notebooks of Tonayuca, drawing by a Native artist, Mexico, c. 1567. Courtesy of the Granger Collection, NYC.

Glossary, Fig. 6, Cat-o-nine tails courtesy of www.free-photos.biz.

Glossary, Fig. 7, *Corma* courtesy of The Bancroft Library, UC Berkeley.

Glossary, Fig. 8, Cudgel courtesy of www.free-photos.biz.

Glossary, Fig. 9, Carmel Mission photograph by C. W. J. Johnson, courtesy of The Bancroft Library, UC Berkeley.

Glossary, Fig. 10, *Neofito*: "Inhabitants of California" by Louis Choris courtesy of The Bancroft Library, UC Berkeley.

Glossary, Fig. 11, Padre: "Franciscan Missionaries As They Came and Went" from Zephyrin Engelhardt, *San Juan Capistrano Mission*, scan courtesy of Pentacle Press.

Acorn courtesy of Florida's Educational Technology Clearinghouse.

Mission image courtesy of www.pinterest.com/PaperModels/california-mission -models.

Vicenta Gutierrez field note from J. P. Harrington Field Notes, Reel 73, side B, April 1935, page 98, consultant Isabel Meadows, in Elaine Mills, ed., *The Papers of John Peabody Harrington in the Smithsonian Institution, 1907–1957,* microfilm (White Plains, NY: Kraus International, 1981).

Isabel Meadows in Washington, DC, courtesy of Smithsonian Institution.

Victor Acedo field note from J. P. Harrington Field Notes, Reel 73, 282 B, consultant Isabel Meadows in Mills, *Papers of John Peabody Harrington.*

Victor Acedo photograph courtesy of the Mayo Hayes O'Donnell Library.

"A Digger Belle" from David Rohrer Leeper, *The Argonauts of 'Forty-nine.*

California Indian Bounty Bond courtesy of The Bancroft Library, UC Berkeley.

"Three Belles of San Luis Rey" photograph courtesy of Braun Research Library Collection, Autry National Center, P.1501.

Burning the Digger: courtesy of California State Parks.

Jacinta Gonzales courtesy of Monterey County Free Libraries.

Joseph Strong illustration of Fr. Casanova's Mass at Carmel courtesy of Monterey Public Library Collection.

José Robles courtesy of The Bancroft Library, UC Berkeley.

"Bad Indian Goes on Rampage at Santa Ynez," *Los Angeles Times,* August 3, 1909.

"J. P. Harrington: A Collage" photograph courtesy of Smithsonian Institution.

Coyote clipart courtesy of arthursclipart.org.

"California Pow Wow" by L. Frank.

Map of El Potrero courtesy of Landcase Map Collection at The Bancroft Library, UC Berkeley.

"No Saint!" courtesy of www.whereismyriver.com.

"Love Is Our Mission" courtesy of the Holy Catholic and Apostolic Church.

Lego Mission post courtesy of Dr. Sarah Culpepper Stroup.

Island Visions image courtesy of Jacob Seigel Brielle.

Author photo by Margo Solod.

"Four Things You Can Do with Your Chart for Calculating Quantum of Indian Blood": charts courtesy of Bureau of Indian Affairs, art by the author.

Quotations

The quoted statements in "Genealogy of Violence, Part II" were assembled from responses to the Interrogatorio (Questionnaire) that the Spanish viceroy sent to California missions in 1812. Since most missions had two priests working together, and they often moved from one mission to another, the quotations cannot be attributed to individuals, but here are the names of the priests working at these missions at the time: San Diego, Fernando Martín and José Sanchez; San Gabriel, José de Miguel and José María Zalvidea; San Miguel, Juan Martín or Juan Cabot; San Antonio, Pedro Cabot and Juan Bautista Sancho.

April Moore's statement in "Digger Belles" is from the PBS American Experience documentary *The Gold Rush* (http://www.pbs.org/wgbh/amex/goldrush/sfeature/natives_03.html)

"Old News" quotes from the collection of newspaper articles *They Were Only Diggers* by Robert F. Heizer.

"J. P. Harrington: A Collage" includes quotations from L. Frank, Ernestine De Soto, and Linda Yamane.

Publications

Publications cited include the following:

California Dept. of Parks and Recreation Office of Historic Preservation, *Five Views: An Ethnic Historic Site Survey for California* (Sacramento: Dept. of Parks and Recreation, 1988). Available at http://www.cr.nps.gov/history/online_books/5views/5views.htm (accessed May 2012).

Elizabeth Cook-Lynn, "Life and Death in the Mainstream of American Indian Biography," *Wicazo Sa Review* 11, no. 2 (Autumn 1995).

Eduardo and Bonnie Duran, *Native American Postcolonial Psychology* (Albany, NY: State Univ. of New York Press, 1995).

O. P. Fitzgerald, *California Sketches* (Nashville: Southern Methodist Publishing House, 1880). Available at http://memory.loc.gov/ammem/index.html (accessed May 2012).

Steven W. Hackel, *Children of Coyote, Missionaries of Saint Francis: Indian-Spanish Relations in Colonial California, 1769–1850* (Chapel Hill: Univ. of North Carolina Press, 2005).

Kristi Hawthorne, *Oceanside: Where Life Is Worth Living* (Oceanside, CA: Oceanside Historical Society, 2000).

Robert F. Heizer, ed., *The Destruction of California Indians* (Lincoln: Univ. of Nebraska Press, 1993).

Kathleen Thompson Hill and Gerald Hill, *Monterey and Carmel: Eden by the Sea* (Guilford, CT: Globe Pequot, 1999).

David Rohrer Leeper, *The Argonauts of 'Forty-nine* (South Bend, IN: J. B. Stoll, 1894). Available at http://memory.loc.gov/ammem/index.html (accessed May 2012).

James Rawls, *Indians of California: The Changing Image* (Norman, OK: Univ. of Oklahoma Press, 1986).

Leon Rowland, *Santa Cruz, the Early Years: The Collected Writings of Leon Rowland* (1940; reprint Santa Cruz: Otter B Books, 1980).

Robert Louis Stevenson, *Across the Plains* (London: Chatto & Windus, 1892), available at http://www.gutenberg.org/ebooks/614 (accessed May 2012).

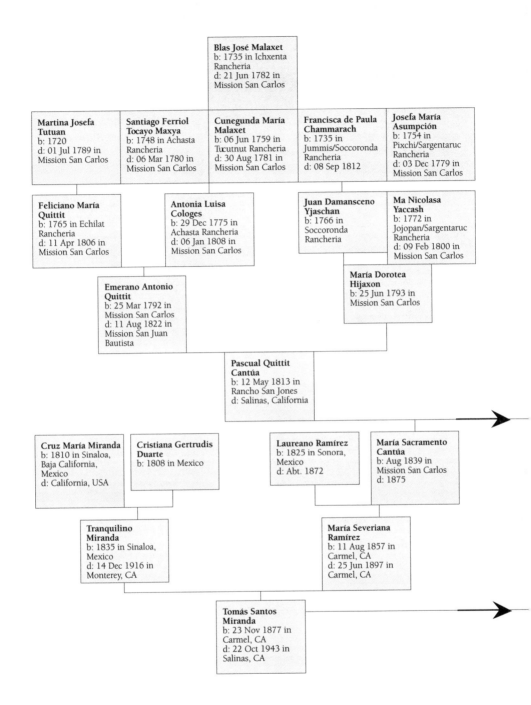

Blas José Malaxet
b: 1735 in Ichxenta Rancheria
d: 21 Jun 1782 in Mission San Carlos

Martina Josefa Tutuan
b: 1720
d: 01 Jul 1789 in Mission San Carlos

Santiago Ferriol Tocayo Maxya
b: 1748 in Achasta Rancheria
d: 06 Mar 1780 in Mission San Carlos

Cunegunda María Malaxet
b: 06 Jun 1759 in Tucutnut Rancheria
d: 30 Aug 1781 in Mission San Carlos

Francisca de Paula Chammarach
b: 1735 in Jummis/Soccoronda Rancheria
d: 08 Sep 1812

Josefa María Asumpción
b: 1754 in Pixchi/Sargentaruc Rancheria
d: 03 Dec 1779 in Mission San Carlos

Feliciano María Quittit
b: 1765 in Echilat Rancheria
d: 11 Apr 1806 in Mission San Carlos

Antonia Luisa Cologes
b: 29 Dec 1775 in Achasta Rancheria
d: 06 Jan 1808 in Mission San Carlos

Juan Damansceno Yjaschan
b: 1766 in Soccoronda Rancheria

Ma Nicolasa Yaccash
b: 1772 in Jojopan/Sargentaruc Rancheria
d: 09 Feb 1800 in Mission San Carlos

Emerano Antonio Quittit
b: 25 Mar 1792 in Mission San Carlos
d: 11 Aug 1822 in Mission San Juan Bautista

María Dorotea Hijaxon
b: 25 Jun 1793 in Mission San Carlos

Pascual Quittit Cantúa
b: 12 May 1813 in Rancho San Jones
d: Salinas, California

Cruz María Miranda
b: 1810 in Sinaloa, Baja California, Mexico
d: California, USA

Cristiana Gertrudis Duarte
b: 1808 in Mexico

Laureano Ramírez
b: 1825 in Sonora, Mexico
d: Abt. 1872

María Sacramento Cantúa
b: Aug 1839 in Mission San Carlos
d: 1875

Tranquilino Miranda
b: 1835 in Sinaloa, Mexico
d: 14 Dec 1916 in Monterey, CA

María Severiana Ramírez
b: 11 Aug 1857 in Carmel, CA
d: 25 Jun 1897 in Carmel, CA

Tomás Santos Miranda
b: 23 Nov 1877 in Carmel, CA
d: 22 Oct 1943 in Salinas, CA

Family Ancestry Chart for Deborah Ann Miranda

(continued on following pages)

unknown

Leonila
b: 1717 in Echilat Rancheria
d: 16 Nov 1782 in Mission San Carlos

Eugenio Joseph
b: San Francisco, Rancheria (Echilat)
d: 13 Dec 1782 in Mission San Carlos

Pulgaria María Yoschal
b: 1747 in Echilat Rancheria
d: 21 Dec 1804 in Mission San Carlos

Diodora María Mihausom
b: Abt. 1728 in Ensen Rancheria
d: 14 Jun 1806 in Mission San Carlos

Patricio José Solol Cholom
b: 1750 in Mission San Carlos
d: 07 Apr 1816 in Mission San Carlos

Felipa María Josefa Chunniron
b: 1755 in Echilat Rancheria
d: 20 Dec 1804 in Mission San Carlos

Moyses José Yunisyunis
b: 1732 in Ensen Rancheria
d: 25 Dec 1803 in Mission San Carlos

Procula María Sommeres
b: 1748 in Ensen Rancheria
d: 13 Nov 1795 in Mission San Carlos

Melchor Martin
b: 1686 in Mexico
d: Juquila, Mexico

Fructuoso de Jesús Cholom-Real
b: 20 Jan 1785 in Soccoronda Rancheria
d: 1840 in Carmel, CA

Yginia María Yunisyunis
b: 1732 in Ensen Rancheria
d: Abt. 1845 in Carmel, CA

Juan Salvada Lugo
b: 09 Oct 1702 in Sinaloa, Mexico
d: Jul 1784 in Los Angeles, CA

María Josefa Francisca Espinosa
b: 18 Feb 1709 in Sinaloa, Mexico
d: 1756 in Sinaloa, Mexico

María Josefa Dolores Cholom-Real
b: 19 Mar 1812 in Mission San Carlos

Felipe Santiago García
b: 1748
d: 1822

Petra Joaquina de Lugo
b: Sep 1756 in Sinaloa, Mexico
d: 02 Nov 1817 in Carmel, CA

Joséf Julían García
b: 1779 in Carmel, CA
d: 17 Jun 1859 in Monterey, CA

Thomas Anthony Miranda
b: 02 Sep 1903 in Monterey, CA
d: 06 Sep 1988 in San Joaquin, CA

Alfred Edward Miranda
b: 19 Nov 1927 in Tuolumne, California
d: 28 Jun 2009 in Arlington, Snohomish, Washington

Marquesa "Keta" Josephine Robles
b: 12 Jul 1907 in Santa Barbara, CA
d: 11 Sep 1950 in Santa Barbara, CA

Deborah Ann Miranda
b: 22 Oct 1961 in Los Angeles, CA

Panna

Culuactes

Chrestina De
Espinosa
b: 1691 in Mexico

Pablo Gonzales

Antonia Garibay

Felíz Juan Alsaldo
Ranchero
b: 1754 in Tucutnut
Rancheria
d: 21 Sep 1782 in
Mission San Carlos

María Francisca
Chimtu Verdugo
b: 1743 in
Tucutnut/Ixchenta
Rancheria
d: 05 Feb 1798 in
Mission San Carlos

Francisco Antonio
Piguani
b: 1739 in
Yippimegesan
Rancheria
d: 26 June 1789 in
Mission San Carlos

José Vicente
González-Garibay
b: 30 Jun 1821 in
Mission San Carlos

María Beatriz
Gertrudis
b: 1767 in Tucutnut
Rancheria

Facundo Huaclanchi
b: 1773 in
Excelen/Excelemac
Rancheria

Carola María Panna
b: 1787 in Escelen
Rancheria

unknown Cueva

Catalina Moraled or
Morales
b: 30 Apr 1818 in
Mission San Carlos

Paula Garibay
b: Jan 1797 in Mission
San Carlos
d: 20 Nov 1878 in
Mission San Carlos

Guadalupe Cueva
b: 1858 in
California
d: 31 Dec 1917 in
Monterey, CA

José Faustino Garcia
b: 1832 in California
d: 1912

María Inés (Agnes)
García
b: 14 Jan 1881 in
Monterey, CA
d: 29 Jun 1966 in
Stockton, CA

Madgel Eleanor
Yeoman
b: 16 Apr 1935 in
Beverly Hills, CA
d: 21 Nov 2001 in
Tacoma, WA

Photo by Margo Solod

About the Author

Deborah A. Miranda is an enrolled member of the Ohlone/Costanoan-Esselen Nation of the Greater Monterey Bay Area in California, with Santa Ynez Chumash ancestry. In addition to *Bad Indians*, she is the author of four poetry collections and coeditor of *Sovereign Erotics: A Collection of Two-Spirit Literature*. She earned her PhD in English literature from the University of Washington in Seattle and was Professor of English at Washington and Lee University, where she taught literature of the margins and creative writing. She retired from her professorship in 2021 to focus on scholarship and poetry involving California mission history and literatures. She and her spouse, writer Margo Solod, live in Eugene, Oregon, a short distance from homelands in California.

HEYDAY · *from* **NATIVE CALIFORNIA**

Heyday's Berkeley Roundhouse program celebrates California's diverse Indian cultures through our quarterly magazine, *News from Native California*, and books on Native life.

Since its origins, Heyday has kept California Indian peoples at the center of its work, beginning with the publication of *The Ohlone Way* by founder Malcolm Margolin in 1978 and the debut of the serial magazine *News from Native California* in 1987. In 2012 the Roundhouse program was developed within Heyday as a place to celebrate Indigenous storytelling and culture-keeping. It's heartfelt, emotional, intelligent work, significant to California tribal nations and friends.

Heyday's California Indian publishing program brings books by and about Native Californians to press. Award-winning and critically acclaimed, publications under the Roundhouse umbrella amplify the traditions, artwork, and insights of the West Coast's first peoples. From tribal memoirs to children's stories to cookbooks, these books preserve cherished knowledge and offer eye-opening perspective with integrity and deep respect.

A quarterly magazine connecting readers to the West Coast's original voices, *News from Native California* publishes essays, news stories, poems, artwork, and tribal histories about and by Indigenous people. Informing and inspiring readers since 1987, this first-of-its-kind publication celebrates and honors the culture, heritage, and social justice work of Native Californians—past, present, and future.

Contributions from friends of Heyday and community organizations make the Roundhouse program possible. Tax-deductible gifts support specific projects and provide funding to support operating expenses for both Roundhouse books and the *News from Native California* quarterly.

heydaybooks.com/roundhouse

newsfromnativecalifornia.com